# The Last Gentleman-of-War

# The
# Last
# Gentleman-of-War

## The Raider Exploits
## of the Cruiser *Emden*

by R. K. Lochner

Translated by Thea and Harry Lindauer

BLUEJACKET BOOKS

Naval Institute Press
Annapolis, Maryland

Naval Institute Press
291 Wood Road
Annapolis, MD 21402

The original German-language edition was published by Heyne-Press, München, Germany, 1979, under the title *Die Kaperfahrten des Kleinen Kreuzers Emden*.

First Bluejacket Books printing, 2002

**Library of Congress Cataloging-in-Publication Data**
Lochner, R. K.
   [Kaperfahrten des kleinen Kreuzers Emden. English]
   The last gentleman-of-war : the raider exploits of the cruiser Emden / by R. K. Lochner; translated by Thea and Harry Lindauer.
   p. cm. – (Bluejacket books)
   Originally published: Annapolis, Md.: Naval Institute Press, 1988.
   Includes bibliographical references and index.
   ISBN 1-55750-538-1 (alk. paper)
   1. Emden (Cruiser)   2. World War, 1914–1918—Naval operations, German.
I. Title.   II. Series.
D582.E6 L6313 2002
940.4'54—dc21

                                        2002070307

Printed in the United States of America on acid-free paper ∞
09 08 07 06 05 04 03 02   9 8 7 6 5 4 3 2 1

In memory of my father,
Professor Dr. Rudolf Lochner
(1895–1978),
who taught me an awareness of history

# CONTENTS

List of Maps                                                    ix
Preface                                                         xi


PART ONE

THE OPENING PHASE

1. A New Hong Kong or Port Arthur?                               3
2. The First Cruiser Success in Tsushima Strait                21
3. Once More in Tsingtao                                        35


PART TWO

THE RAIDER WAR

1. Detached for a Raider War                                    55
2. The First Prize in the Indian Ocean                         75
3. Commerce War off Bengal and Rangoon                         85
4. The Burning Oil Tanks of Madras                            109
5. Off Ceylon and Diego Garcia                                118
6. Again in the Bay of Bengal                                 133

7. The Unbelievable Raid on Penang          145
8. The Last Reprieve                        160


PART THREE

THE END OF A CRUISER

1. The Action near the Cocos                167
2. The Adversary                            193
3. The Prisoners                            206


PART FOUR

THE LANDING PARTY

1. The Landing                              213
2. SMS *Ayesha*                             222
3. The North German Loyd Freighter *Choising*   236
4. Through the Desert                       242
5. At Sea Again                             258
6. Ras al Aswad: Battle in the Desert       264
7. On to the Hejaz Railroad                 274


PART FIVE

EPILOGUE                                    281


Appendix: The Ship                          301
Bibliography                                309

# MAPS

Bombardment of Madras, 22 September 1914          114

Action Against Penang, 28 October 1914          152

Battle off the Cocos Islands, 9 November 1914         176

Route of the *Emden*'s Landing Party Through Arabia,
    8 January–24 May 1915         246

SMS *Emden*         302

# PREFACE

The almost unbelievable story of the adventures and voyages of a small German cruiser named the *Emden* may be, in our highly technical era, one of the last examples of the successful operation of a solitary surface warship. As a final chapter in the brilliant, romantic, centuries-old history of traditional sea warfare, it will assuredly arouse a feeling of nostalgia.

In accounts of naval warfare during World War I, such singular destinies are secondary. More complex questions like overall strategy and political antecedents prevail, as well as analysis of the influence of Tirpitzian theory, submarine warfare, operations of the battle fleet, and economic warfare.

Taken by surprise at the outbreak of war as they were sailing about the world's oceans in the summer of 1914, Germany's few existing cruisers disappeared quickly. It was a war fought by a young, inexperienced German navy handicapped in having as its foe not only powerful Great Britain but also France, Russia, and Japan.

The strategic mission of solitary, foreign-based German cruisers was to interrupt enemy shipping, block and disperse Allied sea power, destroy merchant tonnage, incite oppressed colonial populations to revolt, and lastly, engage in combat with enemy warships. Considering their size, strength, and technical capabilities, the cruisers more than fulfilled this mission. For months on end they sailed all the world's oceans, the thorn in their enemies' side. They accomplished their tasks despite enormous difficulties and with exciting results.

The men of the *Emden* operated entirely alone. They were cut off from support, constantly plagued by doubts about resupply, fatigued by endless watches; they were under pressure to attend to the smallest details, because even a slight error could endanger the speed, combat readiness, and ultimate survival of their ship. It was a dangerous and nerve-shattering war against an enemy blessed with fortified bases, warships, and materiel; fought in constant flight with tenacity and cunning. The *Emden* story is one of initiative, devotion, and will brought to bear in the face of solitude and fear. With astounding effort and an almost anachronistic sense of gallantry, her captain and crew respected the rules of humanity and international law.

This story of a commanding officer, a crew, and a ship that earned the admiration of friend and foe alike is narrated in the simple, sober language of documents and eyewitnesses from both sides. Any dramatized treatment would have made it less credible.

Without the men of the *Emden* who wrote down or otherwise related their experiences, without the postwar book publishers, and without the carefully maintained documents in several archives, it would have been impossible to reconstruct these events. The various sources are catalogued in the bibliography.

In acknowledgment, I owe special thanks to Dr. G. Sandhofer of the Bundesarchiv-Militärarchiv, Freiburg/Breisgau; Mr. N. J. Flanagan, director of the Australian War Memorial, Canberra; Mr. Dieter Kraft of the Kulturamt/Archiv, Emden; Mr. J. S. Lucas of the Imperial War Museum, London; Dr. Bruno Preisler, Wyk auf Föhr; Mr. Khoo Boo Chia, curator of the Lembaga Museum Negeri, Pulau-Penang; Mr. Thiru N. Krishnamurthy, director of information, Madras; and Mr. P. J. Grills, official secretary of the Office of the Administrator, Cocos islands. I gratefully received direction and information from Dr. S. T. Sat-yamurti, director of museums, Madras; Mr. Jasvinder Singh of the historical section, Ministry of Defense, New Delhi; Mr. B. T. Carter of the National Maritime Museum, Greenwich; and Mr. Peter Schönfeldt of Hamburg.

In the procurement of photographs, I had the friendly assis-tance of M. Bernard Rosin of Maison Marius Bar, Toulon; the staff of the Bundesarchiv, Koblenz; Mr. Hervé Cras of the Musée de la Marine, Paris; Mr. L. R. Jayakumar of Madras; Fa. B. Drüp-pel of Wilhelmshaven; Mr. Arnold Kludas of the Deutsches Schif-fahrtmuseum, Bremerhaven; and Mr. Hans-Jürgen Witthöft of Hapag-Lloyd, Hamburg.

I thank my brother, Mr. Dietmar Lochner of Hamburg, for his competent and patient execution of all drawings according to my specifications and wishes.

Above all, I am most grateful to Mr. Rolf Heyne and the Wilhelm Heyne Verlag of Munich for their interest in this proj-ect and their liberal support as its scope continued to grow.

Lastly, my most intimate and particular thanks go to my wife, Mrs. Lucia Helga Lochner. Without her patient understanding and her meticulous attention to and effort with the manuscript, this book could not have been written.

*Hamburg, Summer 1979*

# One

# The Opening Phase

CHAPTER ONE

# A NEW HONG KONG OR PORT ARTHUR?

The city, a green island in the Chinese province of Shantung, could not have been more carefree, more optimistic, more picturesque than it was at this moment. The beaches, the business opportunities, the outstanding harbor facilities on the Chinese coast, a location that was perfect for a naval base—all made it an ideal foreign foothold. The city had not been developed until after 13 November 1897, when three cruisers occupied it after the murder of two missionaries. In less than twenty years this inhospitable, neglected fishing village on the broad and sheltered Bay of Kiaochow had been transformed into a modern trade center and tourist paradise. It had attracted a massive influx of job seekers. The new Shantung Railway had been constructed and coal and mineral mines were operating at full capacity. A true pioneer spirit prevailed. On the heels of such basic economic developments came hospitals and schools; even a high school had been founded. Impressive government buildings with European villas clustered around them rose from the friendly hills. Friedrichstrasse descended from there. It led to the Tsingtao bridge, where the boats of the gray cruisers anchored off the green coastal promenade were tied up. One of them, SMS *Emden,* was a light cruiser under the command of Karl von Müller, who had just returned to his home base from an arduous assignment in China and Japan. Over this whole scene, over the landing bridges and the government buildings, flew the black, white, and red flag of Germany. It was May in the German base of Tsingtao on the China Sea. The year was 1914.

*May 1914*

The men of the *Emden* were disappointed. Their cruiser was scheduled for a trip to either the South Seas or the Dutch East Indies. Then, because of civil disturbance in Mexico, they were to sail to the west coast of America. After much hemming and hawing, the navy accounting office decided instead to send the cruiser *Nürnberg,* which was several hundred nautical miles farther east in Japanese waters. Coal was expensive and the navy had to economize. Later the *Nürnberg* would be relieved by the *Leipzig.*

So the crew of the *Emden* made themselves at home in Tsingtao. For the old hands these were the last few weeks of work. Their relief was due to arrive at the beginning of June. The order of the day was routine duty, which had been largely neglected during the last voyage. The *Emden* conducted landing maneuvers with an emphasis on target practice. They usually ended with a cookout at the beach and a parade homeward through the streets of Tsingtao.

On 23 May 1914 Admiral Graf Spee combined the available ships *Scharnhorst, Gneisenau,* and *Emden* in a squadron exercise in the Bay of Tsingtao. On 24 May, a Sunday, there was a horse race on a track nearby. Some of the best jockeys on the east Asian coast, many of them familiar to the officers of the *Emden,* participated. A number of officers themselves took part. The event drew all the ranks of Tsingtao's high society into the stands. The following day, 25 May, saw the yearly tug-of-war competition and the squadron's sailing races. Lieutenant Robert Witthoeft of the *Emden,* in spite of a break in his mast fitting, emerged the winner.

From 28 to 30 May Ensign Erich Fikentscher, the sports officer of the *Emden,* led the crew's old hands on a three-day excursion into the Lauchou Mountains. It was quite an event, financed by a petty cash fund that had been enriched when the *Emden* earned a salvage fee for towing the steamer *Deike Rickmers.* No expenses were spared. Even the ship's band was taken along. The goal was to reach the Mecklenburg House. A wagon with all sorts of provisions was dispatched ahead. Then, by train, the excursionists went by way of Syphan to the Lizun Valley. There the real march to Mecklenburg House began. They divided themselves into five groups and, though well briefed, became utterly lost on the way. At the time of the evening rendezvous all 160 of them had managed, miraculously, to find their way. For two days the sailors wandered about the beautiful countryside, infused with a holiday spirit. The orchestra played tirelessly in front of Mecklenburg House, once even for the entertainment of a Chinese prince. In the evening the musicians divided themselves among the jagged cliffs surrounding the resort and, with the conductor placed strategically before them, filled the air with inspiring music. The return trip to Tsingtao was accompanied by the sound of stirring marches. Tired and footsore though the sailors were, they delighted in their adventurous outing. A few more days on land and they would be able to board the relief ship at Tsingtao.

On Sunday, 31 May, the old crew members attended their last church service. Those officers who were off duty took one more trip on horseback to the forests of the Iltis Mountains. So ended May 1914.

## June 1914

On 2 June the departing crewmen left the *Emden* and settled with their seabags in one of the barracks on the wharf. The following morning, at 0600, the HAPAG (Hamburg-America Line) steamship *Patricia* made her majestic entry into the inner harbor. She brought fifteen hundred men to the squadron on change-of-duty orders. For the next few days the detailing officer had his hands full with berthing assignments, fire drills, bulkhead in spections, and other shipboard tasks. Lieutenant Hellmuth von Mücke, the navigator, relieved Lieutenant Peucer as first officer. It was Mücke who directed the assignment of the relief crew. The young officers liked working with him, and they appreciated his acknowledgment of their efforts. Ensign Albert von Guérard inherited the post of the homeward-bound adjutant. Ensign Fritz Karl Zimmermann arrived ill on the relief ship and remained temporarily unassigned. As signals officer, Ensign Fikentscher took charge of the division composed of specialists, radiomen, signalmen, and artisans.

The *Patricia* stayed in the harbor only long enough to take on coal. The moment of departure drew closer and the farewell to comrades was at hand. Slowly the ocean giant pulled away from the pier with pennants flying from masthead to water. To the strains of Samoan melodies she glided between the warships and out of the harbor. The ship's orchestra played "How Beautiful Is the World When One Is Homeward Bound." The other ships' bands were also caught up in the excitement of the departure. Left and right they started harmonizing with the traditional melody of "Now That I Must Leave Thee, My Fair City." This was accompanied by shouts of farewell and fluttering waves of goodbye.

The following weeks were most strenuous. The new half of the ship's company had to be hastily drilled and coordinated in the various shipboard duties. Old hands had to do double duty so that new arrivals could be integrated as smoothly as possible. There was also a request from the first officer for a revision of duty assignments and watch bills for the technical personnel. All this had to be done in the space of two days. No one could complain about a shortage of work.

After the change of personnel and the flurry of activity accompanying it, an atmosphere of normalcy descended on the *Emden*. Now she had the more enjoyable task of preparing to receive an important warship. On 13 June the English armored cruiser *Minotaur* visited Tsingtao. For the officers there were banquets, balls, and excursions. For the crew, a sports meet stood high on the list of priorities. The recreation officer of the

*Emden* functioned as umpire in many of the events. Attention focused on the soccer game between the German and English teams. At the end of the second half the score stood 2:2. In the twenty-minute overtime the English showed what a well-trained team could do, driving three more goals into the German net. The German sailors had to be satisfied with their awards in gymnastics and high jumping.

During the warship's visit the German and English seamen became so friendly that at the point of farewell there were joking assurances that they would never fight one another. Even in a climate of political tension, who could possibly imagine armed conflict between the German navy and its admirable British counterpart?

On 15 June Ensign Fikentscher, like so many others, counted the days until his return to Germany. Along with Ensign von Guérard, he was to begin his journey home in the mail boat *Bülow*.

During these June weeks the captain of the HAPAG liner *Staatssekretär Krätke*, Julius Lauterbach, took part in a reserve officers' exercise in the *Emden*. He held the rank of lieutenant (j.g.) in the reserve. Ensign Fikentscher knew him to be an extraordinarily efficient and knowledgeable seaman. Lauterbach had sailed over east Asian waters without interruption for five years and knew most of the traders plying these waters. Fikentscher had befriended him while sailing from Shanghai in the *Staatssekretär Krätke* on his way to the *Emden* at Tsingtao. It was a trying time. Fikentscher had a bout with dysentery, and several other officers and men were on board and in the infirmary in Tsingtao with the disease. The attending doctors had recommended the greatest precaution to keep it from spreading, particularly as the *Emden* was scheduled to sail for Shanghai, Hangkow, and then up the Yangtze River. The invalids were anxious to get back on their feet and board the ship, which was scheduled to depart the beginning of July.

Admiral Graf Spee sailed on 20 June with the *Scharnhorst* and *Gneisenau* on a cruise to the South Sea islands of Samoa. He would not return from this voyage until September. The *Emden* was ordered to lay in a supply of coal and provisions for three months and to be prepared for instant departure if necessary. And so her schedule was delayed. Because of the considerably healthier climate in Tsingtao the men were delighted. Shanghai, as all old hands knew, was a hellhole of heat at that time of year.

The off-duty officers spent their time in various ways: on the beaches, hiking, riding horseback in the Prinz Heinrich Mountains. Some visited the casino or held forth in the German Club. No one thought of the dreaded summer trip to Shanghai. But at the time even Tsingtao was hot. The inhabitants complained that for ten years they had not suffered such an unbearable heat. The gunboat *Luchs* radioed the *Emden* from Shanghai with a plea to relieve her.

The otherwise peaceful midsummer mood was shattered with the arrival of a shocking report. On 28 June the heir to the throne of Austria and his wife had been murdered at Sarajevo. According to the report, sharp notes had been exchanged between the Austrian and Serbian governments.

*July 1914*

In far-off Germany Kaiser Wilhelm II canceled the festivities of the Kieler Woche—the week-long celebration of German naval activities which this year included the unprecedented visit of a British battleship squadron under Admiral Warrander. By 6 July, however, the situation seemed to have stabilized, and in his yacht the *Hohenzollern,* accompanied by the greater part of the High Seas Fleet, the kaiser set sail for his yearly summer cruise to Norway.

From the South Seas Graf Spee ordered the *Emden* to remain in Tsingtao. There began a period of watch and wait. The Far East echoed with rumors in the rising humidity and heat.

On 8 July the orders for the *Emden*'s Shanghai deployment were finally canceled. The next day a warning came from the Admiralty in Berlin about a possible outbreak of war between Austria and Serbia. If that happened, it was certain that other powers would join in. On 11 July the Admiralty sent another warning, this time about possible confrontation with Great Britain. The radio room of the *Emden* filled with the intercepted messages of foreign warships.

On the night of the twenty-second and into the twenty-third, a storm of hurricane force hit Tsingtao. The midwatch duty officer observed that in a short time the wind turned 180 degrees, whipping up until ships lay sideways under the pressure. In the deluge all boats had to be tightly secured, and as a precaution the ships dropped their second anchors. High-pressure steam was raised in two of the *Emden*'s boilers. But the tempest blew over as quickly as it had come. The *Emden* had ridden it out. Once more Tsingtao presented the usual picture of peace.

On 24 July the Austrian cruiser *Kaiserin Elizabeth* arrived in Tsingtao. Everyone was aware of the ominous meaning of this arrival. Several officers from the *Emden* knew the Austrian officers from Pola and invited them to mess. The Germans admired the calm with which their Austrian comrades approached mobilization. For an entire week they seemed to do nothing but entertain on board and on shore. Perhaps the situation was exaggerated.

Soon the following news overtook them: Austria-Hungary had presented Serbia with an ultimatum on 25 July but on 26 July they received the reassuring message that Germany regarded the problem as an internal one, concerning only the nations directly involved. Naturally, should Russia take a hand in the affair, Germany would support Austria. Russia was allied with France, which was allied with Great Britain, which was allied with Japan. Still, the crew of the *Emden* hardly believed that war was imminent, even when they received word that the German High Seas Fleet had canceled its Norwegian summer maneuvers and headed back to home ports.

On 27 July the Admiralty Staff in Berlin reported that Austria-Hungary had broken diplomatic relations with Serbia. A declaration of war followed on the twenty-eighth. It would seem that, all things considered, political developments in Europe were serious indeed.

The Admiralty Staff issued an order to the *Emden* on 29 July: "Attempt to rejoin cruiser squadron." The cruiser *Nürnberg*, returning from her mission on the west coast of America, received orders not to head for Tsingtao but to join the squadron at Ponape in the South Seas. Now the Austrian cruiser *Kaiserin Elizabeth* made serious preparations for combat, removing all unnecessary equipment from her spaces. The *Emden* also went on alert, though there had been no mobilization order. The cruiser squadron was still in the South Seas. Thus the senior officer of the east Asian command was the commander of the *Emden,* a man well apprised of the overall situation. Anticipating definitive orders, he reappraised the possibility of the *Emden*'s involvement and took every practical precaution.

In the summer of 1914 the German navy was not prepared to take on the overwhelmingly powerful Great Britain. War with that country had often been discussed theoretically, and contingency plans had been drawn up, but no one believed it would actually happen. Commander von Müller counted many friends in the Royal Navy. Everywhere abroad, German naval officers looked for contact with their British counterparts, whose professional expertise and sociability they so admired.

Since Nelson's victory at Trafalgar in 1805, the situation at sea had been referred to as the Pax Britannica. Owing to its strong industry, its commerce, and its merchant fleet, Great Britain had acquired colonies, waged small colonial wars, and built strategic support points. Soon other nations followed this example— Germany, in particular, from 1871 on. The British business world was not fond of the idea of strong German competition, and all over the globe German diplomatic efforts began to meet with countermeasures. Yet the crews of German warships enjoyed their camaraderie with Royal Navy counterparts. There was hardly a German naval officer who did not admire and emulate the British. By doing so, wasn't he honoring the hopes and declarations of his emperor, the kaiser, grandson of the great Queen Victoria?

Wasn't it the declared intention of the German "Risk Fleet" to deter war with England? No matter how impassioned the criticisms of "perfidious Albion" leveled by armchair admirals and other naval circles, the German navy did not believe a war with England was imminent. Or had it simply pushed such a disturbing thought into the background?

Was the construction of a mighty German flotilla not chiefly undertaken with England in mind, and therefore vigorously pursued? Still, thought the officers, we have the best of relations with our Anglo-Saxon cousins. As recently as June there had been a British squadron visiting Kiel. Hadn't it been the emperor himself who welcomed the British admiral of the fleet? And hadn't he rendezvoused with the High Seas Fleet for its yearly summer cruise to Norway? Under such conditions, how could a serious threat of war with England develop?

And how would such a war be conducted? English colonies, bases, protectorates, and spheres of influence girdled the globe. The Royal Navy was omnipresent. Even in neutral harbors, the influence of the British would make the support and provisioning of German warships impossible. Great Britain had the tightest network of support in the world; in many countries it even included the press. British, French, Russian, and Japanese warships—whole squadrons and flotillas—would be lurking everywhere. Each one of the armored cruisers belonging to these countries was head and shoulders above the *Emden*.

Germany's only east Asian possession was the base of Tsingtao, and it was easily blockaded. Britain's Weihaiwei and Russia's Vladivostok were not far away. At anchor off the coast of Korea and the Japanese islands was a modern Japanese fleet accustomed to victory. In Africa, German power consisted of four isolated colonies without military significance. Of course, in the South Seas the kaiser retained a wide-reaching protectorate of islands, including Samoa, the Marshalls, the Carolines, Ponape, the Marianas (Pagan), the Palaus (Angaur), and German New Guinea. None of these, however, was fortified.

How could Germany possibly conduct a foreign war without any significant military force? The German squadron with its armored cruisers *Scharnhorst* and *Gneisenau* lay somewhere in the South Seas. On all the world's oceans this task force, under Admiral Graf Spee, was the only serious threat to the British navy. The big question was how this squadron could be refueled and provisioned without bases.

What was the German Reich looking for in east Asia? Certainly not more or less than the other European nations that hustled about that region. The latter part of the nineteenth century was the last phase of classic colonialism. When in 1871 the German empire was born at Versailles, the world had already been parceled out. Under Bismarck, however, Germany did manage to secure colonies in Africa, later adding protectorates in the South Seas and the support base in China. While the European powers sought a foothold to explore the potential of markets in east Asia, their activity, in particular the establishment of bases, was looked upon with suspicion by the developing country of Japan. Meanwhile, the United States pursued its Open Door policy.

None of the great powers would allow another to rise to a dominant position in China. They all carried out their trade policies under the protection of warships for which they needed strategic bases. Through a formal treaty signed with China in 1898, Kiaochow was leased to Germany for ninety-nine years, as Hong Kong had been leased to Great Britain. In 1900–1901 the German fleet was actively involved in the suppression of the Boxer Rebellion, and when that subsided German trade with east Asia was off to a good start. North German Loyd, HAPAG, and other German shipping firms ran regular shipping lines to the Far East. Tsingtao was booming. But it remained the only true German support base overseas. Diplomatic blunders led to intensifying animosity on the part of Japan. When England, now allied with that country, declared war on Germany, the outcome was predictable. Tsingtao would not become the German Hong Kong but sadly echo the fate of Port Arthur.

For waging war at sea, fleet bases and material support were decisive factors. To coordinate the activity of dispersed warships and squadrons, however, close communication was essential. In that department, at least, Germany had the advantage.

Great Britain saw no urgency for new-fangled technologies. For communication it relied on an efficient, tightly meshed submarine cable network. From every corner of the world information could be passed at lightning speed to every British base. Germany's few foreign cable connections, on the other hand, could easily be disrupted in the event of war, and the country had therefore been forced to develop another means of communications technology, the radio. The German empire had developed the strongest, most modern radio transmitters in the world. With only small gaps in the Indian Ocean, the eastern Pacific, and America, German radio waves spanned the once-vast reaches of the globe. There were more radio receivers in German merchant ships than in any other commercial ships of the world. Besides that, the receivers operating in the German merchant and military fleets were much more dependable than those in any other navies. For a war at sea this technology was of the greatest significance. Without it, the German navy would not be able to achieve any success. Even in peacetime it made a difference. The German merchant marine had used it extensively while the British navy still relied heavily on telegraphy.

And how did the German navy picture, if at all, a military conflict with this overwhelming sea power, Great Britain?

The skipper of the *Emden* was familiar with the thoughts and opinions of his teacher and mentor, Tirpitz. After all, he had worked next to the Grand Admiral in the Navy Department for three years, and there the navy secretary had often aired his opinions. Some of them differed considerably from those voiced by the emperor and the Navy League in their frequent public statements. Commander von Müller was an attentive listener, and he considered the admiral his spiritual father. No doubt Müller owed the much-desired command of SMS *Emden* to the recommendation of the Grand Admiral.

As Müller knew, Admiral Tirpitz had taken over the preliminary work for the projected German fleet laws in 1897. At the time an outline had already been prepared by an imperial navy commission. The emperor was particularly impressed with the idea of a large and powerful overseas fleet. With it he wanted to call the world's attention to Germany's might. Tirpitz, on the other hand, hoped for the creation of a strong, well-coordinated battle fleet in home waters. In his opinion Germany could not dispatch a cruiser to protect its interests abroad without the move mushrooming into a major conflict, at least in most countries of the world. Even such nations as Argentina, Brazil, and Chile had modern warships at their disposal. Every overseas cruiser had to be backed up by a powerful home fleet if it were to succeed. Germany did not hold a single usable foreign base to meet an emergency. Tirpitz continually had to battle lay propaganda pushing for the creation of a strong overseas cruiser fleet. He was convinced that an out-and-out war using transoceanic cruisers against England and other great powers was technically impossible because of the lack of German bases and the location of the homeland. Certainly the foreign admiralties were aware of the problem. For him, the objective was a battle fleet that would operate between Helgoland and the Thames in the North Sea. This would keep the Baltic free and abort any enemy landing attempts. As chief of the East Asian Cruiser Squadron, Tirpitz had learned from bitter experience how his squadron could be crippled by the mere refusal of British docking facilities or the delivery of British cargo in territories watched over by the Royal Navy.

Leading circles in the German navy latched on to the theories of the French "Young School," which propagated the theory that a navy's function was to provide coastal defense and impose economic blockades with cruisers (*guerre de course*). Under this influence the German Naval High Command developed the concept of an overseas fleet, and it caused Tirpitz no end of work. For a while the theory was taught at the German Naval Academy, prompting Tirpitz, after some time, to intervene. He thought it was inadvisable for the service's highest training school to criticize the development of the fleet as it was laid down in the naval laws. As he told his colleagues, he deplored the inability of the emperor and leading naval officers to see that their desired buildup of an overseas fleet would pave the way for a total collapse of the naval laws.

For Tirpitz fleet construction was a matter not just of money but of strategy as well. He knew that Germany could not allow itself a single error of judgment if it were to have a strong High

Seas Fleet capable of preserving the peace through deterrence. The emperor and a part of the officer corps—especially those with overseas commands, which were highly sought after but less and less numerous—wanted heavy cruisers for missions abroad. Tirpitz, however, built fast, lightly armed cruisers for reconnaissance, not battle.

Initially, overseas cruisers were the older armored ships and those on permanent station assignment. Later, more modern ships were added, but they did not have the optimal endurance, long range (coal-carrying capacity), or armament (at least fifteen-cm guns) for war on the world's oceans. England and France owned many older, powerful, heavily armored cruisers for the protection of their colonies and sea lanes; Germany could not afford to develop such a specific type of craft for its overseas missions.

Tirpitz wanted to avoid sending single light cruisers and battle cruisers overseas, for in a war with England, without land bases, they would be lost. The solution was a compromise. In 1909–10 the newest armored cruisers, the *Scharnhorst* and *Gneisenau,* were sent off to east Asian waters. Their construction had been planned before England introduced the battle cruiser, which rendered all other armored cruisers obsolete overnight. The deployment of the new German cruisers was cautious and stingy, but a change came about in 1909, when the old station ships were pronounced weak, slow, old-fashioned, and unimposing. The building of battle cruisers, crucial to the mission of the domestic fleet, had begun, and a rotating replacement policy for modern cruisers, designed primarily for duty in the confined waters of the North Sea and the Baltic, had been established. The *Emden* was such a ship. If these cruisers were to defend themselves successfully in an overseas war, it would be through the resourcefulness of their commanders. Regarding the light cruiser, there was criticism in and out of navy circles that it was too lightly armed. One had to consider, however, that Germany could lay the keel of only two ships in any category per year. The navy laws originally called for three cruisers, but the third had been canceled by the Imperial Parliament. Thus the German navy suffered constantly from a lack of cruisers. England, on the other hand, because of its transatlantic commitments, had three or four times the number in production. Because of this the Royal Navy was able, during the war, to place the most modern light cruisers in opposition to Germany's ships, which were fewer and of older vintage. Finally, the German light cruiser had to be viewed as a compromise between the type destined for overseas duty and that destined for home waters. Those deployed with the fleet were fast, faster than the British light cruiser of the same age. But the British type was armed with the stronger 15-cm gun; the German, until the beginning of the war, carried only a 10.5-cm gun.

Tirpitz was more than aware of another nagging problem for the German overseas fleet, that of coal, the daily bread of steam-ships. A single cruiser swallowed several railroad carloads every day. Lacking supply installations overseas, the German navy had built up an efficient, secret supply network. This was a network of citizens, naval officers, and confidential agents in ports the world over who knew everything about international trade and maritime traffic—men who had learned in peacetime how to circumvent the omnipresent British influence. True, theirs were emergency measures, but without them the German overseas fleet would have been ingloriously interned in neutral ports dur-ing the first days of war.

A cruiser like the *Emden* had a normal bunker capacity of 790 tons. Filled to capacity, she might carry 1,000 tons, but combat capability and quality of life on board would suffer. At twelve knots, the speed at which she could achieve the longest range at maximum endurance, her coal consumption was two tons per hour, or forty-eight tons per day. At the high speed of twenty-three knots, consumption was no less than 15.7 tons per hour, or 376 tons a day. Thus, at fuel-saving speed the *Emden* had a staying power of about twenty days and could cover a dis-tance of 5,700 nautical miles, while at high speed her endurance was a little over two days, her range only 1,200 miles.

Another restriction was that cruisers could never use up their total coal supply. At all times they had to maintain a reserve in case of emergencies, such as a long maneuver at high speed or even a raid on a collier. Aside from that, a full coal bunker pro-tected vital machinery and steam fittings against the sort of dam-age these ships, without protective armor, so easily received.

How could an independently operating warship, without a support base, secure the necessary amounts of coal for opera-tions that lasted months? By capturing other ships, obviously. And how could a raiding cruiser transfer its booty aboard with-out cranes, piers, loading gear, lighters, and coolies? Transfer on the high seas? It was a task unknown to cruiser crews. The transfer of coal could only be accomplished when ships were in harbor, at anchor, or tied to a buoy in a quiet roadstead with a coal lighter bobbing alongside, supported by many hands. Ow-ing to this problem of self-supply, the endurance, survival, and with that, the success of a cruiser hung in the balance. All means to a solution had to be researched. Raiding, therefore, meant the military task not only of destroying and sinking enemy ships but also of purloining their cargoes. For sheer survival, cruisers with-out bases had to provide themselves with coal and materiel.

All these technical facts pertaining to warship construction greatly influenced Germany's strategic and tactical situation at the outbreak of war with England. Taken by surprise, the few existing German cruisers were ordered to operate independ-ently. Sooner or later they would be located, pursued by the superior British fleet, and in most cases, after a short but fool-hardy battle, sunk, though not without honor.

Commander von Müller, commandant of the *Emden,* an-chored at Tsingtao in the summer of 1914, did not adhere slavishly to the tactical and strategic convictions of his superi-ors. He supported the Tirpitzian concept of fleet strategy, but his view regarding the ad hoc use of cruisers in war differed, for ex-ample, from that of his squadron chief, Admiral Graf Spee. The admiral, whose armored cruisers represented an impressive fighting force, even against the British, thought along the lines of naval combat, not trade war. Not so Müller. He envisioned the native populations of England's colonies rising in revolt against the iron fist that held them down. He, Müller, would support these freedom fighters. The correct Graf Spee had little patience with "militarily dishonorable" actions like raids, the sinking of unarmed merchantmen, and the fomentation of colonial populations by political agitators. He wanted to exercise tight control over his squadron, meet the mighty enemy in battle, and if necessary, go down honorably.

Müller was familiar in part with the beliefs of Graf Spee. He hoped to convince the admiral of the necessity of acting quickly and independently in a cruiser at the beginning of the war. Graf Spee, being a fair man, could not but listen to the sound opinion of his squadron commander. Before his departure to the South Seas, the admiral left the following orders for Müller: "In the event of War Plan C, the *Emden* will be responsible for supplying the entire cruiser squadron with coal; will avoid being bottled up in Tsingtao; and later, will rejoin the cruiser squadron." When Müller asked the admiral's staff officer, Lieutenant Commander von Bötticher, how he planned to bring coal ships out of Tsingtao, he received the curt reply, "That's entirely up to your discretion." Müller emphasized that the only practical plan would be to attack enemy merchantmen, which would draw enemy combat forces away from Tsingtao.

He was not only to provide for his own ship but to arm available fighting forces in the event of political complications in Europe. The scattered gunboats had to be recalled to Tsingtao. Trading ships in east Asian waters had to be radioed and warned. The speedy mail steamers could be converted to auxiliary cruisers, and the slow freighters could serve as colliers and store ships. Certain German freighters that were no longer able to reach Tsingtao would load up with provisions and coal in Japanese and Chinese ports as quickly as possible before heading for secretly designated rendezvous points on the high seas. They would meet up either with the *Emden* or with Admiral Graf Spee's squadron. Not only the *Emden* but the entire squadron, which was without bases, had to be supplied. All other German and allied merchantmen should be apprised of the political situation and directed to a neutral port.

Facts about the temporary anchorage of foreign warships, imminent enemies, were also important. Cable and radio kept everyone in the *Emden* informed of what was going on. The first-line opponent was the Russian squadron consisting of the light cruiser *Zhemtchug* and a string of torpedo boats in Vladivostok. The heavy cruiser *Askold* was presumed to be at Wusung Roadstead, off Shanghai. The French armored cruisers *Montcalm* and *Dupleix* were apparently anchored at Vladivostok. Concerning the disposition of the British Far East Fleet, the following was known: The armored cruisers *Minotaur* and *Hampshire*, escorted by numerous destroyers, lay at Weihaiwei north of Tsingtao; the battleship *Triumph* was south at Hong Kong along with submarines and destroyers; the light cruiser *Yarmouth* was in Shanghai; and another light cruiser, presumably the *Newcastle*, was at Nagasaki. No one in Tsingtao figured on the belligerence of Japan as yet.

By coincidence the German gunboats *Iltis* and *Tiger* of the East Asian Station and the old cruiser *Cormoran* of the Australian Station were in Tsingtao. Unfortunately the *Cormoran* was not battle ready, being in dry dock for an extensive two-year overhaul. The torpedo boat *S 90* had returned from the Gulf of Pechili only a few days before. The gunboat *Luchs* lay at Shanghai, and the *Jaguar* was on the Yangtze heading downstream to Shanghai. She too was on her way to dry dock, in need of extensive repairs after being rammed by a Chinese ship. The *Luchs* received orders to proceed to Tsingtao immediately; the *Jaguar* was to complete her repairs as quickly as possible and join her. The small river gunboats *Otter*, *Vaterland*, and *Tsingtao* would lay up in designated areas in neutral China and dispatch their crews to Tsingtao. Logistical support had to be initiated that would secure the continued supply of coal and provisions to the squadron. As these steps show, the squadron was not caught unawares.

The extensive measures were undertaken smoothly, thanks to the cooperation of port consulates and most merchant captains. Tsingtao, which possessed an efficient radio transmitter, succeeded not only in bringing the gunboats to Tsingtao in time but also in alerting the colliers and sending them out of Japanese or Chinese ports to rendezvous with the squadron.

The commander of the *Emden* had the following message radioed to the cruiser command: "Propose that the *Emden* in War Plan B (France-Russia) head south to infest Saigon and other ports of Indochina with mines, and to cause general confusion on the coast and raise havoc with the French trade."

*30 July 1914*

The *Emden* followed the example of the Austrian cruiser. At 0630 Lieutenant von Mücke gathered all officers and gave the order to prepare for action. The men were ordered to clear the decks and set battle stations for exercises and maneuvers. The crew was brought up to full strength and more coal and provisions were taken on board. Everyone worked hard. Anything on board intended for use in war had long been inventoried. This saved time and made the preliminary work of disposing of splinter and fire hazards much easier. Many of the treasured objects that made life for the crew comfortable in peacetime had to be left behind.

The captain assembled the officers in his cabin, informing them of the situation and issuing secret orders. In the course of the morning he also had a conference with the commanders of the *Tiger, Iltis, Cormoran,* and *S 90.*

During the afternoon off-duty officers were permitted a last liberty on shore. No one spoke of the trip home that so many officers had dreamed about all summer long.

CHAPTER TWO

# THE FIRST CRUISER
# SUCCESS
# IN TSUSHIMA STRAIT

*31 July 1914*

At 1900 the *Emden* cast off from the coaling mole at the Imperial Dockyard. Soldiers from the marine battalion were posted over the stockpile of *Emden* inventory that had been brought ashore. The cruiser steamed seaward, followed by the collier *Elsbeth*. The minefields anticipated off Tsingtao had not been laid yet. At the onset of twilight all lights in the *Emden* and *Elsbeth* were extinguished.

Because of the tension between Austria and Serbia and the possibility of Russian involvement, the commander of the *Emden* decided to push to the north rather than in the direction of Indochina, where he had originally planned to interrupt French trade. He was determined to act differently from the Russian cruisers *Varyag* and *Koreetz*, which in the Russo-Japanese War had remained in the harbor of Tchemulpo until they were blockaded by the Japanese fleet. Müller wanted to inflict as much damage as possible on his opponents at sea. As protection for the fortress of Tsingtao his cruiser would be a disaster; her ten guns of 10.5-cm caliber couldn't do much against an enemy blockade. The fortress had to provide its own protection. Müller wanted to block the five-funneled cruiser *Askold*'s passage to Vladivostok.

The crew began war-alert watches, which meant battle readiness day and night. Any surprise attack, particularly by enemy torpedo boats and other warships, would have to be met immediately. Half the men were at battle stations—on the torpedo decks, on bridges and in strategic lookouts fore and aft, manning the guns and searchlights. Those not on duty slept in their clothes in hammocks strung in designated areas. In an alert, the men could reach their posts immediately.

War-alert watches put a terrible strain on the crew of a warship. Every man had his duty doubled. Under normal conditions, the watch was divided into four reliefs; under war alert, the watch was divided into two. The men, furthermore, did not come away from sleep feeling refreshed. In the tropics a blacked-out ship with closed portholes became unbearably hot. It was hermetically sealed so no ray of light could penetrate. Of course, air-conditioning was only a pipe dream in those days. But the crewmembers of the *Emden* were technically ingenious. By simply disconnecting some of the electrical circuits they could open portholes and air shafts without danger.

Until 2300 the *Emden* escorted the steamer *Elsbeth* in a southerly direction. Then she detached the ship as she headed toward the cruiser squadron.

### 1 August 1914

The *Emden* steered in a more easterly direction, toward Quelpart Island, off the shipping lanes where, if unobserved, she could await further developments. While she maintained a watch-and-wait attitude, tension gripped the ship. What would the next few days bring? After a whole generation of peace, would there actually be war? It didn't appear so. The weather was glorious, in the beautiful sunshine the sea empty and smooth. There was nothing to see far and wide, not even the small fishing boats that normally ventured onto the high seas in such weather.

At about 1500 Lieutenant von Mücke tested the cruiser's transmitters to see if there were any foreign radio signals. They almost burst his ear drums. Something like this had to be reported immediately. He dashed to the bridge and told the captain what had happened.

A few minutes later the *Emden* passed the turbulent, long-lasting wakes of several steamers. One could attribute the pattern, one wide and several small ripples, to a large unit and several torpedo boats. Because the wakes ran southerly the *Emden* held her position to the east, accelerating in order to hasten past the sea lanes from Weihaiwei to Shanghai. Although war had not been declared, foreign ships would report the presence of the *Emden* in these waters. As Müller found out later, the English squadron, steering in a southern direction out of Weihaiwei, had passed this position just ahead of him.

The *Emden*'s guns were ready. In the evening the cruiser was darkened, as she would be every night from now on, and the battle watches were placed in position. During the day the radio picked up nothing in particular from intelligence, but that evening the order came for mobilization of the army and navy.

*2 August 1914*

On this morning, Sunday, a worship service was held. There being no time to change into clean dress uniforms, the men appeared in soiled work clothes, an unusual sight on a German ship that served as a reminder of the danger that lay ahead. The service closed with the famous Dutch hymn of thanksgiving, "We Gather Together," which would be sung from this day on at the close of every church service on board. Then sounded the command, "All hands aft!" The shrill boatswain's whistle piped every man on deck.

It was now 1400 and SMS *Emden* was in the Yellow Sea. The crew listened attentively to the skipper as he read a communication from Tsingtao:

> His Majesty, the emperor, ordered the mobilization of the army and navy on 1 August. As a consequence of Russian

troops crossing the German border, a state of war exists between our nation and Russia and France. What has been expected for years is now a reality. Without formal declaration of war, the enemy armies have invaded Germany. In the words of the German monarch, "Although there were many timely opportunities to appear as the conqueror, the German sword has been sheathed for forty-four years. Germany never thought to conquer through force. It was through peaceful competition, through diligence and labor, through commercial and industrial ability, through intellectual ability and education, through technology and science, through honesty and reliability, that Germany earned an honorable place among the nations of the world. Here she stands, envied by those who cannot equal her. This envy, this recognition of their inadequacy in the fields of civilized achievement, fields in which the German nation succeeded peacefully, prompts them now to unleash the furies of war. By the sword they hope to conquer what they cannot conquer through spiritual and moral means. It is up to us to prove that this healthy, vigorous German nation can survive the test. The war will not be easy. The enemy has been arming for many years. The watchword for us now is live or die. We will honor our ancestors and our fatherland by our worthy conduct; we will persevere should the whole world stand against us.

"It is our intention," Müller added to the communiqué, "to proceed in the direction of Vladivostok. Our mission is to wage war against merchant ships. As far as we can tell, Russian and French naval forces are gathered in the vicinity of Vladivostok. There is a strong possibility that we may encounter them. In this case, I know I can rely on my crew."

Three cheers for the emperor echoed over the Yellow Sea, every man voicing his conviction. Then orders sounded: "Clear for action! All hands to their stations!" Like clockwork all departments reported, one by one, to the first officer. "Guns ready! Torpedoes ready! Engines and auxiliaries ready! Damage control ready! Signal and radio ready! Bridge is all clear!" A quick check of the ship and Mücke could report to the captain that she was battle ready. At a speed of fifteen knots she steamed toward Tsushima Strait.

In the afternoon the commander granted his crew a rest. Over the last few days they had operated on a demanding schedule trying to turn a peacetime ship into a war vessel. Every man had performed his duty willingly. The skipper could be satisfied with his crew, particularly in light of the fact that half of them had been on board for only two months.

At 0100 radio operators informed Commander von Müller that Russian forces had crossed the German border. War had been declared between Germany and Russia. The long, monotonous wait was over. It was now a hunt for ships and battle.

### 3 August 1914

The *Emden* proceeded from her holding position eastward to the sea lane between Vladivostok and Shanghai. Then she continued in a northerly direction and headed for historic Tsushima Strait. On this course the captain intended to hunt for enemy merchant ships that might be traveling between Shanghai, Nagasaki, and Vladivostok.

That evening the radio reported Germany's declaration of war against France. For the commandant this was not unexpected, and he ordered the crew to be prepared for the belligerent stance of English warships. This made the men reflect. Would Great Britain really join the opposition? Would the respected men of the proud Royal Navy? Meanwhile, from Tsingtao news arrived of three Russian merchantmen at anchor in Nagasaki.

The night was moonless, pitch-black. Even at close range little could be seen. Every light in the ship was covered. Painstaking measures were taken to prevent smoke issuing from the funnels. But light glowed in the phosphorescent sea. The wake created from the turbulence of churning propellers, a light green twirling tail, was visible far beyond the ship's stern. Waves breaking high over the bow and flowing over the sides emitted the same iridescent sheen. The ship seemed to have been dipped in a coat of reddish-green gold. Long glowing strips appeared and reappeared, and the lookouts reported submarines close at hand.

Around midnight, when the *Emden* entered the western channel of Tsushima Strait, she sighted other ships for the first time since leaving Tsingtao. To starboard the men discerned numerous lights that could easily be the stern lights of other warships. Commander von Müller suspected the presence of warships because his radioman had overheard additional transmissions. Were they really warships, or were they peaceful fishing vessels? He decided against a surprise attack on harmless boats to avoid a situation of the sort that had faced the Russian Baltic Fleet in 1903. At the Dogger Bank the Russians had rampaged among the British fishing fleet, an action for which they had to answer in a painfully embarrassing inquiry conducted by an international board. The *Emden* made no attempt to follow the harmlessly shining lights.

*4 August 1914*

A strong wind whipped up, and in the gathering storm all visibility was lost. At about 0200 lookouts thought they saw the stern lights of a steamer, but because of heavy weather the commander allowed it to pass. The sea grew increasingly rough. Between 0400 and 0600 heavy cloudbursts chased the *Emden* further south, where she hoped to find clear weather. The ship turned with a swing southward, setting a course toward the east channel of Tsushima Strait.

Shortly after the change of watch at 0400, in the vicinity of famous Tsushima Island, the alarm bells rang. From the dull thuds and vibrations it was obvious to the crew that their ship had accelerated to maximum speed. In the first light of day, between rain squalls, they could see a large vessel without lights, the outline of a warship. The captain took the conn. At about 0600 the skies cleared somewhat, and from the bridge of the *Emden* they recognized, not too far away, a two-funnel steamer. It seemed to come about before vanishing in a cloud of thick black smoke.

The order to clear for action sounded on the *Emden*. "That's the *Askold!*" shouted the men. But it was not a warship. A gust of wind tore away the smoke and rain enveloping the ship and a black merchantman emerged with two yellow funnels. The vessel, which seemed to recognize the *Emden*, ran at high speed in a southerly direction to reach the territorial waters of Tsushima Island. The *Emden* pursued it, first at seventeen knots, then at nineteen, concerned that she would lose the merchantman. During the chase the *Emden* fired two warning shots, then live rounds. The prey continued running. It was not clear whether the cruiser had scored a hit. Both vessels steamed at high speed against wind and waves. Thick smoke clouds from the merchantman obstructed the *Emden*'s view, making binoculars useless. Spray penetrated the conning tower and soaked the men on the bridge.

After the tenth shot the merchant ship slowed down; after the twelfth it stopped and drew to port. As the *Emden* learned later, the ninth or tenth shell was only a few meters short of its target. That had changed the freighter's mind.

Quickly the *Emden* drew close, flying on her foremast the international signal "Stop immediately, do not signal," for the captured prize was radioing an uninterrupted SOS. Into the heavy sea a cutter was lowered from the *Emden* and a boarding party under Lieutenant Lauterbach of twenty armed men, including a boatswain and machinist, pulled rapidly toward the cornered ship. The *Emden* took position on the leeward side of the vessel, now only about 150 meters away. The boarding party clambered onto the steamer. Immediately the radio operator took over the wireless station, the rest of the boarding party all other strategic posts.

Lauterbach examined the ship's papers. As it turned out, the vessel belonged to the Russian volunteer fleet, a new 3,500-ton, Schichau-built passenger and freight steamer, *Rjäsan* by name. She carried about eighty passengers, no freight, and was on her way from Nagasaki to Vladivostok. On the *Rjäsan*'s stern the imperial war flag unfolded and fluttered in the wind, a sign that she now had a new owner. Thus the German navy took its first prize on the high seas. The *Emden*'s war had just begun.

Because of the *Rjäsan*'s female passengers and high speed, the captain decided to bring the ship to Tsingtao. She was ideally suited to be an auxiliary cruiser, heavy enough for weapons and armaments and with a speed, demonstrated during the chase, of seventeen knots. The *Rjäsan* led the way and the *Emden* followed about three hundred meters astern. That distance allowed the German cruiser to observe her booty closely.

As for Lieutenant Lauterbach, he was to prove himself an outstanding boarding officer during captures. After all, in civilian life he had been captain of the east Asiatic mail ship *Staatssekretär Krätke*, a HAPAG steamer. He knew the most minute details about the merchant ships in his home waters. From afar he could recognize the type of ship heaving into view, and he could identify its company and its customary trade routes. Once on board a captured ship, he would immediately request the correct papers, often withheld by a balking captain, then complete the inspection of cargo and other such duties more quickly and thoroughly than any officer in the *Emden*. As an old China hand he spoke excellent English. Of an easygoing nature, he was able to humor and console the captains of captured ships, even of those that were to be sunk. This experienced and well-traveled HAPAG captain added much to the reputation of the Gentleman of War, as the *Emden* was dubbed by her opponents.

After gently and diplomatically freeing himself of the endless questions posed by passengers and a protesting captain, Lieutenant Lauterbach buried himself in the radio log of the *Rjäsan*. Apparently, that very morning the *Rjäsan* had been in contact with the French squadron which, according to the message, had left Vladivostok in a southerly direction. This was most significant for the *Emden*. She might now meet up with two French armored cruisers. What a triumph it would be for those opponents to chase the German ship away from her prize! To avoid such a disaster, two signalmen with powerful binoculars were sent to the foremast crow's nest.

About an hour after boarding, Lauterbach reported that the crew of the *Rjäsan* refused to work, the captain protesting that the *Emden* was in neutral waters and not on the shortest route to Tsingtao. It was not true that the waters were neutral, but it was a fact that to avoid detection by the Japanese, the *Emden* now and then strayed slightly from her route. The hostile captain hoped with this sort of tactic to change the *Emden* captain's mind. "Tell him that his ship is a prize. He and his crew are under German martial law. Protest denied," read Müller's short reply to Lauterbach. It seemed to work; from that time on there were no more complaints.

In the afternoon, at about 1500, the *Emden* had almost reached the southern tip of Tsushima. A small Japanese steamer, apparently a fishing vessel, let the cruiser pass unhindered. During the course of the day the weather also improved, growing warm and calm. The sea lay still under a beautiful sunset. It was exactly the kind of weather a seaman could appreciate.

At about 1700 the lookout on the foremast crow's nest reported electrifying news: to starboard the smoke of at least five ships was visible. Müller ordered an eight-degree turn to port. He wanted to steam away from the smoke clouds, showing the *Emden*'s small side so that her three funnels couldn't be recognized. There was no doubt it was the French squadron—the armored cruisers *Dupleix* and *Montcalm* and several torpedo boats. They steered southward in a wide formation.

On board the *Rjäsan* came the precautionary order to clear for sinking, which called for the lowering of lifeboats. In the most drastic circumstances the opponent would find only the sinking hull of a ship. It was clear that, until her arrival in Tsingtao, the *Rjäsan* would have to face the possibility of that fate.

The crew was at evening mess when a radioman appeared on the bridge. An intercepted message, not even coded, read: "*Dupleix* to *Amazon* [the mail steamer of the Maritime Messenger Service]: German heavy cruisers *Scharnhorst* and *Gneisenau* occupy Tsushima Strait. Return to Kobe immediately." Now it was apparent that the ships on reconnaissance ten to twelve nautical miles away were actually France's East Asiatic Squadron, and that they mistook the *Emden* for an armored cruiser attached to the German squadron. At sighting the five smoke clouds the *Emden*, south of Tsushima Island, had been steering a southwesterly course toward Tsingtao. The French squadron, after passing the west channel of Tsushima Strait, steered a course diverging about five degrees from the *Emden*'s, apparently toward Shanghai or Hong Kong. The officers had a good laugh over the confusion with *Scharnhorst* and *Gneisenau*. No wonder the French squadron hadn't attacked.

As darkness descended the *Emden,* which at first had headed east, turned to the west, circumventing the French in a wide sweep. The cruiser steered between Quelpart Island and Korea toward Tsingtao. For the successful escape of the German cruiser the first award was made: the signalman responsible for sighting the French squadron was promoted for his attention to duty. By dawn Quelpart Island had slipped behind them.

*5 August 1914*

Toward noon the *Emden,* still holding her westerly course, met two large Japanese freighters that dipped their flags in greeting. The ships, belonging to an as-yet neutral country that was crucial to the maintenance of Tsingtao as a base, were allowed to continue unmolested.

Since 1000 a smoke cloud had been visible north of the *Emden*. In the afternoon, at about 1600, a second one came into view on the port side. It quickly shifted to starboard and sailed past the *Emden*'s bow to the north; the possibility of a warship lurking behind the cloud was not unlikely. As a precaution the *Emden*, for the time being, held to a somewhat southerly course. Both smoke clouds disappeared an hour later in the direction of the Gulf of Pechili.

Just as the officers were gathering on the quarterdeck after dinner to enjoy the beautiful evening, the adjutant, Lieutenant von Guérard, burst in from the radio room and announced that England had declared war on Germany. For a moment there was total silence. So England had joined the side of the adversary. It had actually come to that. Slowly the enemy was gathering force. The young German navy would have to measure up to this all-powerful opponent. The unthinkable specter of war had become a reality.

What thoughts occupied Müller's mind now? Was Tsingtao already blockaded by England? Then the *Emden* would surely lose her prize and herself run into danger. Wouldn't it be better to sink the *Rjäsan* right away? The passengers and crew could get by in lifeboats. If the *Emden* were chased off by superior forces, her only loss would be a sinking ship left behind, but with it would go the boarding party of Lieutenant Lauterbach. Yet, the *Rjäsan* with her tremendous speed would be useful as a converted auxiliary cruiser, and that was worth a risk. If the *Emden* got to Tsingtao with her prize, she could leave again, alone, provided the departure were immediate.

Just how many English naval units might intercept the German cruiser en route to the base could only be guessed, for the English deployment plans were, at best, unknown. Because the distance between Tsingtao and the British base of Weihaiwei was so slight, the *Emden* had to anticipate a clash between herself and the ships stationed there.

The most important enemy forces known to Müller to be in the western Pacific in August 1914 were as follows: the Royal Navy battle cruiser *Australia;* the battleship *Triumph;* the armored cruisers *Minotaur* and *Hampshire;* the light cruisers *Yarmouth, Melbourne, Sydney, Encounter, Pioneer, Philomel, Pyramus,* and *Psyche;* the auxiliary cruisers *Empress of Asia, Empress of Russia,* and *Himalaya;* and in addition to some destroyers, the gunboats *Cadmus, Vernon,* and *Clio.* There was also the Japanese armored cruiser *Ibuki,* the light cruiser *Chikuma,* the French armored cruisers *Montcalm* and *Dupleix,* the gunboats *Kersaint* and *Zelée,* and the Russian armored cruiser *Askold* and light cruiser *Zhemtchug.* In the harbors of the Japanese islands lay the battle-tested and evermore threatening armada under the flag of the rising sun. There were many superior enemies to avoid, but their positions were unknown. The German light cruiser *Emden* found herself alone in Chinese waters. One couldn't count on the old gunboats at Tsingtao, and Admiral Graf Spee and his cruiser squadron were far away in the South Seas.

In spite of Britain's declaration of war, Commander von Müller decided under any circumstance to attempt to bring the *Rjäsan* to Tsingtao. Thus, before darkness set in, he sent Lauterbach the following order: "At approach to Tsingtao close up in the wake of the *Emden*. In case we meet the enemy, attempt a breakthrough to the coast. If that does not succeed, beach the ship." Night descended on the sea.

*6 August 1914*

Around 0100 the lights of Tschalientao, one of Tsingtao Bay's foremost islands, came into view. In SMS *Emden* battle stations were ordered and the entire crew took up position. It was raise steam for high speed. From the location of the lights it was determined that the *Emden,* in strong currents, had drifted north, and so the ship proceeded on a southerly course toward Cape Yatao. From there she intended to run to Tsingtao, hugging the coastline.

Two hours later the bright stern light of a ship appeared. It was Japanese, slightly to the south, steering a southeasterly course.

On the command bridge tension mounted. For some time the *Emden* had been monitoring many, if somewhat unintelligible, radio messages. Considering the strength of the reception the sender could not be far off. From these signals one could surmise the presence of British destroyer forces off Tsingtao.

As happens so often at sea when tension is in the air, two incidents occurred that heightened it. First, refracted light from the planet Venus descended and in the last moments grew so bright that many men swore it was a falling comet. Shortly afterward they observed a shower of shooting stars of an unusual green color. To the men these were omens, and could only mean the presence of enemy ships. Many unblinking eyes strained through the dark of night. In the *Rjäsan,* which as ordered took position in the *Emden*'s wake, the boarding party was suspiciously alert. But nothing happened.

As the *Emden* steamed into Cape Yatao at dawn all eyes fastened on the precipitous coastal rocks nearby. In their fissured inlets British destroyers could be lurking. Shortly the alarm sounded. Dark shadows had emerged from the rocks and were slowly approaching. What looked to some of the excited men like torpedo boats turned out, on closer inspection, to be nothing more than harmless junks.

As morning light fought through the mist, the men of the *Emden* sighted a ship heading in a southerly direction. It was the HAPAG steamship *E. F. Leisz,* vigilantly patrolling the harbor entrance. Tsingtao was on war alert. There were no welcoming fires or lights. A minefield had been sown. For all private homes a blackout had been ordered. The city lay in disquieting dark, so different from the dizzying swarm of lights that used to greet cruisers coming in.

South, off the island of Maitao, the *Emden* halted and sent a Morse signal to the coast. She had notified Tsingtao of her approximate arrival time. Almost instantaneously an entrance fire was lit to show safe passage. The *Emden* spied the gunboat *Jaguar,* which had found her way out of Chinese waters to home port. The old gunboat had sailed close to the coast from Shanghai to Tsingtao trailed by an English cruiser, possibly the *Yarmouth,* which was also anchored at Shanghai. Even before the British declared war, the *Jaguar,* an east Asian veteran of the German navy, must have reached Tsingtao.

Meanwhile it became daylight. A steam launch with the commander of the minelaying operation and his pilot arrived alongside. The *Rjäsan,* which had to anchor outside the minefield for the time being, followed her captor a short while later. During their passage into the harbor, the men of the *Emden* could see naval gunners at the ends of the mole and armed soldiers on the dockyard quay.

Around 0300 the cruiser entered the mined dock area with barriers of casks and chains. A few minutes later she docked at the same spot she had vacated on 31 July. Waiting at the pier were Lieutenant Commander Thierichsens, commander of the *Luchs,* and Lieutenant Commander Adalbert Zuckschwert, commander of the old unarmored cruiser *Cormoran.* "How fast does the *Rjäsan* run?" they shouted to the *Emden* before she even docked. As Müller answered, "Comfortably at seventeen knots," both men broke out in grins. From the first they planned to convert the prize into an auxiliary cruiser. Müller, as senior naval officer, sanctioned the conversion.

The *Cormoran* (ex-*Rjäsan*) would leave Tsingtao on 10 August and by 27 August join the cruiser squadron in the South Seas. The *Emden*'s capture of the German navy's first trophy and her heroic escape to Tsingtao had already paid dividends.

# CHAPTER THREE

# ONCE MORE IN TSINGTAO

*6 August 1914*

After tying up, the men of the *Emden* explored Tsingtao. The war alert had scarred her natural beauty. Land that had for generations been painfully forested was now being cut down to provide clear fields of fire for the artillery. The fortress garrison had obviously not been idle. Directly behind the *Emden* lay the imperial post packet *Prinz Eitel Friedrich,* which belonged to North German Lloyd. She had been almost totally converted into an auxiliary cruiser by the gunboats *Iltis, Luchs,* and *Tiger.* Side by side in the back of the dockyard were the old gunboats, stripped of their guns and masts. The *Cormoran* had been set afloat near a floating dry dock, and the Austrian cruiser *Empress Elizabeth* lay on the other side of the harbor, at wharf 2. After the *Emden* had docked, the *Rjäsan* joined her. At pier 1 rested the steamers *Markomannia* and *Frisia,* owned by HAPAG. There was also a freighter belonging to North German Lloyd at pier 2. The German ships were loaded with coal and ready to debark as the supply ships for the cruiser squadron. The huge stockpile of coal in Tsingtao had melted away.

In the *Emden* a rest period was in force until 0800. The crew needed it. The night watch was long, and during the day much had to be done. Around 0800 they began to load coal and take on deck supplies, more than a thousand tons. The normally willing Chinese coolies, exhausted from the previous day's work, decided on the spur of the moment to strike—this in spite of the promise of higher wages. Although the German sailors implored them for help, the coolies accomplished little. Thus more of the *Emden* crew than could be spared ended up loading, to the neglect of other duties. The torpedo personnel had plenty to do just fetching explosives from the depots. The *Emden* had, after all, been outfitted as a peacetime cruiser. With the imminent voyage, a solitary one of unknown duration, her needs had to be met. There couldn't be enough vital equipment on board. The steward had to take on provisions to feed the crew well in the weeks ahead. The various messrooms had to be refurbished with comfortable fittings left behind earlier—a piano, silver chests, and furniture, including lounge chairs.

Gunnery and torpedo officers were saddled with the biggest task. A hundred hammocks were taken on board as protection against splinters. Forty men came from the *Iltis,* the *Cormoran,* and the river gunboat *Vaterland* to supplement the crew on the *Emden,* and they had to be quartered. Living space also had to be found for a lieutenant from Shanghai, the assistant medical officer, who was an army doctor from Saxon Artillery Regiment No. 77, and twenty-five men from other ships who had been ordered to the *Emden.* In short, the atmosphere on board was one of organized chaos. Lieutenant von Mücke hardly knew where to draw people for the numerous details entrusted to him.

Exacerbating the problem was the fact that the coal carriers were exhausted and not very cooperative. Because of the political situation they were afraid of losing money. One day after the declaration of war they had stormed the German Asiatic Bank to withdraw their savings, only to find payment refused. Tempers flared. Fortunately the bank remained closed on Sunday, and by the time the requests were paid out on Monday the situation had eased somewhat.

At this point it was clear that the coolies were migrating. In

east Asia this was the first sign of an imminent crisis. A group of
workers attempted to leave the protectorate, on foot, by sam-
pan, by railroad. The German administration was able to capture
most of the birds of flight. An incident on the railway amused
German sailors. Runaways and their families were allowed to
board the train, but once on it they were separated. The men
had to ride in the last car. The train moved out, and when it
finally stopped again the men got off, not in China but back at
the dockyards of Tsingtao. At the first stop in Syphang the last
coaches had been detached and switched to a track that returned to the departure point. The astonished Chinese were escorted back to work by soldiers.

The comings and goings on the *Emden* were similar to those
in a train station. All the other commanders arrived for briefings
in the morning. A group of officers and officials visited in search
of information about the *Emden*'s last voyage. In Tsingtao a
rumor circulated that the ship had met the Russian cruiser *Askold* in battle and sunk her. According to the report, the German ship had suffered heavy casualties. The chief surgeon at the
government hospital was surprised that the *Emden* had not notified him of her wounded so that he could have beds prepared.
There were many such rumors abroad.

Reservists came from every corner of China and Japan. Some
came by ship; others, from Japan and the provinces of southern
China, arrived in junks. An adventure brought the crews of the
decommissioned river gunboats *Otter* and *Vaterland* from their
stations on the Yangtze to Tsingtao. In Nanking they dressed
in civilian clothing. The Chinese government didn't want to let
the German seamen go, so they requisitioned a railway car and
attached it to a train bound for a Tsingtao. Chinese railroad
officials in Pukow claimed ignorance of the escapade. Perhaps
money had helped them close their eyes. Chinese officials in
Tsinfu hesitated to let the Germans proceed, so the German government itself sent a locomotive to Tsinfu to pull the unofficial
railway car to Tsingtao.

The incoming "Shanghai-ites" and "East Asiatics" were puz-
zled and depressed by the British declaration of war. On their
departure from Shanghai many had been brought to the station

by then-neutral English friends. German and British shook hands in farewell and assured each other that a war between their nations was inconceivable.

Lieutenant Lauterbach, who after docking the *Rjäsan* had sunk exhausted into his bunk, could find little time for rest. First a representative of the judicial administration appeared for the transfer of the prize ship's records. Then the commander of the *Cormoran* and building inspectors from the docks wanted to examine the *Rjäsan* and judge her suitability for conversion to an auxiliary cruiser. Lauterbach resigned himself to sleeplessness and went on board the *Emden* for some breakfast. Next he had to hurry to the government court for a continuation of the hearing on the takeover of the *Rjäsan*. Finally he and the boarding party returned to the *Emden*. The *Rjäsan*'s crew and passengers had been gathered, fed, and housed in a shed on the wharf. They were later free to travel by railway to Vladivostok. The *Cormoran* men drew watch on the *Rjäsan*, which was tied up under the dock cranes. The *Cormoran* appeared alongside and gave the Russian ship a thorough cleaning. She had been carrying an extensive cargo of Japanese garlic. Then the conversion began.

The new auxiliary cruiser *Cormoran* (ex-*Rjäsan*) was manned by Lieutenant Commander Adalbert Zuckschwert and a crew consisting of personnel drawn from other ships. The old *Cormoran*, coming from deployment in Australia, had been in Tsingtao since June for hull repairs. Her eight 10.5-cm guns and searchlights were transferred to her successor, and later her stripped hulk would be sunk.

The afternoon of the sixth harmony threatened to disintegrate. Like all cruisers of the squadron, the *Emden* had Chinese laundrymen, a "chief" and his three employees. The chief, Joseph, had been with the *Emden* for years and spoke German well. That afternoon the laundrymen declared they would not sail with the ship. It was too dangerous a voyage. With diplomatic cajolery Joseph convinced his people to remain. He promised them higher wages, then visited the officers to settle the grievance.

"Well, Joseph, do you want to desert us?" he was asked.

"No, but I have to give my workers more money. Of course I'll stay. After all, I'm an old *Emden* fighter. I was with her at Ponape and Wuhu. I've been everywhere with her. I'm not afraid."

And so the laundrymen remained, and the crew did not have to worry about clean linen. The Chinese word for laundryman being *si-i-di,* Joseph's three workers became known, somewhat unkindly, as Sidi 1, Sidi 2, and Sidi 3. All three would fall in battle on 9 November 1914. Their true names were never known.

For the next few days the HAPAG freighter *Markomannia,* under Captain Faass and First Officer Bahl, was put at the disposal of the *Emden.* The ship, 4,505 Brutto register tons, was built in 1911 in Great Britain and named *Nigaristan.* In 1913 she was bought by HAPAG. She would serve the *Emden* loyally until 12 October 1914, when near the Simeulue islands, off the west coast of Sumatra, she would be scuttled by her crew to avoid a confrontation with the British light cruiser *Yarmouth.*

The Swan of the East, as the *Emden,* because of her graceful lines, was called by German mariners in the Far East, began her voyage into war not knowing what it would bring. The order came to cast off and the entire crew assembled on deck. Slowly, the *Emden* turned her bow toward the harbor entrance. The crew of the *Empress Elizabeth* cheered the departing cruiser with a threefold hurrah; they were joined by the crew of the *Cormoran* from the wharf. The men of the *Emden* replied with their hearty farewells. The governor of Tsingtao, Captain Meyer-Waldeck, who wanted to inspect the *Prinz Eitel Friedrich* before her departure, passed the *Emden* in his motor launch and gave a friendly salute. His officers waved their caps. In the still, clear air the cruiser slid slowly out of the harbor and set her course toward the sea. The ship's band played "Watch on the Rhine" and the men chimed in.

The city glittered in the sunshine. Many a sailor wondered if he would ever see Tsingtao again. There it lay, jewel of the Far East, red-gold in the radiating sunlight, a picture of peace. On the shore the tidy, charming houses were arrayed in long rows, all of them overshadowed by the single hill. In the background ranged the mountains covered in the bright green of new forestation. The church steeple, with its cross at the top, emerged from the rose-colored morning mist. The trim barracks and the government house stood farther to the right, along with the beaches. The picture was framed by the white surf and the sea breaking against the rocky coast like diamonds and pearls cast from the generous hand of Neptune. Provincial charm and German diligence had conjured up this fairyland in the midst of an otherwise inhospitable region.

The *Emden* steered carefully around Yunnuisan toward the outer roadstead. Suddenly, opposite Tsingtao and over the Pearl Mountains, two rainbows appeared. To the men in the *Emden* it was an auspicious sign. Outside the roadstead, where the *Markomannia* and *S 90* were waiting, the *Emden* dropped anchor for a half hour. During that time the commander joined a brief conference in the *Markomannia*. At Cape Yunnuisan the auxiliary cruiser *Prinz Eitel Friedrich* appeared. Then the *Emden* weighed anchor and, along with the *S 90*, the *Prinz Eitel Friedrich,* the *Markommania,* and a small Japanese steamer, was piloted through the minefields. Another short halt was made when the pilot came on board and wished everyone smooth sailing. At that moment the Chinese laundryman Joseph must have escaped to the pilot boat, for he was missed shortly thereafter. In spite of his bravado, he balked at the thought of another voyage. Thus his three employees went their way to war without him.

The squadron, consisting of four vessels, headed out to sea. Soon they scattered to make it difficult for any shadowing opponent. The *Eitel Friedrich* and *Markomannia* went farther south toward Taikungtao and into the open sea. The *Emden* held close to the *S 90,* headed straight north, and left the bay by way of Cape Yatao. In the interest of Tsingtao's defense, they had to discover if enemy forces were on the approach; Japan's position was still unclear.

A clear, starlit night descended. For a short while the *Emden* held to her old course, but at a higher speed; then she took a turn to starboard. Way out, much farther south, she picked up the *Eitel Friedrich* and *Markomannia* again. Once more the *Emden* had left Tsingtao unmolested. It would be the last time. She was sailing into a war continually waged behind enemy lines.

Soon they detached the *S 90*. She would remain on patrol duty before Tsingtao Bay. Later, during the siege of Tsingtao, under the command of Lieutenant Brunner, she would sink the Japanese cruiser *Takachio* with a torpedo. At a speed of twelve knots the small *Emden* squadron steered south by east into the China Sea. The morning of 7 August all alarms sounded, unexpectedly. It turned out to be only a test, one of many to come. The crew had to be kept alert for enemy attacks that were sure to arrive at night.

During the night both the *Markomannia* and the *Eitel* made their first camouflage efforts. The former chose the disguise of a Blue Funnel liner, although she lacked that type's characteristically high funnel. The *Eitel Friedrich*, according to her rank, turned herself into a P & C liner, no less elegant than before. In the *Emden*, everything that wasn't nailed down, that might bob should the cruiser be sunk, was marked with the name *Nagatu Maru*. Nothing, not even lifeboats or preservers, should survive to identify the sunken cruiser. If any of the objects identified as *Nagatu Maru* spilled overboard, they would add to the rumors spread by sensational news headlines that the *Emden* had sunk several Japanese ships.

The *Eitel Friedrich* practiced mounting her camouflage successfully for the first time. Later on she would conduct frequent raids and the enemy would dub her the Thieving Magpie of the German Corsairs. She would be the only armed ship in the whole Graf Spee squadron to survive the war. The *Eitel Friedrich*, after a successful raider war in the Pacific and the South and North Atlantic in which she sank eleven enemy ships, would be interned on 10 March 1915 at Newport News, on the east coast of the United States.

In the morning, around 1000, a smoke cloud at last came into view. While the *Eitel* and *Markomannia* slowly maintained their course, the *Emden* approached the ship at high speed. It was a Japanese steamer. Disappointed, the *Emden* rejoined her squadron. The *Markomannia* was detached with orders to rendezvous again at a southeasterly point after passing Japan's Ryukyu islands. The *Emden* and *Eitel Friedrich* would embark on a hunt for freighters. The two ships crossed the sea lane between Shanghai and Nagasaki with the *Eitel Friedrich* taking a more northerly position. At about 1400 another smoke cloud was spotted and the *Emden* immediately headed for it. Again the vessel turned out to be a Japanese neutral.

As twilight approached, the *Emden* and *Eitel Friedrich*, having been ordered to join their squadron, took up course without delay for the Ryukyus. Soon they received news reports from Europe. For the first time the men heard something about the fighting in Belgium and East Prussia. They delighted in the adventure of the Helgoland excursion boat *Königin Luise*, which dared to sail into the mouth of the Thames to sow her mines. Unfortunately the feisty little ship was lost, but she took the British cruiser *Amphion* with her. It was a triumph. In the Mediterranean the *Goeben* and *Breslau*, blockaded by French and British ships on both ends of the Messina Narrows, had managed to get away. Even the *Emden* was mentioned. She was cruising in the East China Sea, according to European reports, with two prize ships. The *Markomannia* and *Eitel Friedrich*'s attempts at camouflage had apparently worked.

Foreign radio reports also stated that the mail steamer *Empress of Japan*, of the Canadian Pacific Line, was standing off the southern coast of Japan on her way to Hong Kong. She was a large ship and the *Emden*, hoping to capture her, headed for Colnett Strait. There, just short of her goal, at about 0900, she sighted a ship with so many bright lights that it had to be a mail steamer. Stalking her closely in the dark, the *Emden* suddenly turned a blinding white flood of searchlights on her. But luck was not with the Germans: the steamer turned out to be a Japanese ship, and on top of that, a small one. Nothing could be done. The searchlights were extinguished and the ship released.

The *Emden* passed through Colnett Strait, one of the many passages through the Ryukyu islands. Soon she found herself at the edge of the South Seas.

*10 August 1914*

The day of reckoning had arrived. The officers' mess was to be destroyed. Rough hands smashed the upholstered furniture into pieces, then threw them overboard or crammed them into the fires of the galley. Curtains, rugs, and deck chairs followed. A bulkhead separating the mess from two guns on the upper deck and therefore impeding direct passage was torn down. Anything that added to the danger of splinters and was expendable flew over the side, including the officers' wicker chairs. Cold and bare, that was the new look of the once comfortable wardroom. Where sofas had stood bulkheads now showed, dirty and dull. They had to be painted. Midshipman First Class Prince Franz Joseph von Hohenzollern amused himself by drawing caricatures. Then the crew proceeded to paint the bulkheads in monotonous colors. The job ended with the application of a coat of garish green for what was destined to be their social club. After all, they were at war. Since the crew would be living sparsely, an example had to be set for them.

In the evening came unpleasant news of Japan's position. She might enter the war; if British protectorates in China were attacked, Japanese shipping would suffer. The cruiser *Tone* and four destroyers were southward bound from Japan. The *Markomannia* had failed to arrive at her rendezvous point, so the *Emden* attempted to contact her by wireless that evening. But it was in vain. As was discovered a few days later, the *Markomannia*'s radio equipment was not functioning.

*11 August 1914*

Housecleaning continued until there was nothing left to do. Finally the order "Clear the deck" sounded. The *Eitel Friedrich*, looking for a range for target practice, drew back. The *Emden* continued on her way. Soon the *Eitel* disappeared; after her target practice she took after the *Emden* and rejoined her the following day. In the evening they attempted to contact the *Markomannia* once more. The *Emden* received the following message: "I'm at the rendezvous. State your position." Why would the steamer need the *Emden*'s position? The radioman reported that the message sounded as if it had been transmitted over a powerful transmitter. It was in the *Emden* code cypher. Was the brave *Markomannia* already in enemy hands? Was the opponent, in possession of her code books, requesting the *Emden*'s location? They would not swallow that bait. The *Emden* called the squadron, which was now within radio distance. She received the laconic answer, "Don't radio." The radioman determined that this was the station that had asked for their position previously. Could it have been the *Scharnhorst?*

In the *Emden* they consoled themselves about the fate of the *Markomannia.* The next day they discovered that it was indeed the *Scharnhorst* that had radioed the first time, by mistake. Meanwhile, the *Markomannia* couldn't answer because her radio equipment was still out of order.

*12 August 1914*

The *Emden* drew ever nearer the predetermined rendezvous. Around noontime she passed one of the German Mariana islands to the starboard side. Then at 1500 the crew sighted the highest volcano of Pagan. There they were to join the German cruiser squadron. Excitement over the reunion reached its peak. Since the middle of June none of them had seen their comrades. Under what circumstances would they now be seeing them?

Pagan loomed larger and larger out of the ocean. Soon they could see two volcanoes. The northern summit was hidden under a cloud of smoke. By and by, through binoculars, they were able to make out coconut palms and mangrove bushes, distinguishable from the other tropical vegetation. It reminded them of the beautiful voyage they had taken to the South Seas the year before. That trip had been curtailed because of the unrest in China, just as this year's plans had been aborted at the outbreak of war.

The ships awaiting them were not yet visible. They probably lay off the other side of the island. A jutting cliff edge blocked the view. At about 1700 the tender *Titania* rounded the curve of the island, patrolling the bay in which the squadron was now anchored. Proudly she flew her war flag and pennants. The

*Emden* and *Titania* exchanged recognition signals, the commanders personal greetings by semaphore. Then the ships passed each other. The *Emden* swung around a corner of the island guarded by a huge, odd-shaped rock formation and a full view of the bay opened before her. In the descending twilight the men saw their squadron again. For everyone it was an unforgettable sight. How many ships lay here at anchor! The number of auxiliary vessels showed how well organized the logistics of provisioning was.

Far to port was the light cruiser *Nürnberg,* which the *Emden* men had not seen for many months. Only a short time ago she had been relieved by the *Leipzig* in Mexican waters. The *Nürnberg* had two ships alongside from which she was loading coal. Next to her were the *Prinz Waldemar,* a mail carrier of North German Lloyd, the *Holsatia* of HAPAG, and SMS *Gneisenau,* which was just taking on coal from the *Mark.* The mail steamer *York,* of North German Lloyd, had been sent from Japan. Off to the starboard side rode the flagship of Admiral Graf Spee, the *Scharnhorst.*

The *Emden* was shown her designated anchorage still farther to the starboard side, near the strange rock formation. There was little space for maneuvering, and the danger of coral beds this far out left the navigators uncertain. But with their diligent use of a heaving lead fore and aft they were able to maneuver their ship between the rocks and the *Scharnhorst* and against the currents. Finally the *Emden* took up position and her anchor chains rattled out of their hawses.

The crews of the *Scharnhorst* and *Gneisenau* lined up on deck and welcomed them with the traditional three cheers, returned by the men of the *Emden.* The cruiser already had an established reputation as a noteworthy ship, thanks to the capture of the *Rjäsan.* Aside from that, the squadron had picked up information the day before that a heavy sea battle had taken place between the *Askold* and the *Emden,* and that both had been sunk.

A few minutes later the *Eitel Friedrich* anchored near the somewhat distant *Nürnberg.* Another ship at anchor, the good old *Longmoon* of the HAPAG line, was camouflaged as an English Jardine-Matheson steamer with a red funnel. Lieutenant Lauterbach grinned. He recognized one of the ships alongside the *Nürnberg* as his former command, the *Staatssekretär Krätke.* There was another east Asiatic coastal mail steamer, the HAPAG line's *Gouverneur Jäschke.* The only ships missing were the *Markomannia,* expected the next day, and the *Elsbeth,* which had sailed with the *Emden* and was overdue. In all probability, they thought, she was lost. Actually, she'd been scuttled by her crew as the enemy approached.

No sooner had the *Emden* dropped anchor and launched the steam pinnace that was to take Müller and his adjutant to the flagship than, in the approaching darkness, a cutter from the *Gneisenau* came alongside.

"Ahoy, what do you want here?"

"Did you bring us our mail?"

Laughter rang from the *Emden.* "We're no mail steamer."

The men from the *Gneisenau* pulled back in disappointment. Their mail was with the *Elsbeth,* resting on the bottom of the sea.

The squadron received the following order: "War watch in effect with light duty for the crew, but with full war alert for officers." All ships were blacked out.

The radio room picked up many dispatches that evening, apparently from English cruisers. Everything was passed on to the *Gneisenau,* which held the squadron's night radio watch. Soon the *Emden* received an order: "Sharp lookout seaward." Meanwhile, the *Titania* continued her patrol before the bay. Excited lookouts reported threatening shadows, but their information proved to be unfounded. All remained calm under the tropic skies.

But silence did not permeate the *Emden.* The officers relieved from watch sat in the blacked-out wardroom drinking a glass of red wine. They had cause to celebrate. From the flagship they had learned of the promotion of the German Naval Academy's Class of 1911. Now they were ensigns. This was a long-awaited moment for Midshipmen First Class Prince von Hohenzollern and Robin Schall.

By midnight all that could be heard was the tramping of sea boots on watch and the snores of men in their hammocks. Once more they could sleep soundly without concern. The *Emden* was ensconced in a picturesque bay, securely guarded by the squadron.

*13 August 1914*

The bustle of shipboard life started early in the morning. Lieutenant Lauterbach insisted on bringing his old ship, the *Staatssekretär Krätke,* along the port side of the *Emden.* Later the *Gouverneur Jäschke* came along the starboard side. The *Emden* was coaling from both sides, and all the while the crew groaned and suffered. Soon the sun stood high in the firmament. The decks radiated heat. An amount of 450 tons was to be loaded, bringing the total to 950. Although the crew laid on heavily, the work dragged. This being the first time they'd had to load alone, they were unpracticed. In peacetime it was unheard of for a warship overseas to coal on its own. What were there coal loading companies for? Moreover, both the *Emden* and the *Jäschke* had inadequate equipment. The *Jäschke's* winches gave out repeatedly, which cost time. A light breeze turned into a stiff one, and the swells that resulted rolled under the ship on the windward side, causing her to buck unpleasantly. So the work proceeded, tough, slow, and painful.

Almost all hands participated in the transfer of coal. Only the few off-duty officers made it to Lieutenant Lauterbach's old ship to escape the coal dust. There they drank wine, cool beer, and whiskey and soda, relaxing with the officers on board. The wine was from Lauterbach's private cellar. This popular officer had transferred his extensive library, as well as several luxurious deck chairs from the *Staatssekretär Krätke* to the *Emden.* As the chairs were smuggled on board the first officer closed his eyes. His only stipulation was that the furniture not be placed below deck.

Amid halloos the *Markomannia,* under HAPAG Captain Faass, arrived about 0900. Having been designated the *Emden's* escort collier, she came with five thousand tons in her hold. Because of her capacity and speed of fourteen knots she was highly prized.

The few people not occupied with coaling were dispersed by steam pinnace and tugboat in every direction to restock the *Emden*. From the *Scharnhorst* the cruiser received yeast for baking bread; from the *York,* hospital supplies; from the *Eitel Friedrich,* fruit and drink. The *Holsatia* supplied fresh meat, and the *Gneisenau* delivered soda-water capsules.

Later that morning Commander von Müller boarded the squadron flagship *Scharnhorst* for a briefing. Admiral Graf Spee revealed his views on the situation and most effective employment of the cruiser squadron. He pointed out the threatening stance of Japan, declared that ignorance of the cruiser squadron's plans and movements was tying up a great many enemy ships, and spoke of the advantages of maintaining a tight squadron formation. He expressed particular concern about supplies of coal because of the huge amounts consumed by the *Scharnhorst* and *Gneisenau.*

After much consideration Graf Spee decided to take the squadron to the west coast of America. When he asked the attending commanders for their opinion, Müller said that a squadron sailing several months on the open sea would be almost useless— that it would cause the enemy little harm. Furthermore, he was convinced that the fleet-in-being theory was invalid. With an eye on the difficulty of constant coaling and the huge reserves needed by the squadron in east Asian, Australian, and Indian waters, he proposed that a light cruiser be sent to the Indian Ocean where conditions were ripe for a cruiser war and where the presence of German naval forces would favorably influence the mood of the Indian population. The chief of staff and the other commanders sided with Müller on the issue of dispatching at least one light cruiser to the Indian Ocean. Graf Spee, in reply, said that he had considered the idea of having the entire cruiser squadron operate in the Indian Ocean but found it unsuitable because of the coal problem. The suggestion of sending a light cruiser, possibly the *Emden,* to the Indian Ocean would be taken under advisement. In closing, the squadron chief added that he would be leaving Pagan that evening and that all ships should be ready for departure at 1730.

After the briefing he took Müller aside for final instructions. Then he bid him a sincere farewell.

Meanwhile, the work of loading coal on the *Emden* continued in the glaring heat with undiminished fervor. The afternoon brought a near crisis. All the Chinese cooks and laundrymen from the other ships had been told that Germany was at war. It was recommended that they board the *Staatssekretär Krätke* and head back to Tsingtao. The mass exodus that followed disturbed the laundrymen in the *Emden,* who were already suspicious after the disappearance of their chief, Joseph. They, too, wanted to go. Pleading was to no avail; promises of higher wages didn't move them. They were determined to leave. The men of the *Emden* watched the three Chinese pack. Like it or not, they had to let them go; they could not force the workers to stay. But minutes after the departure they returned, unpacked their belongings, and declared, to the delight of the crew, that they wanted to remain on board. They were enthusiastically praised for their loyalty and courage. What had changed their minds? As it turned out, the diplomatic Lieutenant Lauterbach had taken them aside and explained that, as former captain of the *Staatssekretär Krätke,* he knew firsthand that the ship would not be returning to Tsingtao, much less anywhere else in China. The laundrymen preferred the fate of the *Emden* to the uncertainty of a future elsewhere. It was a real stroke of luck for the crew, who hated to think what would have happened in the tropics without clean linen. Strangely enough, Lauterbach was right. The *Staatssekretär Krätke* was later interned in Honolulu. During the course of the cruise the three hard-working Chinese, seeing the *Emden* sink ship after ship, became so brave that they laughed when told of an impending battle. "Maskee, no matter," they would say, convinced of the *Emden*'s invincibility.

The war log of the flagship *Scharnhorst*, brought from Valparaiso to Germany, has the following entry:

> During the night, a message was reconstructed from a garbled telegram from Tsingtao: "Message from Tokyo . . .

Declaration of war . . . Enemy fleet apparently heading for the South Seas." Thus it was impossible to leave the flotilla anchored at Pagan. Under cover of darkness it would leave port, heading east. That same night it would have to contact Guam for further information. Should the news be confirmed, the ships of the squadron would have to disband to avoid unnecessary confrontation with an overwhelming enemy force. Their function thereafter would be to raid the enemy, appearing here and there out of nowhere and disappearing as quickly as they had come. A thrust toward the Indian Ocean would be impossible for the squadron, even if it could get through the enemy cordon, because it could not replenish its coal. Departing for the west coast of America, it could still find neutral ports and confidential agents. The Japanese would be reluctant to follow for fear of upsetting the United States. It would certainly be to the squadron's advantage.

A single light cruiser that needed much less coal and, in any case, replenished itself by raids on enemy steamers could operate much longer in the Indian Ocean against the combined shipping of India, east Asia, and Australia.

In the afternoon Commander von Müller, by way of a *Scharnhorst* cutter, received the following orders:

Pagan, 13 August 1914

# 151

Accompanied by the steamship *Markomannia,* you are to be detached for deployment in the Indian Ocean, there to wage a vigorous cruiser war to the best of your ability.

Enclosed is a copy of telegraphic communications with our southern supply network during the last few weeks. It lists the amount of coal ordered for the future, an amount that will be turned over to you.

Tonight you will remain with the squadron. Tomorrow morning, this order will be set in motion by the signal "Detached."

I intend to sail with the remaining formation to the west coast of America.

Signed,
Graf Spee

By sundown the *Emden,* finished with the transfer of coal, weighed anchor along with the rest of the German flotilla. Then the squadron fell into formation. One column was formed of the *Scharnhorst, Gneisenau, Nürnberg, Emden,* and last in line, the *Titania,* an old escort ship that because of her service with the squadron was now designated military. The second line formed to starboard. It consisted of auxiliary cruisers and merchant ships in the following order: the *Prinz Eitel Friedrich, York, Markomannia, Mark, Prinz Waldemar, Holsatia, Staatssekretär Krätke, Gouverneur Jäschke,* and *Longmoon.*

Though the merchant ships had never traveled in formation before, they seemed to find their places with notable dexterity. Total darkness, however, brought some confusion among them. After all, steaming in formation is something that has to be learned.

*14 August 1914*

The impressive squadron proceeded for ten nautical miles on an easterly course. The merchant ships had to stay in line, and with all the ships observing blackout it was a difficult task, at least for the unpracticed freighters. As morning dawned the convoy showed itself widespread indeed; in fact, the last three merchant vessels were nowhere in sight. Admiral Graf Spee did not consider it a disaster. As long as they maintained radio contact and kept their escort boats, they would find their way. The problem was loss of time. He ordered a small sweep to gather in the stragglers. When they could not be found he had the squadron proceed but kept the second line steaming behind the *Eitel Friedrich,* on the old course. A short time after the three "small ones," the coastal mail steamers, were located. The squadron reassembled in good order and headed in an easterly direction—an entire German flotilla steaming through the South Seas toward the east.

Two

The
Raider
War

# DETACHED FOR A RAIDER WAR

*14 August 1914*

It was natural for the men of the *Emden* to ask themselves where they were going this time. All night they had steered toward the east, so most likely they were headed for Australian waters, the Pacific Ocean, ultimately the west coast of America. Perhaps even farther, around Cape Horn into the Atlantic. A nice long voyage. But then to their complete surprise, around 0700 the flagship signaled the *Emden* and sent a message: "Detached! Wish you every success."

That meant, without question, that they had been dismissed from the squadron forever. They would be waging war on their own. What could be more welcome? Tensely they waited for orders from the commanding officer. But he semaphored a return message to Graf Spee: "Thank you for the confidence placed in me. I wish the cruiser squadron smooth sailing and great success." That message aroused even more curiosity. Next Müller signaled the *Markomannia* to close with the *Emden*. The latter fell away from the squadron and swung in a wide arc to the southwest. The *Markomannia*, with six thousand tons of the best Shantung coal aboard, left the line of ships and joined the cruiser, which had come to a brief halt. A chief signalman was transferred to the *Markomannia* so that constant communication between the two ships could be maintained. Then came the long-awaited orders: "Set course south, later southwest, twelve knots." A look at the charts showed where they were almost certainly heading—the Indian Ocean.

Commander von Müller was sure that he had been assigned this mission because of the speed of his cruiser. At twenty-four knots, the *Emden* was the fastest ship in the squadron. Such confidence would not be misplaced. Müller wanted to wage his war primarily against enemy trade. His area of operation, therefore, had to be near the major shipping lanes. For his first theater he chose the Bay of Bengal. It promised to bring in a huge booty.

The first task was to get there unobserved; English and French battleships and cruisers covered every step of the way. Not only warships but also neutral steamers had to be avoided. A single radio warning could bring a whole flock of enemy cruisers to the *Emden*'s heels.

The greatest problem was that the German cruiser did not have a single support base in the area. Tsingtao was now irrevocably closed to her. Even if she reached the port, she wouldn't be able to leave it again. The *Emden* was in limbo, a ship without a home. She had the *Markomannia* at her disposal, but once that coal reserve was gone the *Emden* would have to depend on the holdings of belligerent vessels to feed her greedy boilers. Moreover, coal would have to be loaded at sea, a task neither simple nor safe.

*15 August 1914*

For the moment the *Emden* held to her course southward. With the Marianas out of the way she turned westward, toward the Palau islands. The American isle of Guam, where the auxiliary cruiser *Cormoran* (ex-*Rjäsan*) was to end her career, remained to the north. The *Emden*'s destination was Angaur Island, where another collier might be found. She would receive further orders. The Yap islands in the west Carolines had a strong new radio station, but since the seventh of August it had been silent. In the *Emden* it was assumed that the islands had been taken over by the British.

During the trip to Angaur everyone on board was hard at work. General quarters was sounded, and there was a call to clear for action, both exercises to condition the crew for future battles. The *Markomannia* played the role of the enemy. They held realistic maneuvers that made direction and range finding more accurate. And in the normal line of duty all measures were taken to maximize the battle readiness of the *Emden*. Wherever necessary, the ship was protected by strategically placed hammocks and thick, artistically woven hawsers and lines.

The boilers were constantly being repaired. Sleeping spaces for the standby watch were built on deck. In the hot tropic climate it was more pleasant sleeping there, and with the men on watch so close to their battle stations, the new setup increased the speed of response to night alarms.

The skipper allowed lighter watches at night because his men endured strenuous duty by day. Of the gun crews, only one person had to be on alert. And only one had to man the searchlights. Others could sleep at their battle stations. This did not apply to those on the lookout and communication stations. Relief there came from the gun crews, who manned these positions more often. Every man stood duty for two consecutive hours instead of the previous four. Another routine applied to the machinists and stokers who, as in peacetime, had their normal three watches. Nor did the torpedo personnel receive much relief from the strain of constant alert. Every watch was continuously occupied with a full work load. At the same time, the standby watch of torpedo personnel was only required to be present in an emergency. Along with the stokers, they were given more rations than the ordinary seamen.

The *Emden* was still receiving radio messages from Tsingtao. One evening the following message arrived: "In a night attack of German U-boats on the Humber, four English dreadnoughts were sunk and several were heavily damaged. German casualties consisted of only a few torpedo boats. According to Japanese navy circles, German successes dominate the war at sea." On board the *Emden* they were jubilant, but the mood was short-lived. They found out later that the story was pure fiction. Apparently an American news report had started the rumor to manipulate the stock market.

More bad news followed. A garbled telegram from Tsingtao suggested that Japan threatened to attack Germany. A declaration of war by Japan would surely amount to the loss of Tsingtao. The thought of losing her, particularly to Japan, was most distressing. But there was a small ray of hope: the United States, seeing her interests in the Far East threatened, might side with Germany.

### 19 August 1914

On the night of the nineteenth the *Emden* reduced speed so that she would be within sight of the Palau islands at daybreak. It was not known whether the collier she expected to meet, if it was even waiting, had anchored off Angaur or another of the Palaus.

As the island group appeared at daybreak, it was apparent that the current had thrown the *Emden* off course to the north. The development wasn't a crisis, though, for the cruiser could steam along the entire archipelago to Angaur, the most southern island, keeping a lookout. The island remained off the starboard side. Not a steamer was to be seen.

Around 1100 the *Emden* reached Angaur, a singularly beautiful island well known to the crew from a trip the year before. From a distance their German flag was recognized. Because Angaur had a radio station and, furthermore, was a phosphate-loading center, there had been no guarantee that the British had not already paid a visit. That worry was now alleviated.

For the loading of phosphates Angaur had two anchorages, one to the north and one to the west. Depending on wind and sea conditions, they offered relatively safe haven. At both sites were two to three strong, trim buoys, about three hundred meters

from shore. The ships could approach that close to land on account of the coral isle, which dropped into the sea at an abrupt
angle.

It was time for the *Emden* to take on coal. Müller chose the
north anchorage, having his ship circle the island one more time
to make sure that all was clear. And it was—so much so that not
a sign was to be seen of the much-awaited collier. The steam
pinnace, after being lowered, helped the *Markomannia* tie up at
one of the stationary buoys. Then the *Emden* swung to the port
side of the *Markomannia*, coming snugly alongside her. Another
coalfest had begun. In the sweltering heat, working until sunset,
the men took on 250 tons, bringing the *Emden*'s supply of vital
nourishment to almost 900 tons.

Not long after anchoring, they were approached by a boat
bringing the director of the island's phosphate company. Angaur
did not have a district magistrate; as director of the company,
the man also filled the position of government representative. It
was in this capacity that he visited the commander, accompanied by the district doctor. They were followed in another
boat by the island's German merchants, some of whom were
well known in the *Emden*. They were greeted most cordially
and, in spite of the choking coal dust, felt right at home. The
government representative hoped that the *Emden* could provide
the island with certain supplies. He was disappointed to learn
that she could not spare any of her precious provisions; at best,
she could trade some of them. The representative offered nothing
more newsworthy than the deplorable fact that an English phosphate steamer carrying seven thousand tons had departed three
days earlier. She had intended to stay longer, but failing to reach
the transmitter in Yap through the Angaur station, she grew suspicious and disappeared the next morning without taking on
her full load.

The problem of the island's reservists had to be considered.
Those living on Angaur begged Commander von Müller to let
them serve in the *Emden* for the duration of the war. He declined their offer for two reasons: German contacts had to

remain on Angaur, and there wasn't a spare inch of room in the ship. The *Emden* had already received forty extra men in Tsingtao. If anything, she needed seasoned navy personnel, mainly stokers. Some were expected that afternoon.

On the previous afternoon, the radio room had listened as the imperial mail steamer *Prinzessin Alice,* a North German Lloyd ship of about ten thousand tons, tried in vain to raise the cruiser squadron. The *Emden* intercepted and ordered the steamer to Angaur, where she was expected to make contact at about 1500. Indeed, around 1400 the lookout in the crow's nest reported a smoke cloud hanging in the northeast, the direction from which the ship they had so long awaited was expected. Soon the signalman reported a black steamer with two yellow smokestacks. Many in the *Emden* remembered the enjoyable weeks they had spent in the trim mail ship en route from Europe to east Asia. At 1500 the *Prinzessin Alice* bobbed up and down about three hundred meters seaward of the *Emden.* Because of the great depth she could not drop anchor, relying instead on her screws to keep her in place.

Earlier, the steam pinnace from the *Emden* had landed Ensign von Guérard, the adjutant, and Dr. Schwabe, the physician, on shore. Guérard wanted to visit the radio station for the latest news and further instructions. The doctor had to restock his hospital linens and whites immediately. At Tsingtao he had been ordered to take on only enough supplies for a two-day period, and since then he had been functioning under trying circumstances, scrounging from every officer around him.

The pinnace was once more lowered, this time to deliver the commander, the adjutant, the purser, and Ensign Prince Franz Joseph von Hohenzollern to the decks of the *Prinzessin Alice.* Müller wanted to obtain any news her captain had and issue him instructions. About the *Alice* he found out the following: At the outbreak of war she had on board seventeen million shillings in gold owned by the British-Indian government. This was to be delivered to Hong Kong. On the way there she was informed about the war and ordered to neutral Manila as fast as her fourteen knots would take her. With luck, she reached the city and accomplished her mission. After taking on coal in Manila, the *Alice* received orders from the German consulate to take on as much water and as many provisions as possible and head out to sea immediately. She was to proceed to the Yap islands, there to join the cruiser squadron. On 18 August she reached her destination only to learn the squadron was not there. On 7 August, totally unexpectedly, an English squadron made up of the cruisers *Minotaur, Hampshire,* and *Yarmouth* had appeared off the Yap islands. The British informed the radio station that in three hours they would destroy it. At the appointed time the station was demolished, but no landing was attempted. Because of the difficulty of navigating the island approaches, the British never came close enough to search the inlets. So much the better for them: they didn't know that in one of the hidden coves lay the small German survey ship *Planet,* and that the greater part of her crew had been put ashore with all the small arms on board to prevent such a landing. After the British had shot the high radio mast to pieces, an act they could comfortably observe from afar, the cruisers steamed off.

After the *Alice* had arrived off the Yap islands, numerous reservists and volunteers let it be known that they wanted to leave the ship and defend the island against future attacks. The commander of the *Planet* had to turn them down; there were neither the weapons nor the provisions for such an undertaking. The volunteers would have to remain on board. The *Alice* remained anchored for three hours, then departed seaward again. Without definite plans she cruised somewhat aimlessly, trying to radio the squadron to no avail. That is what she had been doing when the *Emden* picked up her message and ordered her to Angaur.

As for war news, the *Alice* informed Müller that Japan had actually given Germany an ultimatum. It was to withdraw all of its troops from Tsingtao and clear east Asian waters of all warships by 5 September. Japan had demanded a reply by 23 August. It was a disastrous report, although many had grown accustomed to the prospect of the eventual loss of the German base.

As no one in Germany had the slightest intention of complying with the demands, war against Japan was a certainty. The *Emden* had made the right choice when she decided to put east Asian waters behind her. Against the powerful Japanese fleet a single weak warship could achieve nothing. In any case her mission was to wage commercial war, fighting off enemy forces only if it was unavoidable.

The *Alice* brought U.S. newspapers from Manila. They contained the wildest rumors imaginable. According to one report, in the North Sea a huge naval battle had been fought in which no less than twenty-eight German and sixteen English warships were sunk, among them the British fleet's flagship with Admiral Sir John Jellicoe aboard. No one in the *Emden* believed the fairy tales being published by the American press. But they were concerned; newspapers appeared to be almost totally unreliable sources of information.

As mentioned, due to lack of space Müller could take very few of the many eager reservists and volunteers on board. The only transfers were Lieutenant Klöpper, an old friend; Quartermaster Second Class Meyer, a reservist; and some ten others. The captain of the freighter received orders to stand by the *Emden* for the time being.

Meanwhile the purser, the first officer, the supply officer, and his stewards searched the *Alice* for provisions. They did not find much. The trader had not yet been equipped for war service, and, complicating matters, the civilian shipowners proved uncooperative. They wanted a strict accounting of all supplies that left their ship, a time-consuming procedure. Thus no noteworthy amount of goods was transferred. And because no one could be spared from coaling the *Emden,* the provisions that were acquired were taken on over one side only. Everyone was angry at the penny-pinching bureaucrats from North German Loyd.

Ensign Prince von Hohenzollern had more luck. As manager of the officer's mess, he went on a beer, cigar, and cigarette foray. His comrades on the merchantman supplied him with ample goods, particularly cigarettes, which were already in short supply.

Coaling and provisioning continued until dark. Then it was time for the *Emden*'s departure. The government boat that had brought Dr. Schwabe back to the *Emden* with his new hospital equipment returned to shore. Quickly the cruiser hoisted her small boats and cast off from the *Markomannia*, which simultaneously fell away from the anchor buoy. In the *Alice* a band played until the *Emden* had passed. Once more the cruiser headed for the dark open sea.

*20 August 1914*

The *Emden* tried again to raise the cruiser squadron and inform it of the Japanese ultimatum. Still the squadron was silent. To her surprise, the *Emden* did manage to pick up a call from the old light cruiser *Geier*. She had reported at Angaur before the *Emden*'s arrival and been ordered to meet her there. But the *Geier* had failed to arrive before the departure of the *Emden*, and so the latter set out to meet her, setting course from the *Geier*'s radioed position.

The captain of the *Prinzessin Alice* wired that he was short of coal and could not possibly make a rendezvous planned for the morning. Moreover, his boilers needed to be overhauled. Reluctantly but decisively Müller dismissed the steamer, which then headed for the neutral waters of the Philippines. Later on the navy would voice sharp criticism of the captain of the North German Loyd liner. Unlike most captains in Germany's wartime merchant marine, he placed the interests of his ship's company above those of a solitary German warship.

His attitude was a vestige of the days before Napoleon, before war was a matter of total annihilation. Then the citizen (perhaps less so the farmer on his land) was only an observer, a spectator at a drama enacted by those of superior rank in the world. He had to protect his possessions, to remain at home and guard house, barn, and attic. Aside from that he waited, uninvolved, almost untouched, for the outcome. And if his king lost a battle or even a war, what difference did it make? Politics and war were the king's business. The ordinary man was only a bystander. He was not part of the process of shifting political power. The civilian could and had to stand apart from it.

Even though it was through the so-called short wars of 1864, 1866, and 1870 that the new Prussian-German nation was established, Germany had enjoyed peace since Napoleon's time. Not even by the year 1914 had the feeling that war was the domain of monarchs, nobility, and the military died out. War should last no longer than Christmas, wrote the newspapers.

No wonder, then, that merchants and shipping companies took the war anything but seriously; no wonder they didn't break out in patriotic fervor. The war of the upper echelon was an irritating interruption of overseas trading and shipping. Businessmen had to protect themselves, making sure that damages were slight. Collective liability, total economic destruction—the citizen had never had to face any of that before. No wonder, then, that large shipowners gave their captains directions to enter neutral ports, guard their ship, and hold their ground. "Sell cargo that might spoil. Sit tight until the storm blows over. And for heaven's sake, no volunteer heroism," the shipowners ordered.

Even without explicit orders governing wartime behavior, the steamship companies could rely on their captains. As representatives of the shipper they knew all too well in whose interest they were dealing and on whose side they stood. Patriotism was one thing, avoiding losses to the company was something else. The first was a personal feeling, the latter a professional, contractual obligation. The Hanseatic houses had always considered agreements, contracts, and exchanges as belonging to a sacrosanct realm high above politics. So it had always been with the "navy that made money," as the merchant marine liked to call itself. It was completely different from the tax-guzzling Imperial Navy. The idea of nation, emperor, German might, yes, that was welcome to the merchants during peacetime. German might should ensure peace, for business was crippled during wartime.

Was it therefore really surprising that a few merchant captains did not enthusiastically support the navy? Merchant ships had already been confiscated and requisitioned. Damages always seemed to result, and the blame for them could never be fixed. "The Gray Steamship Company," that is, the navy, should look elsewhere when it conducted a war. Many self-respecting merchant marine officers with worldwide experience, seasoned seamen, captains and navigators, had suffered the slights of arrogant officers of the naval service. Such snobbery sent tempers flaring. Who earned the money for this expensive navy, anyway?

Curiously enough, though, that summer of 1914 a tidal wave of patriotism swept over what were otherwise sober and industrious businessmen. On the whole, and in spite of differences, the Imperial Navy could not complain about lack of cooperation from the merchant marine. Requests for support in building up staging areas overseas had been met at every turn. The devotion of the navy's seafaring colleagues had proved to be enthusiastic. When a captain or a purser had expressed other sentiments, he was usually swayed by the emotions of his crew. But not always, as we have seen in the unusual experience of the *Emden* when she met the *Prinzessin Alice*.

Today the anger of the *Emden* officers over the conduct of the *Alice* is readily understandable, but so is the position of the captain and the paymaster. No one then was aware that a new age had dawned, an age of blockades, of collective requisitioning and embargoes, of universal destruction of economies, and that eventually, along with his nation, the ordinary citizen, merchant, and shipowner would lose everything. Those were developments no one could foresee.

### 21 *August 1914*

At about 1600 two clouds of smoke appeared in the distance. Presently a large steamer and a very small warship came over the horizon. It was the old cruiser *Geier* being escorted by the collier *Bochum*. The latter overshadowed the cruiser, and the men in the *Emden* laughed at the sight of the once-great ship tied to the apron strings of the steamer. They felt themselves equipped with fighting power immeasurably superior to that of the fragile old warship. Though her battery was not impressive, the *Emden*'s high speed of twenty-four knots exceeded that of most merchant ships she might encounter in the Indian Ocean. It also surpassed the speed of some of the larger enemy cruisers and would allow her to outrun them. The *Geier,* with her antiquated guns and torpedoes and her speed of only twelve knots, would undoubtedly fall victim to any enemy warship she encountered. Hunting for enemy ships, the old cruiser would be reduced to standing by and gnashing her teeth while her quarry took off with scornful laughter. In peacetime the command of such small, old, but comfortable ships serving the African and South Seas stations was most desirable; in wartime it was most ungratifying.

As the distance closed between the two German warships, the other ships stopped. A cutter from the *Geier* transported the skipper, Lieutenant Commander Grasshoff, and his adjutant to the *Emden* for a briefing. At the outbreak of war the *Geier* had lain at anchor in Singapore. She was on her way from east Africa to the South Seas to relieve the old cruiser *Condor,* scheduled to go home. At the first rumor of war the *Geier* and the *Bochum* had crept out of the harbor.

There was great joy in the *Geier* at this meeting, but it ended all too soon. Müller filled Grasshoff in on the latest news and passed on the orders issued by the squadron, then the commander and adjutant left. Soon the ships were in motion again. Sailing apart, both crews exchanged hearty wishes for a smooth and happy voyage.

While the *Emden* set course for the Molucca Straits the *Geier,* rolling in the swells, disappeared in the direction of Angaur. Müller was now doubly sad that the *Prinzessin Alice* was out of reach. How easily the *Geier* could have outfitted her as an auxiliary cruiser. True, the merchant liner made only fourteen knots, but that was decidedly more than the speed of the old cruiser, whose machinery and boilers were no longer serviceable. Even the *Prinz Eitel Friedrich* did no more than fifteen knots. Despite her handicap the old *Geier* performed nobly until machinery and boiler failures resulted in her internment in neutral Honolulu. The American navy requisitioned her in April 1917 and converted her for duty, giving her the name *Carl Schurz*. The ship was lost on 21 June 1918 off the Atlantic coast.

*22 August 1914*

The Molucca islands were spotted on the horizon and eventually the *Emden* entered the straits. That evening she passed the equator for the first time since war began. For half the crew it was the first time ever, but there was no baptism, as in peacetime. The old hands remembered sadly how in the year 1913, on a splendid South Seas voyage, they had crossed the line between Angaur and Aitape (New Guinea). What a merry baptism they had had, what fun! No matter; even though they had to forgo the ritual celebration, the honor of having crossed the line now belonged to everyone. Even the first officer, who, despite long service, had never been stationed overseas, exclaimed at mess that he was highly satisfied. "Now my last wish, to cross the line, has been fulfilled, and I can die happy," he said. Everyone pensively nodded their head.

During the night the *Emden* made radio contact with the German steamship *Linden* and, over the Batavia station, ordered a collier to meet her at Langini Harbor (Sumatra).

*23 August 1914*

At 0800 the crew was thrown into great excitement by the report that a smoke cloud had been sighted. They would finally get to capture a freighter. It was about time. The commander ordered the helmsman to stand by, but to the disappointment of all, the ship turned out to be a Japanese steamer of the Manila Austal Line.

Müller found himself in an awkward situation. This was 23 August, the day Japan expected the German answer to its ultimatum. In spite of the threatened position of Tsingtao, Germany would almost certainly not comply with the outrageous demand. The steamer belonged on the bottom of the ocean. But what if Berlin was negotiating to save Tsingtao with delayed replies or counteroffers? The *Emden,* by sinking the steamer, would aggravate the political situation and, possibly, counteract unknown diplomatic maneuvering. Müller could not take that kind of risk. With a heavy heart he let the ship proceed. It made him feel even worse to suspect that the Japanese didn't recognize the *Emden* as a German cruiser. The advantage would have been his.

Just before dark, as the *Emden* passed the Amboina Narrows on the south exit of the Molucca Straits, she sighted the lights of two steamers. Since they were probably Dutch coasters, the *Emden* slid out of their way. Every measure had to be taken to ensure that she entered the Indian Ocean unobserved. She would have to operate there by total surprise.

*24 August 1914*

In brilliant sunshine the *Emden* steered toward the eastern point of the Portuguese island of Timor. During the day preparations were made for taking on coal the following morning. Müller was hoping to find the ship *Tannenfels,* with five thousand tons of good coal on board, waiting for him in Nusa-Besi Strait. The stores in the *Markomannia* were a precious reserve to be tapped as seldom as possible. Five thousand tons was a huge amount, but it wouldn't last forever in the hungry mouths of the boilers. Even though the cruiser steamed with great economy, consumption was enormous.

Their experience at Angaur was destined to be replayed. At daybreak, as the *Emden* steamed toward the strait, all eyes were fastened on the horizon. There was no collier in sight. The *Tannenfels* had been driven out of neutral waters by Dutch warships. Later, on 20 September 1914, she would be discovered by a British destroyer and conducted to Hong Kong. So once more the German cruiser had to rely on the *Markomannia.* That dependable HAPAG steamer anchored around 0800 with the *Emden* alongside her. Another day was to pass in the fatiguing work of coaling. Just short of nightfall 420 tons had been loaded. Once more, the *Emden* had 950 tons of the precious black diamonds on board. The boilers, despite the ship's economical speed, ate up an unbelievable amount of the costly material—four to five railroad cars a day.

To the provisions in the *Emden* belonged a stately herd of six oxen and two pigs; a few sheep sailed the seas in the *Markomannia*. In early afternoon the steam pinnace and a cutter, armed with a machine gun against native attack, were sent ashore to cut fodder for the livestock, a duty for which numerous volunteers, hoping to avoid the rigors of coaling, had clamored. Only a few were lucky. They waded in to shore and gathered forage for the menagerie. They couldn't stray too far from shore, so while their coal-loading comrades worked themselves into a red-hot frenzy, the members of the "fodder expedition" bathed leisurely in the sea. They were fervently envied.

At 1700 Müller discontinued the coaling operations. The *Markomannia* weighed anchor and the *Emden* cast off, heading out of Nusa-Besi Strait on a northerly course alongside Timor. Originally, for reasons of safety, Müller wanted to continue his voyage to the Indian Ocean south of Timor, but because the expected collier failed to show and he hoped to meet another German collier, the *Offenbach,* at Tana Djampeja, he chose the northerly route. During the night they passed a small island off Timor where blazing forest fires lit up the tropic night with eerie flames.

*25 August 1914*

The *Emden* steamed through a tropical paradise, the blue sea scattered with palm-covered volcanic islands. The route through the Sunda islands to the Indian Ocean belonged to that group of the world's beauty spots which have special appeal to romantic yearners. Luxuriant tropical forests covered the hillocks, and smoke billowed from volcanoes into the clear blue sky. In the midst of such natural splendor the men of the *Emden* bemoaned the fact that, had it not been for the war, their ship would have stopped sooner or later in this area. A trip to the Dutch East Indies had indeed been planned.

Everywhere there were islands, many of them inhabited. How easily the cruiser could be spotted and recognized. How easily messages could find their way to the British. But dangerous passages could not be avoided, and during them an atmosphere of ready alert pervaded the ship.

In the evening the *Emden* intercepted strong radio signals being transmitted between Dutch warships. The Siamese station, Singora, blared in English for all the world to hear that Liège and Namur had been captured. This met with great jubilation in the *Emden*.

At night the lonely ship passed the Tiger islands, on the way picking up the Japanese declaration of war on Dutch radio. There were now four world powers and some of the Balkan states at war with Germany and Austria-Hungary. By radio the men learned additional details: the French government had relocated its seat in Bordeaux, and near Tannenberg a bloody battle was in progress. So German soldiers were fighting the enemy on all fronts. Everyone in the *Emden* hoped to see action again, soon. Until now they had not seen one puff of smoke. It seemed as if ships were fleeing from the German cruiser whose legendary capture of the *Rjäsan* had long circled the globe. No one knew the whereabouts of the *Emden*.

### 27 August 1914

At daybreak the island of Tana Djampeja came into view. The radiomen were receiving such strong signals that the signal officer reported to Müller the presence of a warship in the immediate vicinity. Presumably it was a Dutch ship. The *Emden* approached the island from the south. To the northeast lay a small island which, along with Tana Djampeja, formed a narrow crossing channel. The cruiser managed to navigate it. She turned slowly to port and passed the northern exit in order to round the northeast corner of the island and enter a bay opening to the north. There they were to meet the collier *Offenbach*. Presently, over a spit of land, the *Emden* spotted a warship steaming toward her. At first glance the ship was only partially visible and her nationality unknown. "Clear for action!" sounded the alarm. "Hoist the top flags!" Müller commanded. They were expecting a Dutchman, but they had to be ready for anything. The radiomen could be mistaken.

The approaching ship flew ensigns on her topmast, the signal of all warships in battle. If this was an enemy ship the situation was serious indeed. It was impossible to get out of her way. At first sighting the distance between the two ships, at most, was three thousand meters. The men of the *Emden* waited for orders to open fire. At the last moment those on the bridge recognized the war flag on the other ship. It was Dutch. The sailors remained at their gun positions.

The *Emden* turned further to port, while the Dutchman, the coast defense ship *Tromp,* held steady course and drew close to the bow of the *Emden.* Then she turned starboard and followed the *Emden* into the north bay of Tana Djampeja. There the German cruiser saw a collier which she took to be the *Offenbach,* but on the approach the crew realized with disappointment that it was the Dutch steamer *Batavia,* the collier for the *Tromp.* This was the first time the *Emden*'s awaited collier had failed to arrive. The situation could become precarious.

Both warships watched each other suspiciously as they anchored in the bay. Soon they were joined by the *Markomannia.* The *Tromp* sent an officer on a courtesy call to the *Emden.* Müller informed him that he would return the complimentary call. Quickly, and out of view of the *Tromp,* the *Emden*'s sailors ceremoniously readied the steam pinnace. They took meticulous care with the appearance of the courtesy boat. No one wanted to bring disgrace to his ship. The crew even appeared in dress uniform. Müller crossed over to the Dutch ship in his spruce pinnace. There he was told by her commander that, it appearing as if the *Emden* had selected the bay for a coaling operation, he had sent the *Offenbach* away, having her escorted to the neutral three-mile limit. While he and his officers were sympathetic to the plight of the Germans, they nevertheless had strict orders to observe neutrality. The Netherlands would allow ships of warring nations a twenty-four-hour coaling operation in Dutch waters once every three months. A friendly invitation extended to the officers of the *Emden,* who were asked to join their Dutch counterparts in a glass of beer, was politely declined by Müller.

In the *Emden* the first reaction to the step taken by the Dutchman was rage. Their ship had lost her coaling opportunity. At the moment they needed coal more than sympathy, and the wonderfully calm Tana Djampeja Bay was ideal for loading the precious fuel. But then one had to understand the Dutch position. What was the small nation of Holland to do? Hadn't Japan with its superior fleet been casting a covetous eye on Dutch possessions? Naturally, Holland had to avoid what would appear to the enemy to be the slightest gesture of good will toward Germany; it must avoid open disregard of neutrality regulations. Above all, it must avoid any situation that might tempt others to snatch the rich Dutch Indies. So now Müller had to reconsider his plans. There might be an opportunity to coal in Dutch waters secretly. Then the *Emden* could still perform the one coaling per three-month period allowed by the Dutch government.

The *Emden* and the *Markomannia* weighed anchor promptly and the *Tromp* followed. As the warships passed each other, a friendly exchange of salutes took place. The German ships steered to the northwest, a false course to mislead the Dutch ship just in case it wanted to reveal their position to the enemy. The *Emden* ran so fast that the *Markomannia,* in spite of her fourteen knots, could hardly keep up. Observing the rules of neutrality, the *Tromp* followed them just beyond the three-mile limit and then turned sharply away to starboard. As soon as she was out of sight the small German convoy changed to a southwesterly course.

In the evening an uncoded Dutch message was intercepted. It mentioned the presence off Batavia of a white torpedo-boat destroyer with four funnels, very possibly British. Fortunately the nights were bright with moonlight so that no destroyer could creep up on the *Emden* and attack.

*28 August 1914*

They faced danger on the night of the twenty-eighth. The *Emden* had to push through the southwesterly string of Sunda islands to the Indian Ocean. The passages might well be blockaded by an enemy who had learned something of the cruiser's approach. Müller selected Lombok Strait for his breakthrough. The transit was scheduled to take place after nightfall.

Müller was uncomfortable at the thought that the *Emden* could be recognized from far away and that she had been seen by a lot of sailing ships. English cruisers had two or four funnels, not the *Emden*'s three. The first officer, Mücke, remembered the idea Ensign Fikentscher had had in the China Sea. It wouldn't hurt if the *Emden* camouflaged herself before passing through a narrow strait on a clear night. Without loss of time runners were brought in, strips of sailcloth about two meters in width that covered the linoleum deck during coaling. Sailors used them now to improvise a smokestack before the foremost funnel. Now if an enemy destroyer spotted the *Emden* she would be mistaken for a British or Japanese cruiser. The fourth funnel was hoisted into place not a moment too soon. In the failing light of late day the lookout spotted a number of small fishing boats crisscrossing the entrance of the strait. They undoubtedly saw the *Emden*.

At some distance from the entrance to the strait the *Emden* halted until total darkness fell. Then, with the crew at battle stations, she steered through the strait at fourteen knots so that the *Markomannia* could easily follow. The steamer stayed close on the heels of the cruiser, doing an impressive job of navigating in formation. In case they met the enemy the collier would, according to orders, fall off the *Emden*'s course at a right angle and then try to break through to a rendezvous on the high seas.

During the passage, at about 2200, they noticed a steamer on the starboard quarter that had most likely come from Batavia. Shortly thereafter a large sailing ship passed on the port side. But nothing suspicious or hostile was to be seen. At 0015 Lombok Strait lay astern of the *Emden*. The first destination of the voyage had been reached, the Indian Ocean. Shouts of joy rebounded through the ship. The fox had broken into the chicken yard. Tension built up over the last few hours, over the last few days, fell away. Now their raider war would start, a war for which destiny and the squadron chief singled them out. The trim, friendly Swan of the East would soon be a feared but respected Flying Dutchman.

# CHAPTER TWO

# THE FIRST PRIZE IN THE INDIAN OCEAN

*29 August 1914*

Now that the *Emden* stood in the broad Indian Ocean Müller had much to think about. The ramifications of international law as it applied to the type of war he planned to wage had to be carefully considered. The central document formulating this law was the Declaration of Paris signed in 1856. In course of time it had been accepted by all maritime powers except Spain, the United States, and Mexico. The first sentence of the declaration abolished privateering, that is, the practice of taking prizes by private ships. The second and third covered the treatment of enemy goods under a neutral flag and neutral goods under an enemy flag.

Of importance to cruiser warfare, the Second Hague Conference of 1907 had offered solutions to many problems, reaching agreement in the following areas, among others: the start of hostilities and the handling of enemy merchant ships at the outbreak of these hostilities, land bombardment by naval forces in wartime, and the application of the Geneva Agreement to warfare at sea. But issues such as the conversion of a merchant ship into a warship, the restriction of raider rights in sea warfare, and the rights and duties of neutrals in the event of naval war still needed addressing.

The agreement reached at the Second Hague Conference, an agreement signed but not ratified, called for the creation of an international prize court as the highest court of appeals in matters pertaining to plunder. This resulted in the convening of the London Maritime Rights Conference of 1908–9, designed to establish a court whose decisions would codify the generally accepted rules of international law. The outcome was the ratification of the Declaration of Maritime War Rights (1909), which adhered to generally recognized international laws. While England, which had issued the invitation in the first place, could not decide on ratification owing to strong opposition in Parliament coming from trade and shipping interests, Germany, in 1909, had accepted the final decisions of both the Hague and London conferences on prize arrangements. It issued an imperial decree to all commanders at sea, thus establishing the basis for German cruiser warfare.

The London declaration encompassed the following areas: blockade in wartime; contraband of war (absolute and relative); conduct violating the laws of neutrality; destruction of neutral prizes; misuse of flags; enemy property; convoy resistance to boarding and search; and restitution and compensation. For the practical execution of trade war by overseas cruisers, the following was of particular importance:

1. The legality of taking enemy or neutral prizes was decided by the prize court, which had to consider whether an action constituted seizure or voluntary cooperation, with or without compensation, and in case of destruction, what restitution should be made. The commander could only capture a prize; but, because under certain circumstances he was forced to destroy it, the court had to anticipate such action and judge each case individually.

2. The destruction of enemy booty was permitted if a commander decided that bringing it into port was "impractical and unsafe." The same rule applied to a neutral ship whose illegal support of an enemy proved it unconditionally guilty. The de-

struction of a ship engaged in contraband trade, blockade running, or other nonneutral activities was legal if bringing it in exposed the cruiser to danger or jeopardized the success of its operation.

3. A commander was entitled to use a captured enemy ship as a merchantman. The conversion of such a ship into a warship was bound by the regulations and agreements on warship conversion reached in 1907.

4. A captain could commandeer the cargo and supplies of hostile ships for his own needs, provided it was proven unconditionally that the goods were not the property of a neutral country. Commandeering the goods of a neutral ship was permissible only with the consent of the neutral ship's captain or if the goods seized were contraband. The foregoing regulations were most important to the captains of Germany's overseas cruisers. These men lacked support bases. They lacked the opportunity to bring prizes to their own or allied ports. They were thoroughly apprised of the laws concerning the destruction of a captured ship, which could be an important source of supplies, including precious coal. These provisions could subsequently be supplemented by international agreement.

The orders to overseas ships in war emphasized that while the commander had the right to inflict as much damage as he wanted on enemy shipping, he was duty-bound to inflict the least possible on neutral shipping. Neutral ships as a rule were only to be pursued and destroyed if they broke their pledge of neutrality or transported absolute or relative contraband, such as food and provisions destined for fighting forces or government offices. This applied to any fuels, lubricants, or equipment that might be used in war.

The *Emden* steamed sixty to seventy nautical miles off the coast of Sumatra. Nothing unusual had happened for days. Most of the time the crew was on work detail. The ship's hull demanded much more attention in the tropics than in temperate zones. Upkeep was difficult, the time and energy expended enormous. Though everything was done to keep the *Emden* neat and trim, she slowly deteriorated from the wear and tear of repeated coaling operations. The transfer of coal from deck to bunker was continual, and coal dust coated everything. The act of trimming attracted dirt like a magnet. During peacetime the wooden decks were blossom-white, the pride of every sailor and officer. Now, even after scrubbing, they were never lighter than an ashen gray. The oil paint on the superstructure turned a shabby rust color, and paint for touchups ran out. In many places on the quarterdeck, cabin decks, and crew deck, linoleum broke. Railings that had once shone like bronze swords were, for the most part, bent, dirty, and rusty. About the hull of the ship, the less said the better. It was an indescribable patchwork of cheerless hues, giving way below the waterline to a thick, stubborn crust of barnacles and other marine life. In short, the trim elegant *Emden* of the Far East had entered the Indian Ocean a battered, seedy-looking fighter.

The first officer was still not pleased with the fourth "funnel." Seen in silhouette, it was most convincing, but the view head on left much to be desired. Only a few millimeters thick, it lacked the fuller dimension of its stepbrothers. Mücke suggested to the skipper that they build a better one, and soon an elegant smokestack had been constructed from laths and sailcloth. Once it was in place, an untrained eye could easily mistake the *Emden* for the British cruiser *Yarmouth*. The funnel was oval in shape, that being the design of the *Yarmouth*'s. The *Markomannia* was ordered to come alongside the *Emden* and, according to her semaphored instructions, assist with the alignment of the fourth funnel. Now all they had to do was rig it so that, night or day, it could be hoisted quickly and efficiently. Off Penang the improvised camouflage—something still unknown in naval warfare—would prove itself an outstanding success. The men thought it was a superb device. With a boiler installed it would puff away like a real funnel. The chief engineer joked about setting a "smoking watch" under it; the stokers would light up cigarettes and contribute to the billows pouring from their funnel.

The cigarettes! It looked as if the supply would run out. Even cigar smokers had to conserve. The number of matches was dwindling. For that matter, almost everything in the canteen was in short supply. A goodly amount of sparkling water bottled in the ship was still on hand, but fresh food had run out and the cook was reduced to serving canned goods. For a while the crew reveled in delicacies that were formerly served only on special occasions; no one objected to pâté de foie gras. But the supply did not last long. Next came an endless assembly line of corned beef. At every meal it appeared in different guise. Most troubling, however, was the shortage of soap. It was used as sparingly as possible: soapsuds were used to wash the crew, then the laundry, and finally the ship. The Chinese laundrymen, held to a tiny ration, turned out uniforms in an unsightly gray color, like that of the wooden decks.

### 30 August 1914

It was Sunday, south of Java. The commander held muster, and afterward there were church services. In the evening, radio traffic between warships was heavy. The vessel that transmitted the most and passed on orders for others to follow signed itself *QMD*. Was it the British armored cruiser *Hampshire*? War bulletins from the Dutch coastal station and the Siamese station at Singora could be heard almost nightly. Some of the news from neutral Siam was cause for joy. Due to rapid German advances the French government had to relocate to Bordeaux. The army was making progress. When would the men of the *Emden* get the chance to do something useful themselves?

### 3 September 1914

In the evening twilight two small islands appeared to starboard, and shortly thereafter the southern tip of the large one, Simeulue, rose ahead. Under the protection of these islands the *Emden* would take on coal the following day. Müller hoped to meet the German supply ship *Ulm* in Langini Harbor.

Simeulue was shaped like a kidney bean. The concave part faced east, in the direction of Sumatra. In the middle of the curve was a bay with a narrow entrance. In the bay itself there was a small island, a forward breakwater. It had to be passed either to the north or to the south. Behind it stretched a chain of even smaller pieces of land; navigating them was like driving down a sinuous road. The islands, aside from lending protection from curious eyes, prevented swells from reaching the middle of the bay. There the water was smooth as a duck pond. This well-sheltered inlet, called Langini Harbor, was ideal for taking on coal. It was chosen by Müller for exactly that purpose.

As the southerly islands lay at an oblique angle in relation to Simeulue, the *Emden* turned starboard and pushed between them to the east. During the night she cruised back and forth off the eastern shore of Simeulue under light steam, waiting for daylight to enter Langini Harbor. Portside, between the islands and the southern tip of Simeulue, the crew could make out several lights coming from the main port of the island, not to be confused with Langini Harbor.

What continued to puzzle the crew was the loud radio traffic from the so-called *QMD*. The ship had to be in the immediate vicinity. Later they learned that that evening was the second time the *Emden* had escaped enemy forces by a hair's breadth. The first had been in the Yellow Sea when the *Emden* churned in the wake of the French squadron. The second had been when the *QMD* apparently searched Langini Harbor as the *Emden* was navigating the islands. What unbelievable luck that the British ship had been twenty-four hours too early.

The commander of the *QMD* had orders to search the waters of the Dutch East Indies for German warships and freighters. He interpreted his orders literally, and would remain on the heels of the *Emden* for over thirty thousand nautical miles. The German cruiser would all too often be plagued by the *QMD* commander's good tracking instincts. But the British ship would never capture the *Emden*. It wasn't until much later that she would be snatched away, and by a vessel that just happened to be passing by.

### 4 September 1914

When daylight came the *Emden* ran into Langini Harbor from the north. It was allotted to very few seamen to see such a breathtaking sight. The shore was hemmed thickly with mangrove bushes. Behind them, slender coconut palms stretched to the sky. To their rear came the jungle, a wall of giant old trees matted with climbing vines in bloom. But natural splendor did not make up for the climate. It was humid and oppressively hot, real malaria weather. The staff doctor wanted to give everyone quinine pills. Even early in the morning the heat was enervating. How would it be later, during the coaling?

The two ships steered cautiously into the bay, the *Markomannia* holding a precise course in the cruiser's wake. To their great disappointment the steamship *Ulm,* carrying coal and provisions, was nowhere in sight. When they reached the harbor the cruiser dropped a buoy for the *Markomannia* indicating the position where she was to anchor. In the absence of the *Ulm,* the *Markomannia* again had to offer her supply of coal. The *Emden* maneuvered into place and lay alongside her. Clearing the buoy, the crew lowered the steam pinnace. Later, during coaling, the men in the pinnace would have the pleasant duty of retrieving coal baskets that had fallen overboard.

The hard work began at 0900. The lookout in the foremast crow's nest was strengthened. From sea level the trees ringing the harbor made it almost impossible to detect a ship's masts. The *Emden*'s coal reserve had dwindled considerably. It was to be replenished to a weight of one thousand tons. Originally the skipper had intended to coal without pause, but in the debilitating climate productivity declined and the job had to be continued the next day.

In the immediate vicinity was a village of native huts perched on poles. On the shore below them a whole row of fish nets hung unused. The natives, awed by the impressive ships, were sequestered in their huts. In early afternoon, however, three of them gathered their courage and rowed out in canoes. They brought oysters and coconuts to sell. For reasons of health the ship's doctor forbade the purchase of oysters, much to the consternation of the crew. But cigars and empty bottles were exchanged for coconuts, which the crew cracked open with hatchets. They greedily sucked up the milk. The meat, being unripe, was thrown overboard.

At 2300 the coaling was interrupted. A total of 450 tons had been taken on, all delivered in baskets. The workers, men and officers alike, were in great need of rest. That night, there being no fear of enemy attack, watch duties would be lighter and everyone who could be spared would be sent to sleep.

Many could no longer sleep in their quarters. They were too far removed for instant response to night alarm and, moreover, it was uncomfortably hot in the tightly sealed ship. The officers, for the most part, slept on deck or in the wardroom, in hammocks or on mattresses. That is how Ensign Schall slept in the wardroom that night, on a mattress. He woke up the next day surrounded by laughing faces. During the night the ship's mascot, a cat rescued from drowning in Tsingtao, had given birth to five kittens between Schall's legs. According to German laws of citizenship, the war kittens were now members of the mess. Where there had once been a sofa the men built a wooden crate for their bed. From that day on, thanks to careful rearing by both officers and men, the kittens thrived. After a short time they found their sea legs and staggered about on exploratory trips. Anyone entering the wardroom did so with greatest caution, as the animals managed to be underfoot most of the time. This was especially so at night. The wardroom was placed off limits at that time so the men would not be delayed by kittens in their rush to nightly drills. When the kittens grew larger the problem was more than their being underfoot. Their favorite pastime turned out to be climbing desks, upsetting pictures, and scattering the contents of the first officer's wastebasket.

### 5 September 1914

At 0600 the dreaded coal operation started again. Full advantage of the relatively cool morning hours had to be taken before the mounting heat that came with the day slowed everything down again. Müller hoped to finish the task unobserved so as not to forfeit his official allowance of coaling once every three months. Therefore his annoyance was not small when, at about 0800, the crow's nest announced that a white steamer flying the Dutch flag was steering into the northern entrance. A short time later the trim ship reached Langini Harbor and anchored along-

side the German cruiser. A rowboat brought a government representative from the main port of Simeulue aboard. When Müller
tried to explain that he had arrived at 0900 the day before, the
representative replied, laughingly, that the *Emden* had in fact
been there since 0700. The allotted time of twenty-four hours
had been more than used up. He requested that the *Emden* and
her collier depart as soon as possible. Thus informed, Müller
sent for the duty engineer and asked him in the Dutchman's
presence when the ship could get up steam. Chief Engineer Ellerbroek immediately read the situation. His boilers were ready,
but he answered that it would take at least two hours for the
*Emden* to get under way. So departure time was set for 1100.
Having done his official duty, the Dutchman showed a more
human side and, over a glass of whiskey in the officer's mess,
proved himself an easygoing character.

By 1100 the *Emden,* with the necessary amount of coal on
board, cast off from the *Markomannia,* which then weighed anchor. Out on the open sea the German cruiser embarked on a
false course, southeast in direction, with the Dutchman close
afoot. After the German ships had disappeared into a rain squall
out of sight of land, they swung in a wide arc to port and struck
a northwesterly course leading deeper into the Indian Ocean.

*9 September 1914*

Just before reaching the freighter route between Colombo
and Calcutta, at about 2300, they saw a white light to the north,
four degrees to starboard. Finally! The *Emden* pressed toward it
at high speed, ordering the *Markomannia* to follow at fourteen
knots. General quarters sounded. The alarms blared. Such precaution was necessary. Behind the stern light they were chasing
could be a warship, and for her survival the *Emden* had to get in
the first shot. Tension heightened. The night was dark. It was
some time before the ship began to take shape through their
binoculars. What they finally saw was a merchantman with one
funnel.

With steam up, the crew of the *Emden* discovered with mis-
giving that their "smokeless" Hungshan coal issued a veritable
rain of sparks from the funnels, spoiling their chance of remain-

ing undetected until the last minute. The freighter, however, didn't seem to notice what was coming up aft. The *Emden* fired two warning shots to remind the ship that, even here in the Indian Ocean, a war was on. Then the cruiser blinked a message in Morse: "Stop your engines. Don't use your wireless." For the first time in the Indian Ocean Lieutenant Lauterbach and his boarding party, armed with rifles and pistols, pulled alongside another ship. A radioman, a signaler, and a clerk were all part of the group. Tensely the officers of the *Emden* waited for Lauterbach's signal from the boarded ship.

The minutes passed slowly. Finally the message arrived: "Greek steamer *Pontoporos*." Bad luck again—after such a long wait to come across a neutral that they would have to release. Worse, tomorrow or the next day the whole world would know that the *Emden* was in the Indian Ocean. But the signal lamp continued: "Loaded with 6,500 tons of Indian coal, destined for the British, en route from Bombay to Calcutta." Now that was a catch, a coal ship destined for the British. Müller decided to seize the cargo as contraband. A prize crew for watch and engine duty was dispatched to the *Pontoporos,* where Lauterbach remained in command while the cutter with its search party returned to the *Emden.* On orders from Müller, Lauterbach proposed to the Greek captain that he join the *Emden* under a German charter with generous compensation. The captain heartily agreed to that. Our cruiser now had a lot of coal, and her presence in the Indian Ocean would not be revealed. All was well, indeed. If only the *Pontoporos* weren't so slow. She made less than nine knots. Still, it was a fortunate day, a most promising beginning for the cruiser war of the *Emden.*

# CHAPTER THREE

# COMMERCE WAR OFF BENGAL AND RANGOON

*10 September 1914*

The heavy tropic air seemed to be pressing the sky right into the ocean. Beads of sweat clung to the bulkheads below the *Emden*'s waterline. Not even the flow of air created by the ship's movement brought relief. The swirling wake glowed in the darkness. Now and then a short rain pelted the dirty, littered deck, washing away the grime and coal dust. The sharply arched bow of the cruiser cut through the swells, accompanied by the *Markomannia* on her starboard side and the *Pontoporos* on her port quarter. With that formation the *Emden* could keep an eye on both escorts. The small convoy held a course west by northwest to reach the sea lane between Colombo and Calcutta.

At about 0900, from the north, a smoke cloud rose into view. Immediately general quarters was sounded. A hundred booted feet thundered over the deck. The cruiser accelerated to top speed, the *Markomannia* and *Pontoporos* trailing behind. Shortly, under the cloud and against the horizon, a steamer appeared in dark silhouette. On its masts radio antennas could be made out and white structures on the decks that, from afar, looked like gun emplacements. Was it an auxiliary cruiser? A blue British flag belied that possibility. Auxiliary cruisers were warships that flew a white ensign. The *Emden,* prepared for anything, steered toward the ship without approaching too close and before hoisting her flag. First she had to determine if the freighter was armed, and as long as possible she should be taken for a British warship. The freighter held course and steered unsuspectingly toward the *Emden.*

Presently in the *Emden* they decided that the curious white installations on the freighter's deck were not gun emplacements. Exactly what they were was as yet unclear. One of the cruiser's bow guns fired a warning shot while the German war flag rose on the gaff. On the foremast fluttered the international signal "Stop, do not radio."

The steamer stopped. The *Emden* approached to within shouting distance. The message not to use the wireless was repeated with a megaphone. Out of the stern porthole of the freighter burning, smoking papers flew overboard. The captain was, no doubt, destroying his secret orders.

On the British merchant flag the sign of the Indian government grew visible. That was curious. The ship had presumably been chartered by the Indian government.

A board and search command under the leadership of Lieutenant (j.g.) von Levetzow, along with a prize crew led by Quartermaster Second Class Meyer, pulled over to the steamer. According to its papers, this was a British ship, the 3,413-ton *Indus* built in 1904 and plying a course between Calcutta and Bombay. Property of the shipping company James Nourse, the *Indus* had been chartered by the Indian government to take on troops in Bombay. She was already converted for troop duty. The curious white structures were horse stalls.

The sea, which the night before and during most of the morning had been rough, grew calm, and, taking advantage of this, Müller ordered the loading of provisions from the freighter. The *Emden* was short on everything. Meanwhile the *Markomannia* and *Pontoporos* caught up.

For the officers on bridge duty, the hour-long pleasure of maneuvering on a "serving tray" began. Though the prize ship no
longer maneuvered, it lay in a crosswind. The *Emden* had to remain close to communicate with the boarding crew. When the
steamer, because of heavy cargo, lay deep in the water, the
*Emden* had to run her engines faster. She could not turn into
the wind because her lee side had to be kept free for boat traffic.
If the steamer was empty, it had to turn faster than the *Emden*
because of the greater wind drag. The ships rarely drove their
propellers at the same speed.

In the future this procedure—a difficult one that sailors
dubbed sawing—would be standard for the *Emden*. A challenged freighter would slow down and, by reversing its engines,
come to a dead halt. Then it would turn its stern into the wind.
The *Emden* would approach her prospective prize and, once
abreast, come up aft on the ship's weather side. The cutter with
the search and prize party would be lowered on the lee side—
the side toward the steamer—and then in turn be made fast on
its lee side. Because boarding had to be supervised, the *Emden*,
right after the cutter was dropped, would maneuver in gradual
leeward steps toward the steamer. This happened as quickly as
possible, since cutter and prize had to be kept in constant view.
By this time the steamer, too, would be in motion, while the
*Markomannia* and those ships captured earlier closed ranks and
formed a semicircle around the cruiser. Their slow-moving machinery made skillful maneuvering difficult. The *Emden* remained the focal point of the scene. She had to make sure that
the cutter crew expended no more time and energy than was
necessary in rowing to and from the prize ship. The boat, remember, always had to use its lee side for the operation. This
meant that the cruiser was constantly maneuvering in a con-
stricted space. Despite her two propellers, in a brisk wind matters
did not always go according to plan. For officers on the bridge
and engine personnel the task required hours of intense concentration. It also consumed a tremendous amount of coal. In a
calm sea everything was much simpler.

The *Indus* had a heavy load, and the second cutter had to be lowered. Besides taking on provisions, there was to be some shuffling of personnel. Müller wanted to send the slow-footed *Pontoporos* to a far-off rendezvous. The Greek captain, although ready to cooperate, had to be kept under supervision, so the first officer of the *Markomannia* was given that role, as regular naval officers couldn't be spared. Lieutenant Lauterbach was transferred from the Greek ship to the *Indus*. With his experience as a merchant marine captain, Lauterbach would be invaluable to the men unloading the *Indus*. Lieutenant Levetzow was relieved of duty in the *Indus* and returned to the *Emden*. The original crew of the *Indus* was transferred to the *Markomannia*. A guard detail was necessary to watch over them. That duty fell to Lieutenant Klöpper. All these exchanges demanded much crossing back and forth of boats. Cutter crews kept busy. Everyone had to pitch in, at the same time keeping a sharp lookout for intruders.

The first officer of the *Emden*, Lieutenant Mücke, was elated. As "housekeeper" on the ship, he was responsible for furnishing all sorts of provisions and equipment. The soap supply had continued to dwindle. Two more weeks and washing would have become a luxury. Earlier, in jest, Mücke had proposed that they pick up a soap ship. Now they had soap, soap in abundance. The ship would be supplied for months. After stowing cutter-loads of the precious cargo on board, the crew turned to other matters. Unloading a captured ship was an art that had to be carefully learned. The *Emden* men didn't seem to know what to take first. Every item of cargo was so coveted that they wanted to take it all back to their ship. Who knew when another such opportunity would present itself? Lieutenant Lauterbach tried to stop the men from taking superfluous supplies, but he wasn't always on the loading platform to prevent it. Hence all sorts of trifles landed in the cutters. The men in the cruiser laughed as every load came alongside. The shipped goods included beautiful blue silk kimonos and huge bundles of stationery fetchingly tied up with pink ribbons.

Around 1200 Mücke crossed over to the *Indus* with captain's orders to finish the provisioning posthaste. But the temptation of remaining cargo to be had for the taking pushed the operation well beyond 1600. No first officer's heart could be left untouched by the sight of piles of large and small towels, so suitable for cleaning and polishing. There were canned goods and preserves from the best English companies just waiting to be unloaded. The *Emden*'s officers justified the seizure of delicacies such as brandy-filled bonbons on the grounds that they were not really unfit for the stomachs of sailors. The stockpile of goods "catered by India" grew: slickers with which even the men on watch duty had never been adequately equipped; charts, chronometers, binoculars, an entire radio station, flour, potatoes, fresh meat, twists of tobacco. The deck of the *Emden* looked like the annual county fair. In a specially designated spot on the quarterdeck sausages and hams were strung in rows. Chocolates rose in mountains from the deck and bottles with three-starred labels marked "Claret" and "Cognac" adorned the drains. A herd of grunting, squealing livestock was corralled in a temporary pen. The mess officer and his men listed everything on hand and then distributed it to the men, who stood in a large circle, talking and smoking, waiting for their share. It took some time before each sailor had his delicacies carefully tucked away. Now, with their coffee, they had chocolates and candy. That night hundreds of cigarettes were lit up on deck, making the ship look as if she was infested with glowworms. And now, at meals, the men enjoyed excellent bread baked from English flour. With such an abundance of foodstuff the ship's cooks had to be careful not to overfeed the crew.

In the carefree days to follow the men of the *Emden* would pity their pursuers. For weeks on end they would live on hard tack and corned beef and could only dream of beer, wine, cognac, fresh eggs, juicy roast chicken, tender ham, chocolate, candy, and cigarettes. Dozens of enemy ships voraciously consumed coal, their crews wracking their brains trying to capture the elusive cruiser, while the Germans lived the life of kings.

After the off-loading the *Indus* was to be scuttled. A party consisting of an engineer, a technical petty officer, and three stokers rowed across to the freighter. Seacocks in the engine room were opened and water shot into the boiler rooms and bunkers in fountains as thick as a man's waist. Then the scuttling party returned to ship and the gunnery experts had their opportunity for target practice. The *Indus* swallowed six shells, the *Emden*'s guns firing only one shot at a time, fore and aft, into the hull. A real salvo was never unleashed on a prize ship, for they had to be careful about not wasting ammunition, which was something captured vessels could not replenish. The *Emden* drew within a few hundred meters of the sinking hulk to make sure every shot had scored where it should have.

Ships don't die easily. The crew of the *Emden* would soon discover that almost no freighter sank in less than half an hour. The *Indus* required more than an hour. For a long time she looked as if she were not sinking at all. Then the hull started slipping through the water's surface, slowly at first, the motion gradually accelerating. With a heavy plunge into the swells the ship took water over her railings and through her side portholes. After that she went quickly. Water rushed into the previously opened loading hatches. The steamer settled on her side. Escaping blasts of air forced large columns of water out of the openings on the port side. Then, finally, going bow first, the ship vanished. A cloud of black coal dust surged into the air. With loud groaning noises the funnels were rent apart, and, after a deep rumbling crescendo, the engine broke loose. When the last waterspouts sank back into the ocean there was only flotsam to mark the spot where the ship had once been. A few moments later large heavy beams that had torn loose underwater pierced the air and tottered back onto the water's surface. Had men gone down with the steamer, these slashing beams would have posed a great danger, as would the sucking whirlpool that followed in the wake of the sinking ship.

In stunned and painful silence the men of the *Emden* and *Markomannia* witnessed, for the first time, the death of a ship. It affected them like the death of a human being. For a few moments they continued to stare silently at the empty sea where only minutes before a moving ship had been. Many turned reflective; even the usual wags and self-styled cynics lost their glib, frivolous tongues. It was war, and thus their duty to bring harm to the enemy who, undoubtedly, brought the same to their ships. Still, none of the men in the *Markomannia* could forget the face of the captain of the *Indus,* who watched with tears in his eyes as his ship went down.

In the *Emden* the men were busy once more. Lifeboats from the *Indus* were drifting alongside regulation life buoys, and the raider was trying to ram them and shatter their air chambers. But the lifeboats were constructed to survive. They wouldn't sink. The cruiser tried to run over them, but waves created by the slicing movement of her bow pushed the buoyant boats away at the last moment. Peacefully they bobbed alongside the ship, teasingly defying her. They weren't worth destruction by gunfire, and so the crew finally gave up, beaten by the harmless white lifeboats. It didn't actually matter that they remained afloat. By the time they were found, the freighter would already have been missed, the enemy already alerted to the action of the German cruiser *Emden.*

The *Emden,* with the *Markomannia* and the *Pontoporos,* continued her voyage in the direction of Calcutta. The sea was as calm as the night. They could remain undisturbed in the area for the time being. The *Indus,* which was to have reported by radio to Point de Galle, south of Colombo, could not have arrived there before 12 September, and anyway reports were sometimes neglected. Suspicion would be aroused only when the ship failed to show up off Bombay after 15 September. Until then, the *Emden* could bide her time.

### 11 September 1914

At about 1400 the *Emden*'s lookout spotted a smoke cloud ahead to starboard. The cruiser immediately steamed toward it, the *Markomannia* and *Pontoporos* following as fast as possible. Approaching, they made out the typical white superstructure of a passenger ship. The blue flag of an English merchantman fluttered aft. Perhaps it was another troop transport. The *Emden* sounded her warning shot and hoisted the German flag, but the admonition against radioing was not necessary this time. The steamer had no antenna on its mast.

Again Lieutenant Lauterbach and his boarding party took over. Soon he relayed that their newest prize was the 6,012-ton British freighter *Lovat*, built in 1911 and owned by the J. Wavrack shipping company. She too was outfitted as a troop transport by the Indian government and en route from Calcutta to Bombay. Her fate, too, was sealed.

The crew of the steamer had ample time to gather their personal belongings, for the transfer of cargo to the *Markomannia* wasn't finished until after sunset. The entire time the *Emden* remained close by the *Lovat*, dangerously close, so that the bow of the cruiser almost rammed the stern of the steamer. After the boarding party opened the seacocks the *Emden*'s cutters were hoisted back on board. The *Lovat* came under fire, taking as long to sink as her predecessor. Darkness set in, and the *Emden* left the ship to her fate. Again jubilation reigned, but the captain of the *Indus* did not partake of the emotion. He welcomed his colleague from the *Lovat* with open arms, happy to have a companion in misery.

This time Lieutenant Lauterbach had orders to return to the *Emden* with newspapers only. They were priceless sources of information, even though they gave one-sided reports of Allied successes and German defeats. This surprised no one in the *Emden;* the English press had been serving palatable fictions to its readers since the beginning of the war. To explain the latest situation to the crew the first officer took charge. A large map of Germany and countries bordering her was posted and the actions were traced. It was not easy to decide what to present to the men and how. The news was largely distorted or nonsensical: large German armies had been destroyed, leading everywhere to collapse, famine, revolution, and the suicide of army generals; the crown prince had been killed; the emperor had been wounded; Bavaria had seceded from the German empire; and similar such nonsense. Lieutenant von Mücke prepared a report avoiding the most outrageous lies, trying to present a fair

picture of what had happened to date. The crew's morale would
suffer if reports from home were continually disheartening, but
on the other hand, the contents of newspapers could not be kept
from the men. When the briefing officer read reports in the pri-
vacy of the wardroom stewards were usually around, and they
listened in. Should there be a discrepancy between these reports
and the official statement, the crew would get the distinct feeling
that news was being sugarcoated. That development had to be
avoided at all costs. So Mücke decided to read the papers word
for word, reserving commentary for later. It was a fortuitous
event, then, when a telegram arrived in the first days of August
revealing the Reuter's news agency's method of reporting. It
read: "Official: *Emden* in battle with *Askold* undisputably
sunk." This swept all doubt from the minds of sailors that reports could be grossly exaggerated. Whatever followed thereafter from Reuters would be regarded with skepticism.

Then came a map of Germany on which the English press had
partitioned the country. France extended to the Weser-Werra
area and to the borders of Bavaria. Denmark reached the
Wismar line and included Wittenberg, Magdeburg, Hanover,
and Bremen. England swallowed Oldenburg. The territory east
of the Elbe, including Saxony, was Russian domain. Bavaria was
independent. Only a small area, Thuringia, still existed as Germany. Crew members born there held their heads especially
high, regarding themselves as the true standard-bearers of the
German empire.

More and more, the ship's complement looked forward to
their reading hour. If, after a capture, more newspapers arrived,
every face wore the question, When is the next briefing going to
be? Up to this point there had been no quarreling about who
had the watch duty, but now no one wanted to miss a briefing
and an undercurrent of complaining could be heard by those
who did. When "All hands to the forecastle" was piped, a roar
of approval echoed from stem to stern.

### 12 September 1914

On this quiet night the small German convoy neared the Calcutta lightship. A suggestion made by the captain of the *Indus* in

jest, that they capture the pilot ship off Calcutta, was actually being considered by Müller. He had been toying with the notion of destroying the lightship's radio installation, bringing a temporary halt to ship traffic to and from India's main city. No ship could enter the difficult waters of the Hooghly River between Calcutta and the open sea without a pilot. In the *Markomannia* the detained captains were looking forward to additional companions in disaster or, perhaps, bridge partners. At least three more freighters had been on their way downstream, they revealed, even naming them. Since these vessels had to cross the *Emden*'s path, the cruiser took her time on the way to Calcutta.

At 2200 the lights on the first-awaited ship appeared. The *Emden* approached her and soon the freighter was halted. So as not to alert other ships with the muzzle flash of a warning shot, the cruiser sounded her sirens. With a signal lamp the order was sent to stop and maintain radio silence. Again Lieutenant Lauterbach took command of the prize ship. Ensign Gyssling and the combined search and prize party boarded her. Built in 1907, she was a British freighter, the *Kabinga*, of 4,657 Brutto register tons. Her owner was Bucknall SS Lines. She could make ten knots and was equipped with a radio. The radio room was immediately placed under guard. The *Kabinga*, with her valuable cargo of yard goods which belonged for the most part to an American, was on her way from Calcutta to New York, via Bombay, Port Said, and the Mediterranean.

Müller could have sunk the *Kabinga* as an enemy ship, but who the American consignors were, and what part of the cargo was theirs, could only be determined after a lengthy examination, for which there was no time. He wanted to avoid later American claims for restitution. Besides that, it was time to rid himself of the numerous involuntary passengers in the *Markomannia*. He couldn't afford to enter port, and hence the occasion had arisen to dismiss one of the captured ships. The captain of the *Kabinga* traveled with his wife and child aboard. Müller decided, then, to turn that ship into a depository for released passengers. The decision did not have to be acted on immediately. First, the *Emden* would wait and see if other ships could be caught in her net.

Three hours later a light was visible to port. With all hands manning their battle stations, the *Emden* bore down on the ship at high speed, a train of vessels following. Soon they could make out a steamer with one funnel lying dead in the water. Lieutenant von Levetzow had the pleasure of boarding the prize, along with Ensign Zimmermann and the search and prize detail. This ship, too, was to follow the *Emden* until the next day, a thorough search being delayed. She turned out to be a British collier, the *Killin,* built in 1908 and owned by the Connell Brothers. Loaded with six thousand tons of Indian coal, she had been on her way from Calcutta to Bombay.

The *Emden* had accumulated an impressive squadron of four ships. The entire convoy now proceeded toward Calcutta, very slowly, because the *Killin* could make only eight knots at best. The *Emden* took the lead, with the *Pontoporos* and *Killin* on her port side, the *Kabinga* and *Markomannia* on her starboard side. All the ships were blacked out. In their nightly raids, it was always the first duty of the prize officers to extinguish all lights on the captured ships. No one knew what darkness might bring, and English warships were always presumed to be nearby. For the merchant ships it was hard sailing in convoy, particularly behind a blacked-out leader. But the formation allowed the *Emden* a good view of the convoy.

### 13 September 1914

It now became apparent just how much the cruiser's crew had learned. The sea was by no means smooth. The calming northeast monsoon had not yet blown over the Indian Ocean, but despite this the transfer of the *Killin*'s crew to the *Kabinga* (which was to be spared), the transfer of the scuttling detail, and the removal of provisions from the latest victim ran quickly and smoothly. The *Emden* steamed first to one and then to another of the ships, as the commander did not want boats rowing too great a distance. When the cutters approached her, she would halt to create a lee for boarding.

At 1000 the *Killin*'s seacocks were opened and the *Emden*'s guns sent her plunging. For a few seconds she stood upright in the air from funnel to stern, then quickly shot to the bottom.

The sinking was watched with a considerable amount of pain. After all, six thousand tons of coal went down with her. As a supply ship, however, she was much too slow. The only speed she displayed was in being scuttled. Finally, a ship that sank rapidly.

The little convoy continued on its way, direction Calcutta. Soon another victim stood before them, to the starboard side. The drama played as before: first the smoke cloud appearing; then the spiderweb of riggings, masts, funnels, and superstructure growing over the horizon; and finally the entire massive hull heaving into view. The *Emden* approached at a sharp angle so as not to be recognized. By and by the crew saw what a beauty the ship was, and not only in size and appearance; she seemed to be absolutely new. At the approach she hoisted a red British merchant flag.

Lauterbach and his party boarded the vessel and reported back almost immediately. Named the *Diplomat,* the freighter, of 7,615 Brutto register tons, was built as recently as 1912 and was owned by Charente SS. Bound from Calcutta for England with a cargo of ten thousand tons of tea, the prize carried the largest amount of booty the *Emden* was ever to take, if not the most valuable. Müller decided to sink her then and there, with explosive charges. The torpedo officer, Lieutenant Witthoeft, crossed over with his demolition squad. On board he heard a conversation between Lauterbach and the traffic manager of the ship's company. This high official had arranged for an extensive home leave in England. Now he was requesting, in none too pleasant tones, that Lauterbach furnish him with a few sailors to fetch his silver golf and racing trophies from the luggage hold. The German officer explained politely that his men were not porters; they had come to destroy the ship.

After the torpedo officer had planted his explosives and appeared back on deck, the *Emden* was nowhere in sight. Lauterbach pointed to the horizon. "She's caught another one over there," he said. The cruiser could be seen in the distance, returning with a brand new victim.

With work on the *Diplomat* completed—the crew and passengers, including the insulted traffic manager, clutching his golf clubs, had been transferred to the *Kabinga*—the ship's seacocks were opened, the demolition charges set. The cutter with its demolition party cast off. When the boat was about two hundred meters from the ship, the blast occurred, ripping off a large chunk of the hull. Later the charges would be placed below a ship's waterline. This had not been possible in the *Diplomat*, with her cargo hold crammed full. The seamen's storage and chain lockers, about level with the waterline, had had to suffice.

Meanwhile, the *Emden* wasn't idle. The ship she had taken, another Calcutta-bound freighter, had appeared on the southern horizon. She was a neutral ship, the *Loredano*. Lieutenant von Levetzow and Ensign Prince von Hohenzollern had boarded the dilapidated vessel, which belonged to the allied Italians and was now accompanying the *Emden* and the rest of the train on their way back to the *Diplomat*. It was suggested to the skipper of this newest acquisition that he take all the crews from the captured ships to Calcutta. After all, that is where he was headed. He would receive provisions for all the unwilling passengers and later be reimbursed. The captain hesitated, quoting the laws of neutrality. Müller grew angry; unless he agreed, the *Kabinga* might have to be sunk.

While this fruitless discussion continued, the *Diplomat* was slowly sinking. With her bow blasted away, she settled her nose deep in the water and lay that way for some time. Every wave that washed over her stern tore hundreds of tea boxes from the cargo holds. They danced in circles on the surface of the water. A few minutes later the ship's elephantine stern jutted straight into the air. After a loud crash, water sucked the mangled hull into its depths. After witnessing this drama, the captain of the *Loredano* decided it might be best after all to take the crews of the captured ships with him. But it was much too late, with night settling in, to transfer two hundred odd prisoners from the *Markomannia* and *Kabinga*. After the *Loredano*'s captain had pledged not to bring any hostile action against the *Emden*, his ship was dismissed. She proceeded toward Calcutta, stopping long enough to pick up some of the bobbing tea containers.

The *Emden* and her entourage set off again, the captain of the *Kabinga* relieved to learn that his ship was still among the living. To confuse the *Loredano*, the convoy steered a southwesterly course. Once out of sight of the Italian steamer it shifted to the south, then slowly to the northwest, pushing toward the sea lane between Calcutta and Madras.

At about 2200 the lookout on the foremast reported a light to starboard. A steamer was approaching from the north. The escorts received orders to follow the cruiser, which pulled hard to starboard and under general quarters held course directly toward the newcomer. The signalman sent a message in Morse: "Stop your engines. Don't use your wireless. What ship?" It was the *Dandolo,* another Italian ship. The reply from the *Emden* was short and sweet: "Thank you. Have a good voyage."

Quickly the German cruiser was swallowed up again in the darkness of night. This time too she steered a deceptive course. The Italians should not be able to report her movements. But decoy maneuvers in the impenetrable darkness lost the *Emden* her convoy. Morse code or signal rockets would only have given her away, and so a green light was illuminated on her starboard side, away from the view of the *Dandolo,* to give the convoy ships a locator. Presently the *Emden* ran across the *Kabinga* leading the way for the other ships. The latter mistook the cruiser for a sailing ship, seeing only the green running light. Fearing that a port turn would result in collision with the ships she was leading, the *Kabinga* cut to starboard in hopes of avoiding what she took to be a slow sailing ship. When the *Emden* spotted the *Kabinga,* the latter was athwart the cruiser's bow. "Back engines, full speed!" came the order in the *Emden,* preventing collision at the last minute.

The convoy, in line once more, took a west-northwesterly course to reach the Madras-Calcutta sea lane. They met nothing else that night.

*14 September 1914*

The *Kabinga* was finally to be released. The convoy lay to at about 1500 and the exchange began. The crews of the *Lovat* and *Indus* were brought from the *Markomannia* to the *Kabinga.* Before leaving their temporary ship, they broke into three cheers for the commander of the *Emden.* This astonished the men of the cruiser, for, after all, they had scuttled the *Lovat* and *Indus*. Lieutenant Klöpper returned with the watch to the *Emden;* so did the prize crew in the *Kabinga,* but not before destroying that ship's radio equipment.

The transfer of so many people took time and the cutters kept busy. As they were working against the advancing darkness that threatened to abort the work, a smoke cloud was spotted to the south. Leaving the ships and cutters behind, the *Emden* steamed full speed toward the new arrival, which showed the English flag. The cruiser and her latest victim returned quickly to the *Kabinga*. Lieutenants Lauterbach and Levetzow and Ensign Fikentscher and their details boarded the captured steamer, the *Trabboch,* which had been on her way out of the Indian harbor of Negabatan, en route to Calcutta. She was an empty collier of 4,028 Brutto register tons. Soon her crew was aboard the *Kabinga,* the seacocks were opened, and the demolition charges were set. It was now routine for the *Emden* to scuttle ships with gunfire by day, explosives by night, the latter to avoid the highly visible flashes that shot from the muzzles of the ship's guns. This time, however, the plan backfired. The detonation set off a coal dust explosion and towering jets of flame turned night into day.

Finally the *Kabinga* obtained her freedom, steaming off toward Calcutta. That action, the release of a ship carrying so much human cargo, would bring the *Emden* and her commander favorable world press. When the *Kabinga* arrived in Calcutta the passengers would recount wondrous tales of the courtesy extended to them, of the consideration shown for their personal belongings and the benevolence of the captain who had spared a ship because he did not want to expose the wife and child of its skipper to the dangers of a transfer in high seas. The Indian newspapers immediately ran these stories, and the *Emden* and her commandant, despite the damage they had done to British shipping, became famous and beloved overnight.

No sooner was the *Kabinga* out of sight, the *Emden* and her small convoy—now the *Markomannia* and *Pontoporos*—on their way, than a ship's light was spotted in the distance. The *Emden* accelerated toward it but it ran. The chase lasted for some time. Apparently the ship had noticed the explosion from afar, seen the many ships, and tried to escape. Neither the blasts of sirens nor warning shots slowed her down. Only after a live shell was laid across her bow did she let up steam and stop. The *Emden* approached, asking in loud megaphone voice, "What ship?" Answer: "*Clan Matheson.*" Question: "English?" Answer: "No, British!" The almost insulted tone of this last evoked laughter in the *Emden*. The freighter, it turned out, happened to be a ship of the Clan Lines with a Scottish home port and a Scottish captain on board. It would be sunk immediately, punishment for its stubborn defiance at being challenged. Lauterbach and Schall and the combined search and prize crew crossed over to secure the captured ship.

The *Clan Matheson,* on her way from England to Calcutta, was a ship of 4,775 Brutto register tons with a valuable cargo of motor cars, locomotives, steam engines, bicycles, typewriters, and other machinery. Her only passenger was a race horse, apparently a favorite in the Calcutta sweepstakes. It was killed with a pistol to spare it a painful drowning.

The preparation for sinking now followed the regular routine. The British crew was transferred to the *Markomannia* under a guard detail led by Lieutenant Klöpper. Then the demolition squad did its work, which wasn't easy. First they looked for the most suitable spot to place their explosive charges. Usually that was the ship's hold. Next the scuttling party opened the valves in the boiler and engine rooms. In the cargo space the men laboriously groped their way below, shoving aside heavy crates and bundles that barred passage. To speed up the sinking, not only did the holds have to be shattered, but the adjoining compartments had to cave in quickly. The charges were placed so that at detonation a part of the hull exploded and, simultaneously, a piece of the bulkhead shattered the sections adjoining. Then the water could flood both compartments at the same time.

Even by day, the lowest cargo holds were pitch black. While the demolitions officer looked for a place to attach his explosives, the men assembled all the lanterns they could find. They brought ropes and ladders to make the passage topside a quick and comfortable one. Then the charges were attached. At this point everyone departed, all but the scuttling party, prize officer, demolitions officer, and his aide. As they left from the lee side, the explosives, for safety's sake, were always placed on the weather side of a doomed ship. The scuttling party opened the seacocks, smashed them, then hurried into their cutter, leaving behind only the demolitions officer and his aide. These two ignited the fuses and, after making sure they were burning properly, joined the others in the cutter. It pulled away quickly in a race against the few minutes it took for the fuses to burn.

The *Emden* continued on an easterly course. Originally, Müller had intended to head for the Balasore roadstead where, out of sight of land, he would take on coal, but the monsoon had not set in and the strong southeasterly wind was not conducive to his plan. The *Emden* could not lay alongside a collier under those conditions, nor could she afford to remain in the area around Calcutta.

That night radiomen intercepted a message from the Calcutta lightship: "According to Italian vessel *Loredano*, German cruiser *Emden* sank steamships *Diplomat*, *Kabinga*, and *Pontoporos*, 86°24′ E, 18°1′ N." The "allied" Italian captain, in spite of his emphatic assurance of neutrality, had used the first opportunity to rat on the *Emden*. As the crew learned later from newspapers, the Indian government rewarded him with a gold watch and chain for his dutiful breach of neutrality. And the *Kabinga*, her radiomen back at work, wired that night: "German cruiser *Emden*, with coal ship *Markomannia*, sank *Indus*, *Lovat*, *Diplomat*, *Trabboch*, and *Killin* off Calcutta. *Kabinga* and all crews released and safe." Now the arrival of the German cruiser in the Bay of Bengal was known to all. The planned attack on the Calcutta lightship was canceled. It was high time to hunt for another theater of operations.

### 16 September 1914

The *Emden* steamed into the haven of the Andaman islands, en route to Preparis North Channel. When the sun rose the sea was smooth as a duck pond. The perfect opportunity to take on coal could not be overlooked. To conserve the supply of the *Markomannia,* the *Emden* drew alongside the *Pontoporos.* Once more the tedious work began. The cruiser ran on one engine slowly; the *Pontoporos* lay dead in the water. That way both ships remained capable of maneuver and at the same time kept rolling to a minimum. The transfer lasted from morning until 2300. An amount of 440 tons was loaded, almost filling the bunkers to capacity. The sailors of the *Emden,* as always, suffered from the heat. Their eyes and mouths were black rings of sweat-clotted coal dust. Thus the help of sixty Indians, formerly stokers and trimmers in the *Clan Matheson,* was appreciated. They were hired with the promise of free room and board and the going wage in Mexican dollars.

Among the sun and coal-darkened men on deck roved the occasional painfully scrubbed, ghostly gray figure of a stoker. No one envied the stokers. It was a miracle that they stayed at their work, for it was living hell. In the narrow boiler rooms twelve boilers spit, raged, and blustered in concert. When the fire doors flew open ashes charged out and were doused with hissing water, an action that spread a sickening odor throughout the ship. Black as night, plastered with sweat, the stokers toiled for six hours to satisfy the greedy mouths of the boilers. Working in the infernal confines of the fireroom in the tropics could become unbearable. The heat rose to 60° or 70° Celsius. Every wrong move meant a terrible burn, every mistake in loading coal, a catastrophe.

The *Pontoporos* carried Indian coal, out and out poison for a warship. The *Emden* could not enjoy a smokeless passage using it, and this was the first and last time she would. After twenty-four hours of steady operation, the boilers would be covered in soot and flue ash. The coal would be spread over the grate like garbage. During the firing, a great deal of it fell right onto the ashes. It required fifty-five percent more Indian coal than Cardiff, the best in the world, to perform the same work. Indian coal did only seventy-five percent of the job done by an equivalent amount of Chinese Hungshan coal from Tsingtao, the kind the *Markomannia* carried. Usually six boilers were operating to keep the *Emden* at eighteen knots. The boilers required constant attention because of faulty pipes, and off-duty stokers and the standby watch had to work on those not in use. Four unused boilers had to be fire-ready at all times, as it took about thirty minutes to get up steam. Under the direction of the duty engineer, the remaining two boilers were cleaned. If a boiler were to be kept in good working order, it had to be scrubbed every five days. Soot was removed from the outer walls, the grate and insulation were reinforced. And every ten days a boiler's water had to be changed and its zinc panels purged of corrosive material. Every twenty to twenty-five days a more thorough scrubbing of the inside walls took place. A wire brush attached to a line was pulled through all fourteen hundred pipes of the boiler. The stokers performed these tasks in addition to regular duties. In emergencies, other sailors assisted. The cleaning was never accomplished according to schedule; operational necessity interrupted the routine all too often.

Unscheduled cruising accelerated the deterioration of pipes. Already in the winter of 1913–14, pipes in two of the boilers had to be replaced. The following winter, six more boilers needed new pipes. The great demands made on the pipes during chases put many of them out of service. All told, some two hundred would fail to function. Over fifty times the stokers had to shut a boiler down, then empty, open, and reinsulate it. The malfunctioning pipes were sealed with steel plugs. To do that, the men had to climb into a boiler roasting at temperatures of 80° to 90° Celsius.

Steaming was not the only activity that devoured coal. Water replenishing was another. Every day the cruiser used twenty-five tons or more of water in the boilers, and four tons was needed for drinking. If the *Emden* remained separated from the *Markomannia,* in whose holds the wash water was stored, she had to lug around seven to nine tons of that. In all, the cruiser carried about forty tons of water. Ten tons of coal per day was needed for distilling. Though the rest of the crew did not envy the stokers, they themselves were not much to be envied during the coal-loading operation. The bunkers, where the trimming took place, were unbearably hot. Needless to say, clothing was kept to a minimum. The so-called coal packet was an old, worn uniform, used only for this detail. After repeated coaling it was reduced to rags and could not be replaced. The pants, which were long, grew theadbare at the calf and knee, exposing the shorts underneath. Before long the uniform was good for nothing but swimming, and eventually the men had little more than coal dust to cover their modesty.

The work was particularly hard in a high sea, when the *Emden* and her coaler ground against each other. The original fenders having long given way, new ones had to be improvised. In Tsing-tao 150 hammocks had been taken on board. Originally they had been intended for use in damage control. Not any longer. The men constructed fenders out of tree trunks wrapped in the hammocks and hung over the sides of the ship. From every coaling they surfaced somewhat battered, but with mending they were ready for the next time. A better and more original fender was the automobile tire, of which a number had been seized from one of the captured ships. They hung evenly distributed over the ship's sides and did an excellent job of protecting the hull.

One particularly laborious stage in the coaling process was the actual transfer of fuel from one ship to the other. The ships, tied together, rolled heavily in the swells. After the men had hoisted the coal sacks, they had to await the moment the ships rolled in unison. At that instant, a rope was released and the sacks careened over to the *Emden*, crashing wherever on her decks they willed. The men had to run out of the way of the charging black masses.

It was only natural that the constant chafing and battering, and the continual raining down of heavy coal sacks on her deck, would take a heavy toll on the *Emden*. She had one gun each in blisters fore and aft. The action of the ships rolling against each other put the foremost gun blister in constant danger. It was dented several times. And then coal sacks often banged into the railing. Soon there wasn't a single undented upright left on the starboard side. The linoleum deck suffered terribly. In a short time areas of it were worn through to the steel plates beneath.

Steel was slippery, and in a rolling sea it was not uncommon to see men stumbling over the deck. After every coaling, the metal had to be roughened with chisels that cut small grooves so that shoes could grip the deck. Every time sailcloth and tar were discovered in a captured ship, the *Emden*'s decks received a protective new coat.

In addition to the cruiser's usual bunker supply of coal there was a deckside supply on hand. On the forecastle, on the middle deck, and on the poop deck lay hills of coal that impeded traffic. When someone wanted to cross the deck he had to press himself through narrow gorges. Quite often after a violent roll the coal would slide about, rearranging itself into a plateau that barred the entire deck.

The hours when the *Emden* and her ships lay alongside each other transferring coal were dangerously crippling. During that time the ship was not battle ready. The enemy lurked all around, liable at any moment to materialize on the horizon. The crew knew it and did their utmost to speed things along. And every means was employed to lighten their workload. In the bow ice-cold tubs of lemonade awaited their desire, mug after mug of the drink being filled and handed out. The band played a continuous stream of uplifting melodies. A slate, visible to all, hung amidships to record the number of tons taken on every fifteen minutes in large chalk letters. No watch wanted to fall behind another. Fervently, and with doubled effort, each worked to overtake the others. Competition was fierce.

Once, after a strenuous ten-hour shift, the usually strict Lieutenant von Mücke suggested to the commandant that he let a sighted freighter escape. Müller consented. When word got around the next day the men grumbled, "We still could have managed that one."

The crew knew exactly what they had in their skipper. They were proud of him, and of the ship he commanded so successfully. All racket and singing stopped immediately when they were told their commandant was tired. During maneuvers or coaling, an encouraging word from him was all that was needed to overcome discouragement and drive them to superhuman

efforts. In spite of the hard work and restricted living conditions, the world still seemed orderly aboard their cruiser. The
captain spent most of his time on the bridge. There they had
placed comfortable chairs so he could sleep when necessary but
be alert when the situation demanded it. He spent most of his
days studying maps, sailing manuals, and news reports. It was
only through hours of painstaking deliberation that he drew up
the plans that led to the successful ventures of the *Emden*.

During the coaling the *Pontoporos* received new orders.
Though her cargo was anything but good and she was too slow
for operations with the *Emden*, she could not yet be released.
The cruiser needed her for emergency reserves in case the *Markomannia* ran out and nothing better came along. And so the
Greek ship was sent to a rendezvous, there to wait until the
*Emden*, with or without the *Markomannia*, could meet her. The
commander of the prize crew, the first officer of the *Markomannia*, Quartermaster Second Class Meyer, would take the ship
along with fourteen men. The Greek captain was promised that
his ship would be released when coal was removed from the
*Markomannia* once again. Furthermore, he would receive handsome compensation for his troubles. The bargain satisfied him
completely.

Once more the *Emden* followed her course toward Preparis
North Channel. The two steamers took their accustomed positions in the convoy, the *Markomannia* to starboard, the *Pontoporos* to port. Slowly the Greek vessel fell back until she vanished into the night. Then she took up a southerly course toward
the designated rendezvous. It was a precautionary move. The captured crew of the *Clan Matheson*, still on board the *Markomannia*, should not guess where the *Pontoporos* was heading.

### 17 September 1914

At about 1400 the *Emden* reached the entrance to Preparis
North Channel, crossroad of the sea lanes between Calcutta and
Singapore, Madras and Rangoon. Here they cruised until dark-
ness. Not a trace of smoke was seen. During the night they

headed in the direction of Rangoon. There, off the main port city of Burma, they hoped to catch a few ships. This hope was to be shattered.

*18 September 1914*

Their binoculars searched the sea for victims. The *Emden* lay close to Rangoon so no ship could pass her undetected. But traffic was sparse. In so important a harbor, that could only be ascribed to the spreading fame of the German cruiser. Finally, at 1600, six degrees to starboard, a cloud of smoke came into focus on the horizon. It appeared to be a freighter arriving from the Malacca Strait. The ship sailed on a course converging with that of the *Emden,* so that for the time being the cruiser was not forced to exceed her fuel-saving five knots. It was not until three hours later, shortly before dark, that the ship approached the *Emden* close enough to reveal a yellow funnel and a white poop. Lieutenant Lauterbach concluded that it was a Dutchman, as they were not too far from the Dutch East Indies. But when the *Emden* stopped the freighter, abruptly, it was discovered to be Norwegian. The German ship came within hailing distance, and soon Lieutenant Lauterbach was climbing the gangway to the new arrival.

The captain of the *Dovre,* a former officer in the Norwegian navy, was friendly. He spoke German fluently, and offered to take the crew from the *Clan Matheson* to Rangoon without payment. When prevailed upon, he accepted one hundred dollars for the service. As the transfer of personnel progressed, the captain, newly out of Penang, told Lauterbach a lot of interesting news. In the Malacca Strait he had met auxiliary cruisers. According to him, both of France's armored cruisers, the *Montcalm* and *Dupleix,* whom the men of the *Emden* knew well, were anchored at Penang. News of their presence there started Müller thinking of a surprise attack on the harbor. They wanted to disappear from this stretch of the Burmese coast, Lauterbach told the Norwegian captain, who obligingly promised to delay his entrance into Rangoon until daylight, giving the *Emden* a solid headstart over the crew of the *Clan Matheson*. That ship's crew would tell all once in port.

During the night the *Emden* intercepted heavy signal traffic. The shore station Diamond Point reported cannon fire near Akyab, a story that could only be ascribed to nervous awareness of the German cruiser's presence. Other stations answered, among them her old friend *QMD*. One shore station asked who *QMD* was; the answer came in obligingly plain language: "*QMD* is the *Hampshire*." So finally they knew in the *Emden* what they had long suspected. Additional information came from newspapers that the Norwegian captain had considerately left behind. The *Emden* learned that the German freighters *Elsbeth* and *Fresia,* designated supply ships for the squadron, had been sunk near Yap Island in the East China Sea. Long articles were devoted to the *Emden's* actions in the Bay of Bengal. In spite of the Indian government's assurances that the sea lanes were secure, and that the German ship would meet her fate if she had not already, insurance rates rose alarmingly.

# CHAPTER FOUR

# THE BURNING OIL
# TANKS
# OF MADRAS

*19 September 1914*

The crew felt something special in the air as the *Emden* steadily pushed westward. Again the seas were mirror smooth, an opportune time for another "coal fest." It began at about 0700 and lasted until 1500, whereupon the *Emden* cast off and renewed her westerly course. In late afternoon the decks were thoroughly swabbed, the next day being Sunday. The cruiser headed for Preparis South Channel, which ran through the Andaman islands. She reached it at 2200.

That night the crew was on sharp alert, for radio transmissions from the *Hampshire* were uncommonly loud, placing the armored cruiser undeniably in the vicinity. When her signals were at their clearest, the *Emden*'s radioman calculated the British ship's position as being no more than ten nautical miles away. Utmost caution was the order of the day.

*20 September 1914*

During their short exhausted sleep the men dreamed of black coal. The night passed without anything unusual happening. At

0100 the *Emden* had already left Preparis South Channel behind, steering a course for Madras. At a speed of twelve knots the cruiser pushed through the quiet, dark sea toward the west.

Müller had planned something different. For the first time during the cruise he was going to undertake an operation against a city, to create panic and confusion among the inhabitants, to disrupt the life and commerce of a strategic British possession in India. He was going to impair the prestige of the Royal Navy. He was going to attack Madras. Perhaps such an exploit, rendering the British impotent, would spur subversive Indian elements into action.

*22 September 1914*

Following an uneventful night the dawn broke, the start of a day on which the virgin cruiser and her men would undergo their baptism of fire. Madras was a fortified city and, without a doubt, its land-based batteries would answer the bombardment. There was also the distinct possibility that enemy warships lay anchored off the shore.

Müller had planned the attack for that evening. The *Emden*, in all likelihood, would be able to approach the city undetected. Final preparations for battle were made during the day. The awnings and deck hammocks indispensable to life near the equator were removed from their riggings and stowed below deck. Ammunition, waiting in readiness beside the silent guns, was doubled. The war log was placed under armored protection. In a briefing the first officer described to the ship's other officers first the overall war situation, then contingency plans for command should both the commanding and executive officers fall in battle. The crew was ordered to bathe in fresh water and don clean uniforms to prevent infection in case of injury. Every detail was rehearsed.

At 1700 Müller ordered the *Markomannia* to detach. Offering his wishes for a successful encounter with the enemy, the loyal Captain Faass turned his ship and sailed toward a southern rendezvous. The *Emden* hoisted her fourth "funnel" and slowly steamed into the tropical night, cutting through the opaque blackness. Then speed increased to seventeen knots. In the distance, sheet lightning skittered across the firmament. The harbor beacon of Madras flashed into view, unexpectedly. Didn't the port authority know anything about the war, or did Madras feel itself so impenetrably secure that it could flaunt precaution? The city's bright lights made the approach easier. The *Emden* drew closer and closer, as if stalking a prey. At dockside not one light aiding a ship's entry to port was out. Automatically the men of the *Emden* remembered Tsingtao. The moment war was declared, all fire and lights had been extinguished. Those who didn't comply were subject to strong reprimand. Here in Madras, the enemy must have assumed that no opponent would have the audacity to attack the coast of India, which since time immemorial had remained almost untouched. The last skirmishes had taken place between England and Portugal in the seventeenth century, between England and France in the eighteenth.

It was all for the better; the surprise attack would succeed. The navigation officer could calculate the ship's bearing by landmarks so that her fire would rake either the oil tanks of the Burma Oil Company, the main target, or the fifteen-cm batteries near the new lighthouse behind them. The guns could finish their job by hitting the blinking tower of light dominating the main approach to the harbor. The chances for success were excellent.

As tension mounted, the panorama of Madras grew. Were there enemy warships lying outside her harbor?

Shortly before 2100 Müller ordered the men to battle stations. The lookouts were posted. At 2145 the cruiser stood directly before the city, 2,800 to 3,000 meters offshore. The men were ready for any unpleasant surprise. It could come from the fifteen-cm guns in the harbor perimeter. Gliding silently, the shadow of the German cruiser closed in on the capital city of Madras.

The *Emden*'s target run was angled so that even an inaccurately aimed shell would not fall in the narrow streets. This was carefully calculated to quell propaganda reports about German bestiality.

The command from the bridge sounded: "Stop engines!" and the ship came to a halt. Another moment of suspense passed. The *Emden* turned to the south, three thousand meters before the piers. Then the long-awaited command rang out: "Search-lights on, open fire!" A blinding light pierced the darkness, il-luminating the target with an eerie, stabbing finger. Immediately the first salvo was fired. Long red flashes tore from the guns. The sound rolled like giant boulders through the tropic night, startling the giant city out of sleep. More salvos were quick to follow. The massive guns discharged their blades of fire, and soon a heavy layer of smoke had settled over the ship, momen-tarily blotting out everything. From their breeches spent car-tridges clattered to the deck. Then, with a hard, metallic rhythm, the mechanisms locked in for the next volley. Again the sound of rolling boulders shattered the stillness.

The cruiser had fired her starboard battery. The first salvo had overshot the oil tanks, although several hits were scored on the coastal batteries. Quickly the gunnery officer had shortened his range, until a salvo landed before the tanks at the water's edge. Adjusting the range, he targeted one of the largest tanks. "*Fire!*" The metal exploded, black oil poured out, and the air erupted in red flames. The men in the *Emden* let out a roaring cheer, as if their favorite soccer team had just scored a winning goal. The tank was now a kaleidoscope of fire. A huge flame cleaved the air, followed by a larger one. At this point the *Emden* could have turned off her searchlight, the burning tanks supplied so much illumination.

Tank number two came under attack, but in the white light of battle all that could be seen were the black holes where the shell had penetrated. The tank was empty. The third one, when it was hit, ignited immediately. Bright flames shimmered on the dark waters.

Meanwhile the surprised British batteries had opened fire. Ap-parently they had difficulty calculating the range of the *Emden,* for out of nine shots directed at her, only three impacts were ob-served. One shell dropped a hundred meters short and the other two overshot by a wide margin, in spite of the short distance between the guns and their target.

The *Emden* had fired between 125 and 130 rounds when Müller ordered cease fire. His sole intention was to destroy the oil tanks and create panic among the inhabitants of Madras. Ammunition could not be wasted, as no one could predict where and when it might have to be used again. But these few shells, according to the Indian newspapers, had inflicted great damage: five thousand tons of precious oil was destroyed. And while the wind, blowing seaward, had saved the city itself from burning, the psychological impact of the attack was tremendous. Newspapers reported that citizens had deluged the railroad station. They no longer felt safe under British protection, and British prestige sank. The purpose of the undertaking had been justified, the goal achieved.

The appearance of the *Emden* in the Indian Ocean and the bombardment of Madras set the whole subcontinent in an uproar. On 29 October 1914 the newspaper *Calcutta Capital* reported the following:

> The damages inflicted by the effective plundering expeditions of the *Emden* are most depressing. The wildest rumors circulate in the bazaars like whirlwinds: The dreaded German naval squadron is about to bombard the city. Even on those who are not agitators, who do not wish to embarrass the government, the successful raids of the *Emden* have made a deep impression. It will not be easy to erase this impression. In connection with this, it must be noted that merchants in the bazaars have been dissatisfied because cheap German and Austrian merchandise is no longer available. German iron and hardware, haberdashery, yard goods, notions, and dry goods sell well everywhere. The embargo of these goods has filled Chukla, Rahman, and Sheik Memon streets with numerous Othellos who brew mischief and discontent. These circles shed no tears for the British. The stories told in the streets of the bazaars are less than flattering to British ears. What good has it been to analyze the failures of German war strategy when the successful ingenuity of a small cruiser has allowed it to pounce on large ships unpunished and to demonstrate directly to the population what German might can do? One cannot deny the continued freedom of the *Emden*. The British are embittered, and for good reason: All the Indians they are in contact with have overblown ideas about Germany's might. The assurances of the sahibs that Great Britain and her

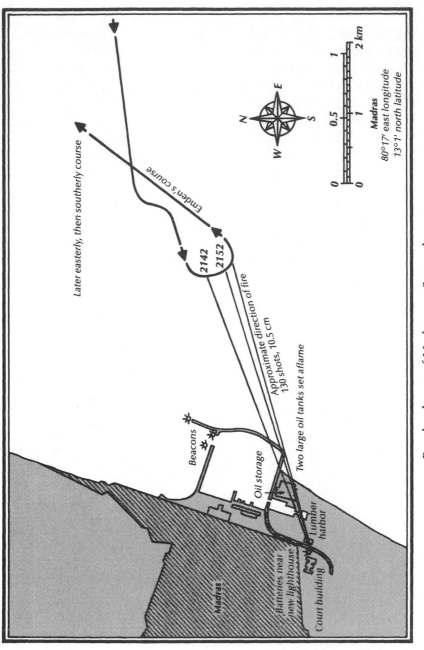

Later easterly, then southerly course

Emden's course

2142
2152

Approximate direction of fire
130 shots, 10.5 cm

Two large oil tanks set aflame

Beacons

Oil storage

Lumber
harbor

Batteries near
new lighthouse

Madras

Court building

N E S W

Madras
80°17' east longitude
13°1' north latitude

0    0.5    1    2 km
0    1

*Bombardment of Madras, 22 September 1914*

allies are slowly heading toward victory have found doubtful acceptance by the native population.

Throughout India millions spoke the strange name of the foreign ship. *Emden* was handed from that generation to the next,
eventually becoming absorbed by one of the languages of the subcontinent. Today, in the local dialect of Tamil, the word *emden*
signifies a cunning, resourceful man, in complete control of himself and his surroundings.

The commanding officer of the *Emden* could not foresee the
day his ship would be a legend. At the moment he was concen-
trating on withdrawal from Madras. As the ship departed her
lights remained illuminated. All the world could see her heading
north. When Müller was certain she had receded from view, he
ordered the portside and stern lights extinguished. The ghost
ship vanished into the night, changing her course south for the
rendezvous with the *Markomannia*.

The air crackled with intercepted radio reports. The *Emden*
had had luck on her side, and not only in eluding the coastal
batteries. There had been another, more serious, threat. The
British armored cruiser *Hampshire,* the *Emden*'s old friend, lay
nearby. During the Chinese Revolution, in 1913, she had anchored alongside the *Emden* at Nanking. This is what had knit-
ted the two crews in tight camaraderie. The *Hampshire* was now
the backbone of the Allied pursuit force. Her commander, Captain Grant, understood the mentality of his German opponent.
He must have stood off Malacca Strait or Singapore after receiving news of the *Emden*'s exploits in the Bay of Bengal. He
was unerring in his assumption that his adversary would choose
the large, open port of Madras as his next target. Grant had
steamed ahead to protect the town and capture the *Emden,*
meanwhile alerting a Japanese cruiser to the chase in hopes of
cutting the German ship off. The fate of the *Emden* seemed
sealed.

During the night of 18–19 September, the *Hampshire* picked
up a message from shore station Diamond Point reporting gunfire over Akyab, Burma. Diamond Point, which had received the

message and dutifully passed it on, was an innocent bystander in an outrageous hoax. The commander of the *Hampshire,* who up to now possessed a sixth sense for tracking, had no choice but to change his course and proceed to Akyab at high speed. By the time the trick was exposed, it was too late for the *Hampshire.* The *Emden* had already attacked Madras and disappeared into the broad expanse of ocean.

Where had the Japanese cruiser *Chikuma* gone? She could have brought the *Emden* to her knees. As it turned out, the Japanese ship had stopped for a leisurely coaling operation, thus missing her chance to capture the German raider.

Meanwhile, the *Emden,* having unwittingly slipped through this Scylla and Charybdis, steamed happily southward. Instead of being the hunted, she was the hunter once more.

Thus, in addition to the war on merchant shipping, Commander von Müller had set himself the task of demoralizing his opponents. There he found himself in agreement with the deliberations of the Admiralty Staff, which had drawn up plans to encourage India's movement to liberate itself from England. The head of the Dresden police force, Dr. Robert Heindl, had planned such an undertaking for the Foreign Office in the fall of 1914. A few years before the war Heindl had visited the penal colony on Andaman Island and reported back that the release of political prisoners there, whose number he estimated at fifteen thousand, might fan the flames of revolution. He suggested that this be done by a surprise attack from a German cruiser. First, he envisioned, Ross Island should be shelled. Then a landing party would be put ashore to take the small police force by surprise and notify all prison camps. After they had been armed and organized, the revolutionaries would be carried from the penal colony to the mainland in small boats.

On 30 September 1914 the Foreign Office had approached the Admiralty Staff in Berlin: "Experts recommend SMS *Emden* be directed to free Indian revolutionaries . . . and, if possible, transport them to India." The actual instructions were sent off on 2 October 1914 to all naval attachés and stations: "Order

SMS *Emden:* Free imprisoned revolutionaries on Andaman Island." The difficulties of this undertaking soon became apparent to senior officers on the Admiralty Staff, and on 7 October 1914 the orders were recalled: "Order #87 for 562, concerning Andaman Island, has been rescinded. SMS *Emden* must act at her own discretion."

# CHAPTER FIVE

# OFF CEYLON AND DIEGO GARCIA

*23 September 1914*

At 0500 the *Markomannia* met up with her cruiser again and they proceeded on a course southeast. Müller hoped to retreat from the Bay of Bengal, where his cruiser's presence was well known, by heading around the island of Ceylon. Things would be different off the western coast of India, should the *Königsberg,* unbeknownst to the *Emden,* not already have picked it clean. There ship traffic from the Red Sea to Bombay and Colombo remained heavy. A surprise appearance might prove fruitful, and thus speed was crucial. The *Emden* had to pass around Ceylon quickly and thus forgo coaling.

*24 September 1914*

The *Emden* navigated the coast of Ceylon at a carefully measured distance, some sixty to seventy nautical miles off shore, to avoid detection. During the day the cruiser intercepted lively radio messages being transmitted between warships and land stations. The *Emden* was on everyone's mind, much to the satisfaction of her crew.

*25 September 1914*

In the morning the cruiser drew closer to Ceylon. At about 1100 the island's south coast appeared to starboard. She passed on a westerly course about thirty miles off shore, ample distance to avoid detection from land. In her coat of gray war paint, and now burning a beautiful smokeless coal, the ship could hardly be recognized.

The coast seemed clear for traffic between Colombo and Singapore, Madras having reported that the *Emden* had headed north. Indeed, at 1300 a smoke cloud appeared, behind which loomed a freighter. The *Emden* did not have to change course to meet it. The vessel assumed that the cruiser was an English warship. What else could she be? No enemy ship would dare come that close to Colombo. The freighter hoisted its English flag, whereupon the *Emden* raised her German ensign, requested the freighter to stop engines, and dispatched the search party and demolition and scuttling squads.

The prize was a 3,650-ton English freighter, the *King Lud,* which had traveled directly from Suez and was headed for Calcutta. She was empty except for provisions. The food supplies were most welcome. They could be taken on in a leisurely fashion, over several hours. The *Emden* was not far from Colombo, but the harbor should not be approached until dusk had settled in.

The crew of the *King Lud* packed their personal belongings. Lieutenant Klöpper boarded the *Markomannia* with a guard detail to receive the new guests. The *Emden*'s mess steward was sent to the *King Lud* to pick out flour, potatoes, fresh meat, and canned goods. Once that was completed, at 1600, the English crew crossed over to the *Markomannia*. The captain and his men, having been consoled by Lauterbach with news of the fate of their predecessors, seemed to be in fair spirits.

The seacocks were opened and the ship was detonated. It sank rapidly. In the *Emden* they watched the procedure, then took up a westerly course. By dusk the cruiser stood thirty nautical miles south of Colombo. Evidently the shelling of Madras had made an impression there: four crisscrossing searchlights covered the entrance to the harbor.

Now they steered a course toward the sea lanes between Colombo and Minicoy. Minicoy, to the west of Ceylon, had a beautiful lighthouse that was used as a guide by all ships traveling
between Aden and Colombo. As early as 2200, to her starboard,
the *Emden* sighted a ship that appeared to have just left Colombo. As the cruiser wanted to capture ships as far from Colombo as possible, she pursued the ship on a very gradually converging course, intercepting it, about an hour later, head on. The
search party, under Lieutenant Lauterbach and accompanied by
Ensign Prince von Hohenzollern, conducted itself quietly. It was
unusual to take a prize within reach of the searchlights of an enemy port.

The captured freighter was an English ship named *Tymeric*.
She had been destined for England with a valuable cargo of four
thousand tons of sugar. Müller decided to take the ship along
for the moment and sink her later, some place far out of sight of
Colombo. Meanwhile, the British crew had time to prepare
their personal effects for transfer. But plans had to be altered.
The English captain was furious at having fallen into German
hands, and right under the noses of the British. British naval intelligence had assured him that the sea lane between Colombo
and Aden was safe, and the good captain had run out a day
ahead of schedule. He forbade his men to lift a finger for a
bunch of "damned" Germans. This was the first and last time
the prize officer of the *Emden* would encounter such strong opposition. The usually easygoing Lauterbach was incensed over
the remark about the Germans and passed it on to the captain
along with a suggestion that they sink the ship then and there.
Müller concurred. He dispatched a boat with reinforcements to
the freighter. The captain and his equally rebellious engineer
were placed under arrest. The cutter scurried over to the *Tymeric*,
bringing the demolition and scuttling squads. Within ten minutes the English crew had to leave their ship, keeping their personal effects to a minimum. That was a blow; the *Tymeric* had
just been to Japan and everyone had bought expensive souvenirs. The crew was furious—not at the *Emden*, but rather at
their captain, whose recalcitrance had precipitated this unfortu-

nate end. A few swore to get even once they got hold of him. Unlike the captain, they had not insured their purchases for one hundred pounds.

When the English captain climbed aboard the *Emden* he did not deem it necessary to discard his cigarette. He did not even wish anyone good evening. Once again, he came up against the wrong man. Lieutenant von Mücke ordered the offending cigarette extinguished immediately and in no uncertain terms spelled out the behavior expected of a prisoner of war. Then both the captain and his engineer were taken to the port bulwark, where a guard was posted. Later they were locked in the mine storage room.

From Minicoy new lights appeared, those of a brightly lit mail steamer. The *Emden* took no notice of it. The radioman had picked up a message reporting that the Dutch postal steamer *Queen Emma*, in need of a pilot, was due to arrive in Colombo at a specified time. Patiently the *Emden* waited for the vessel to pass before proceeding with the demolition of the *Tymeric*. The demolition squad made a connection between a shaft and the cargo holds above it, placing the charges between them. Then the seacocks were opened. The last of the boarding party returned to the *Emden*, bringing with them a few hens and fresh eggs for which they would find excellent use: Engineer Stoffers had been very ill and was in need of fresh food.

### 26 September 1914

Without waiting for the *Tymeric* to go under, the *Emden* resumed her course westward in the Colombo-Minicoy sea lane. It was about 0300. Lauterbach had brought valuable newspapers along. Besides the world situation, which interested Müller enormously, they carried news of ship movements to and from India, listing both arrival and departure times. From that the captain could draw all sorts of conclusions. The papers from the *Tymeric* were the most recent, as the ship had left Colombo only hours before. Among other things, it gave a thorough description of the shelling of Madras, reporting damage and the ensuing breakdown of morale. One article was favorably slanted toward the *Emden* and her commander, referring to him as a fair sportsman. And a firm responsible for the soap found in the *Indus* had placed the following advertisement in a section of the paper: "Our superb soap is even used in SMS *Emden.*"

No sooner had the cruiser embarked on her course toward Minicoy than she encountered a new victim, a freighter, which was stopped and ordered to follow the convoy. Lauterbach and Ensign Zimmerman took their combined search and prize party to the ship, a 4,437-ton British vessel bound for Colombo. The *Gryfevale,* her cargo holds empty, was designated a "rag collector." The captain and crew proved cooperative.

Over the course of the following afternoon the Danish motor launch *Fionia,* an old acquaintance from China, radioed Colombo for a pilot. Just after the message was intercepted, a ship came from Minicoy all lit up. In the *Emden* they were convinced it was the *Fionia.* So as not to give themselves away, it was decided to let her proceed unchallenged. While the vessel passed the *Emden* men tried to identify her with binoculars. This proved more difficult than expected, her lights were so blinding. Although she passed very close, no funnels were discernible and they felt it was the Danish ship. In the *Gryfevale* a different opinion prevailed. There the captain remembered a Bibby Liner at Suez that had laid at anchor to his stern. Half jesting, he asked Lieutenant Lauterbach, "Why do you capture only us poor freighters? Why not one of those fat and sassy mail steamers? That Bibby Liner, for instance?" Lauterbach, seeing the high speed and the many lights, immediately signaled the *Emden:* "This ship is a Bibby Liner." The *Emden* disagreed. In the meantime the unknown vessel had passed her by, running at high speed. Chasing her would have lured the German cruiser back into Colombo waters, and the captain did not want that. Later, Lauterbach and the rest of the people in the *Gryfevale* swore that they had seen a thick funnel. The question was never satisfactorily answered. In any case, the sinking of a mail steamer carrying a lot of passengers would have caused all sorts of difficulties. There were other successes in store for the *Emden.*

*27 September 1914*

At 0200 another steamer crossed the *Emden*'s path. Within a half hour it was halted. From the *Emden,* a dark outline without lights could be made out beyond the vessel. Immediately general quarters was sounded and the cruiser braced herself; a blacked-out warship might be accompanying the steamer. But the warrior turned out to be nothing more than a dense smoke cloud from the freighter.

No prize was ever more happily greeted than this. The *Buresk,* an English collier of 4,350 tons, hauled no less than 6,600 tons of first-class Cardiff coal, 1,600 more than the *Markomannia* had originally started out with. She had been chartered by the British Admiralty and was en route from England to Hong Kong. Now, in one stroke, the *Emden* was free of worry for a long time to come.

*28 September 1914*

After such a fortunate night it was only fitting to wake to a beautiful Sunday dawn. The long-awaited northeast monsoon had finally arrived and they had nothing but clear days and calm seas.

After the Sunday church service ended Lauterbach sent a message from the *Gryfevale:* "Captured crew creating problems with drunkenness and disorderly conduct. Had to place several men in irons. Send reinforcements." The *Emden* signaled back: "Take away all alcohol immediately. *Gryfevale* close up with *Emden.*" Originally, on leaving their ship, the crew of the *King Lud* had been given generous permission to take along some of their whiskey supply. Now, ready to celebrate their so-called English Sundays in style and encouraged by the beautiful weather, these decent seamen overdid it, drinking themselves into oblivion. For no reason at all, one of them took it into his head to waylay a Chinese. The unfortunate man, burdened with a soup tureen, saw no way out of his trouble but to empty the pot over the head of the drunken sailor. The rest of the crew got into the action. Several men shattered the tureen over the skull of the

Chinese. Others piled on with a wild roar, and knives flashed in the sun. At that moment the alert German guards jumped in and parted the fighting cocks. Lauterbach placed the most drunken among them in irons, isolating them from the rest. The least involved of the troublemakers were taken to the forecastle and locked up. Every door and stairwell was guarded. The captain of the *Gryfevale,* an energetic man whom Lauterbach had entrusted with command over his crew, gave sharp orders which he reinforced by waving a pistol. Slowly sleep descended on heavy heads. Peace had been restored.

Sunday rest ended at 1300. About that time more smoke appeared, and a steamer was discovered directly in the path of the *Emden.* It took only a hoisted signal flag to invite the vessel to linger. She was an English ship, the 3,500-ton *Ribera,* on her way from Aden to Batavia. Though empty, she had provisions on board that helped the *Emden* considerably. Some were sent to the *Gryfevale,* along with the ship's crew. One hour later, the naval engineer set his charges, and the scuttling party sent a few well-aimed shells in her direction. Lieutenant Gaede never missed his mark. The ship found an early grave.

The carefully kept signal log of the *Ribera* proved interesting, the captain informative. Apparently, on a previous trip in the Indian Ocean, she had met a convoy of Indian troops traveling from Bombay to the Red Sea. The *Ribera* exchanged signals with both escorting warships, the English battleship *Swiftsure* and Russian cruiser *Askold.* She also exchanged messages with other enemy ships between Suez and Colombo.

After scuttling the *Ribera* they continued their voyage toward Minicoy. The coal supply in the *Emden* had diminished, for the first and only time, by more than half.

The *Emden* had to leave the area, for by now the *Gryfevale* and *Ribera* would have been missed in Colombo. The bloodhounds would be on their heels in no time. Müller wanted to discontinue his raiding operations for a while, letting the grass grow over his victories. But at 2100 another prey appeared on the scene, the 4,147-ton English freighter *Foyle,* without cargo, bound from Aden to Colombo, and presently the combined prize, demolition, and scuttling parties were at work. The *Foyle* was to receive short shrift. While the boarding parties were busy, a second ship showed its lights from the same direction. The *Foyle* received orders to follow. Meanwhile, the boarding crew readied the provisions for takeover, placed charges, and ordered the British crew to pack its belongings. Everything would be accomplished in record time.

The *Emden* sailed to the newcomer with her proud squadron of four ships: on one side the *Markomannia* and *Gryfevale,* on the other the *Foyle* and *Buresk.* They determined by its lights that the ship was a passenger and mail steamer. In Morse code the cruiser ordered it to stop. In the *Emden* there was a great delight at the news that they would capture and sink a mail steamer. Such a handsome ship, with so many expensive fittings and comforts, was a much better prize than a simple freighter with its cheap cargo. The psychological impact of scuttling a mail steamer was also greater: the many passengers would not hesitate to deliver breathless accounts to the press of their vessel's demise, and the stories would spread far and wide. An added boon might be gold. Mail steamers often carried it. But their hopes were soon deflated. The vessel, the *Djocja,* was Dutch, a neutral. Besides that, she was empty; she had neither mail, gold, nor passengers on board. They had to let her go.

In the *Foyle* everything was ready. No more than half an hour later provisions were transferred to the *Emden;* another fifteen minutes and the crew was safely aboard the *Gryfevale.* With the explosives in place, the party returned to the ship. The *Emden* did not stay for the sinking.

The two unwilling guests in the *Emden,* the captain and chief engineer of the *Tymeric,* were moved to the *Gryfevale,* which was setting off on her own. They had finally decided to cooperate and were treated accordingly, but when they departed it was with icy expressions. Not a word of farewell issued from them.

The cruiser steered as close as possible to the *Gryfevale,* keeping her guns trained on the ship. The withdrawal from the English ship of Lauterbach and his men had to be covered; because of the recent incident of insubordination there, the *Emden* had to be prepared for anything. Thus it came as a total surprise when the English crew broke out in nine shouts of hurrah— three cheers for the commanding officer, three for the officers, and three for the crew. Tension evaporated into cordial fare- wells, and the *Gryfevale* was sent off at 2300 with sincere wishes for smooth sailing. She headed immediately for Colombo. The *Emden,* for her part, altered course until 0100. It was not until the *Gryfevale* had completely disappeared that the *Emden* set course for the Maldive islands. This, then, was the lucky conclusion to another of her days as a modern corsair. With her she took 6,600 tons of the best Cardiff coal. That, in the final analysis, was most important of all.

The *Emden* continued to follow a southerly course, slowly leaving the danger zone with any pursuing warships behind. Once more she reached the shelter of land. East of the Maldives the crew was to take on the coal their ship so needed. The swells created by the last southwest monsoon on the western side of the archipelago ruled that out as an area of operation. Coaling was scheduled for the next day; in the afternoon they made ad- vance preparations.

During their approach to the islands the crew saw an unusual natural phenomenon. The cruiser passed a spot where a hot spring reached all the way to the surface of the ocean. Steaming hot water gushed toward the sky and then traced an arcing path back to the sea. There being no record of the spring on any map, they decided they had chosen the wrong anchorage. The *Emden* stopped and turned sharply, passing within no more than fifty meters of the spring. The *Markomannia,* which could not change course quite so fast, steamed right through it and was deluged by hot water.

### 30 September 1914

The twenty-ninth passed in coaling, and on the thirtieth the *Markomannia* was to turn over all the additional coal the *Emden* could stow before leaving on a resupply mission. The *Buresk,* the new milk cow, was to draw alongside the *Markomannia* and take from her all the oil and water she could carry.

Shortly before noon mess the men of the *Emden* were engaged in what was, for them, an unusual pastime, that of letter writing. The *Markomannia* was to take along mail and forward it. They could not write much: there wasn't enough time and censorship was tight. Nothing in the letters should lift the *Emden*'s curtain of secrecy. For the officers who had to scan the letters, it was a pleasure to discover with what spirit the crew had adapted to hardship. There were no complaints about strenuous duty or short provisions, only expressions of pride and joy in their ship. Between officers and men a bond existed, one of understanding and humor, strengthened always by an awareness of the absolute necessities of the moment. Yes, morale ran high in the *Emden*. The ship, with her luck, would survive no matter how long the war lasted. Little did they know that, when the letters were being read on the receiving end, many of the senders would be dead.

But to return to the *Markomannia*: a further 150 tons of coal had to be removed. As this task was being completed, the captain of the *Markomannia* received written orders for his upcoming mission. He should avoid busy sea lanes, meet the *Pontoporos* at the designated rendezvous, and, having met her, take on as much coal as possible. The *Emden* boarding party was to transfer from the *Pontoporos* to the *Markomannia*, and the Greek freighter, after receiving the promised compensation pay, would be free to depart. At this point the *Markomannia* was to enter a harbor in the Dutch East Indies, quietly buy provisions for the *Emden*, run out undetected if possible, and then rendezvous with the *Emden*. The designated meeting time was set for the beginning of November.

When the coaling was finished, and the coal sacks, shovels, and loading gear had been transferred to the *Buresk*, the *Emden* cast off from her loyal companion, the ship that had provided her with life-giving black nourishment for two months. It was an emotional farewell. The band played. Three cheers echoed on both sides. Goodbyes, good luck, and wishes passed from one ship to the other. At 2030, empty and riding high in the water, the HAPAG freighter took up an easterly course. With sweet sadness the men of the *Emden* watched her vanish. The fourteen-knot *Markomannia* was fast for a collier and had operated smoothly with the *Emden*. On top of that, she was a German ship; a deep camaraderie had developed between her crew and that of the cruiser. The men of the *Emden* had grown fond of the considerate and industrious Captain Faass and his men. It was not much consolation to think of the *Markomannia*'s replacement—an English ship, and one that was slower by some four knots.

The farewell would have been even more heartrending had the men known that their ships were seeing each other for the last time. The fate that so many English vessels had suffered at the hands of the *Emden* would soon overtake the *Markomannia*.

To keep her destination secret at any cost, even from the German crew of the *Markomannia*, the *Emden* steered a deceptive course until the other ship had disappeared. Then the cruiser headed for the Chagos Archipelago. There the crew would rest and recuperate while the cruiser received much-needed repairs. If it so happened that they met traffic—the archipelago lay at the crossroads of a sea lane between Australia and the Red Sea, and of another between Capetown and Colombo—they wouldn't hesitate to perform the job at which they now had so much practice. From the newspapers they learned that reinforcements were to be sent from Australia to England. In view of the information obtained from the *Ribera*'s captain, these might be the same transports that had brought Indian troops to the Mediterranean; now they might be on their way from Suez to Australia via the Chagos Archipelago.

The trip to Diego Garcia, port of the Chagos Archipelago, took more than a week. The days, spent searching for likely victims, ended without results. First the *Emden* steered, at low speed, toward the sea lanes between Australia and Aden, and between Mauritius and Calcutta, lying south of Diego Garcia. There she cruised back and forth for two days, finding nothing. She proceeded to the intersection of the sea lanes Australia-Aden and Mauritius-Colombo, again to no avail. Meanwhile, the crew had a chance to relax. Aside from the thorough overhaul of engines and boilers, whose steam pipes had to be fitted with tight plugs to halt recurring damage, the duty was light and there was ample time to mend and launder uniforms.

After the first three days, the honing of professional skills recommenced. In addition to division duties, the men participated in infantry exercises and calisthenics and attended briefings. Small arms stowed under the armored deck were carefully cleaned, as were machine guns. The gunnery officer ordered a subcaliber target practice in which the *Buresk* served as target tow. Particular attention was paid to the performance of prize crews and landing parties, men most likely to see action. Battle drills, some under general quarters, were conducted with Müller himself in command. Even the stokers were instructed in the handling of guns. Before long the *Emden* resembled the taut warship she had once been.

*9 October 1914*

At 0600 the *Emden* reached Diego Garcia. A "comedy on the high seas," thus did a large English newspaper later refer to the cruiser's short visit to this enchanting, secluded island. The harbor in which the *Emden* and *Buresk* anchored was protected by coral reefs that assured a safe berth. The isle was small and circular, thickly ringed with coconut palms that provided its sole industry. Coconut oil and copra were the only exports. Every three months a sailing ship with mail and provisions arrived and left laden with the products of the little paradise.

Immediately after dropping anchor, the crew began work on the *Emden*'s hull. She started to list as compartments were flooded, and soon loud scraping and scratching noises followed by a harsh, energetic *whoosh* could be heard. The ship had left the docks of Tsingtao in June. Since then marine life of every description had stubbornly attached itself to the area below the waterline. Even if the entire hull couldn't be cleaned it would at least help to remove the encrusted growth, for every square foot of clinging life reduced the ship's speed.

Shortly after they anchored the first guest arrived. It was the French-speaking assistant director of the island's oil installation.

After talking with the commander he was taken to the mess, where in spite of the early hour he accepted a few rounds of whiskey and soda. No one in Diego Garcia knew anything about the war. The sailing vessel that was their only link with the world had left just before its outbreak. For some time the guest actually assumed that the *Emden* was a British warship; he apologized profusely for not speaking English. In time he discovered the true nationality of the cruiser, the crew having forgotten to exchange the portrait of the kaiser for that of Britain's King George. He was greatly surprised to find himself on a German ship. Her neglected condition, the officers explained at the behest of the captain, was the result of an extensive world cruise that left little time for upkeep. Naturally they had no news from home. Had Diego Garcia received any news, by chance? The good man laughed at this, saying that if the gentlemen knew nothing, they still knew more than he.

The assistant director had been on board only a short time when he was followed by his chief, who was taken directly to Müller. As a representative of the government he was even more inquisitive than his underling, wanting to find out all that had happened in the world during the last few months. Regretfully, Müller said, he had been on the high seas too long and didn't know a thing. His aid was of a different sort. The visitor owned a motorboat that, due to a mishap, had been out of commission for some time; something was wrong with the motor and no one on the island understood anything about motors. The senior machinist, Petty Officer Kluge, who in peacetime operated the *Emden*'s motor launch, returned with him to land. In no time, to the delight of the director of the oil company, Kluge had solved the problem, and before a day had passed Müller received a letter of thanks, an invitation to breakfast, and a boat loaded with fruit, a pig, and a huge pile of fresh fruit. In return the commander and his officers sent numerous bottles of wine, cognac, and whiskey as well as several boxes of cigars, all rare and welcome items on Diego Garcia. The *Emden* and her crew were not going to be indebted to their unsuspecting enemy.

After noon mess the ship weighed anchor and drifted along-side the *Buresk* for coaling. In great alarm the English captain expressed his concern. The Royal Navy, he explained, did not even allow a small torpedo boat to draw alongside a merchant ship. If it was absolutely necessary to coal at sea, the merchant ship would come alongside the warship; that was the rule.

Their stay in the harbor offered the men an opportunity to hunt. Something floating in the water which at first glance looked like dirty rags thrown overboard started to move, exposing two flashing silver bellies. They turned out to be stingrays, about four to five square meters in surface area. The fish had wide, menacing jaws that snapped at the little fish around them. Rifles were immediately brought on deck and aimed at the fish. At the opportune moment, when they broke the water's surface with their arching backs, shots were fired. One was hit in the broad expanse of the back. He reared high in the air, his strong fins flipping back and forth like a pair of powerful bird's wings. But the men could not get a closer look. It was impossible to haul the fish on board.

The time at anchor was also used for fishing. Lines hung out of every porthole. The harbor brought a rich catch of the most incredible shapes and varieties of fish. Every color of the rainbow showed up—pink, green, blue. There were fish wide, flat, or rounded, with eyes on top or below, with or without stingers. The doctor had to examine every one before declaring it fit for consumption; many were known to be poisonous. And then there were the eels, but they could not be caught. They jumped out of the water, two meters in length, whipping themselves into an almost upright position before disappearing beneath the surface.

The coaling was suspended at midnight. Only four hundred tons had been taken on; Müller wanted a thousand total.

### 10 October 1914

By 1000 the crew had completed the coaling operation, taking on less than they had hoped. At noontime the *Emden* departed from Diego Garcia, the remote island so protected from the turbulence of world history and, so it seemed, from time. She steamed away on a northwesterly course and once out of sight changed course to the northeast. Müller planned to proceed from Diego Garcia to Penang. For a time the cruiser traveled east of the Chagos Archipelago, along the sea lane between Australia and Aden. This she did in hopes of catching an unsuspecting freighter, but luck was not with her. The *Emden* radiomen, meanwhile, intercepted a message sent to Colombo by a steamer that wanted to know if the way between Aden and Colombo was safe. The answer was yes—in other words, the *Emden* was no longer thought to be in the area. With that, Commander von Müller shelved the advance toward Penang and once more took up the hunt around Minicoy.

As the hunter, the German cruiser did not always meet with success; as the pursued, it was a different story. After the sinking of the *Emden*'s latest victim, HMS *Hampshire* conducted a search around the Maldives to no avail, then turned south and continued her pursuit in the direction of Diego Garcia. The British warship must have been acting on some sort of uncanny instinct, for the assumption that the *Emden* could have gone to Diego Garcia was by no means logical. But by the time the *Hampshire* appeared off the tiny island, accompanied by the auxiliary cruiser *Empress of Russia,* the *Emden* had already departed. The good man who directed the oil operation on Diego Garcia must have been shocked to learn just who it was he had treated as honored guests. When asked the direction and time of the *Emden*'s departure, he readily supplied the information. From experience, though, the British captain knew not to take the reported departure course of the *Emden* as her actual one. Now he would have to start the painstaking work of tracking all over again. For so long he had been so close on the heels of his erstwhile friend from the Yangtze days. But once more the elusive *Emden* had slipped back into the safety of the vast ocean. The hunt continued.

CHAPTER SIX

# AGAIN IN THE BAY
# OF BENGAL

*15 October 1914*

The *Emden* approached Miladu-Madu Atoll, a northerly island in the Maldive group. For three days she had steamed at slow speed on the east side of the islands, heading north. Now she had to take on coal. She came alongside the *Buresk*, but because of the shifting sea bed she could not drop anchor and so drew slowly ahead on one engine, dragging the collier along with her. In the transfer of 280 tons of coal the crew achieved its highest productivity rate, 90 tons per hour. As early as 1400 the cruiser was able to leave Miladu-Madu and set course for Minicoy. At 2230 an illuminated beacon started growing in the darkness. A half hour later Müller could see that the area he had left just two weeks earlier was still rich in booty. At 2300 the lights of a ship from Aden appeared to port. The *Emden* and her escort, coming from the south, increased their speed, the *Buresk* following as best she could.

A dense smoke formation and the shadowy silhouette of the island gave the impression of a warship lurking beyond the steamer. The *Emden*, the crisp order "Clear for night action" ringing from her decks, turned hard to port. The torpedo officer had his starboard tubes ready to fire when, a few seconds later, the warship dissolved. The *Emden* turned again on the unsuspecting freighter, stalking slowly to avoid giving herself away. At about midnight the helpless prey was ordered by megaphone to stop. A few minutes later the prize detail took over.

The *Clan Grant*, built in 1902, was the second freighter of the Clan Line of Kayser, Irwin, of Glasgow. She was the first of the final series of the cruiser's conquests. On her way from England to Colombo and other Indian ports, the 3,948-ton ship carried mostly solid cargo like typewriters and porcelain. She had a lot of livestock, including a miniature antelope, as well as flour, canned goods, beer, and cigarettes. Intending to transfer all of this to the *Emden,* Müller decided to take the ship along until the next day. The *Emden* then steered a course for Colombo at reduced speed.

*16 October 1914*

Long before daybreak the *Emden* turned again, passed Minicoy with a large sweep to the south, and steamed toward Aden. The departure was timed so that by dawn the cruiser would be out of sight of Minicoy.

At 0700 the work began. Both cutters and the cruiser's steam pinnace were launched. It was light work, thanks to the northeast monsoon which kept the sea smooth and still as glass. The mess steward, along with fifteen men and the cutter crew, climbed aboard the *Clan Grant*. In a short time the transfer of goods and supplies was in full swing. On the cruiser deck goods of every variety piled up. First the livestock and provisions arrived, then came flour, cigarettes, biscuits, machinery parts for the engine room, and fireproof bricks for the engines and boilers.

At 1000 hours the work was temporarily interrupted. In the direction of Aden a smoke formation had been spied. A new prize was beckoning. The steam pinnace and a cutter stayed behind with the *Clan Grant,* as did the *Buresk,* whose provisioning needs were organized by Ensign Schmidt. During the *Emden*'s absence she was to take on as many supplies as possible.

The *Emden* hoisted the second cutter and steamed head on to meet the newcomer. It was never clear what lurked behind a smoke formation, so Müller staged the encounter as far from the other ships as possible. As soon as a masthead could be seen piercing the horizon, general quarters sounded. The mast rocked back and forth heavily, like the mast on a torpedo-boat destroyer or a cruiser such as the *Fox* or *Pyramus*. It turned out to be a dredger—that they hadn't expected, not in the middle of the ocean. As the crew was dismissed from battle stations, the curious vessel rolled terribly. The *Emden* signaled her to follow and they returned to the *Clan Grant*. There, with great difficulty, Lieutenant Lauterbach and his men boarded the awkward, pitching crate. Much to their suprise they were greeted by a laughing captain and jolly crew. The ship, named *Ponrabbel*, had come from England and was proceeding on a straggling four-knot course to Tasmania. Her predecessor had not completed the voyage, sinking somewhere en route. The men were delighted that circumstances beyond their control had cut short a miserable passage; the fact that they had demanded pay before embarking left them with nothing to regret. Now, fully approving the raider's action, they stood ready with their packed gear when the prize party arrived. Some leapt for joy—a real feat on the rolling, heaving platform. With tears of thanks making a crooked path down his weathered cheeks, the captain exclaimed, "Thank God I'm rid of this piece of junk, and that I got my five hundred pounds sterling in advance!" The men of the *Emden* sympathized with him and his men for having put up with so much hardship.

While the cutters and the "little *Emden*"—that's what the sailors had dubbed the pinnace—were busy transferring crews and provisions, the large one wasn't idle. She opened fire on the dredger, and as soon as the shell exploded the *Ponrabbel* turned canary yellow. As if that weren't curious enough, after the second and third explosions she capsized with a sudden sweeping motion. The hull of a dredger usually consisted of two separate parts, and as a result the *Ponrabbel* had been expected to turn over slowly, on the side facing the *Emden*. The sudden flip trapped air in the ship's compartments and she floated like a huge red whale, belly up. It seemed as if she had a sense of humor; she was going to the gallows laughing. Müller was considering whether to lob another shell her way when the good vessel decided to oblige him and, like her unfortunate predecessor, gurgled her way into the ocean deep.

Now attention was focused on the already low-lying *Clan Grant,* which had absorbed a few well-aimed shells. Soon she did her death dance, capsizing, resting a few moments on her port side, then literally spinning into the depths to the loud cheers of her animated crew and the excited chatter of a flock of ducks and geese. These last passengers, escaped from the confines of their pens, preferred the uncertainties of their accustomed wet element to the inevitability of the mess cook's knife.

The *Emden* recalled the cutters as well as the pinnace and, with a swing to the east, resumed her course. At 2300 more lights were sighted to port. The *Emden* headed for them with the *Buresk* following close behind. The captured ship was a British freighter of 4,806 tons, the *Benmohr,* built in 1912. Owned by the shipping firm of W. Thomsen, Leith, she was carrying cargo to the Far East, valuable cargo: machine parts, a motor launch, bicycles, motor vehicles, and the like. Her crew joined the others on the *Buresk* and shortly thereafter she was blown up. The heavy cargo sent her to the bottom rapidly, and when she had disappeared the *Emden* set course at low speed to the west of Minicoy.

### *18 October 1914*

The seventeenth had proven uneventful and so the *Emden* proceeded north of Minicoy, out of sight of the island. The beautiful Sunday morning of the eighteenth augured well. At about 1130 hours, the *Emden* sighted a wisp of smoke to starboard. An hour later a thick gray funnel appeared which, on approaching, slowly turned blue. It appeared to be a Blue Funnel liner, the best in the business. The *Emden,* which had gradually fallen away to port, now closed the ship and was soon in its vicinity.

Lieutenant Lauterbach's crew reported that the magnificent prize was a brand new 7,562-ton British freighter, the *Troilus,* of the Blue Funnel Line, Holt, a Liverpool company. She was on her way from Colombo to England with a superb cargo—copper, rubber, and zinc to the tune of about twenty-five million marks—as well as several passengers, including a lady. She astounded Lauterbach, approaching him with a friendly greeting and addressing him by name. Having once sailed in one of his HAPAG liners in the Far East, she remembered him well. She seemed delighted with her "romantic capture" on the high seas. Happily she paraded on deck, distributing cigarettes and chocolate to the surprised men of the corsair cruiser. Everything was absorbed with sportsman-like nonchalance; disruptions caused by the *Emden* were nothing new to her, she said. On a journey from Hong Kong to Europe, her ship had been forced to turn back to Hong Kong on account of the outbreak of war. There she wasted away for weeks, informed that the *Emden* was lying in ambush at the gates. She managed to get to Singapore and even a bit farther, but again the specter of the *Emden* turned her ship back. After a few more weeks of waiting in Singapore, she pressed on to Colombo. From there she'd embarked on this latest leg of her journey, only to run into the arms of "her *Emden.*" The detainment she took philosophically, even if it did mean returning to India with the rest of the "ragtag mob." A real lady, the men of the *Emden* decided, full of admiration.

The captain of the *Troilus,* on the other hand, was furious. "As long as I've been sailing to India," he exclaimed, "I've used the regular sea lanes. This time the naval intelligence officer in Colombo advises me to travel thirty nautical miles to the north, and I fly right into your arms." That was interesting information—the *Emden* had only to steer east to collect more booty.

Initially, to save time, Müller had the *Troilus* follow along. Then the *Emden* steered an easterly course, with the *Troilus* off her port quarter and the *Buresk* off her starboard quarter, to the new sea lane between Aden and Colombo.

At about 2100 ship lights were sighted off the port bow and the *Emden* steamed directly toward them. The ship showed no directional lights, but as a precaution general quarters was sounded. Carefully the cruiser drew up to the stranger, until it was obvious even in the dark of night that it was only a harmless freighter. By signal lamp the vessel was requested to stop.

This time it was the 5,596-ton British ship *St. Egbert* that had fallen into their hands. She was carrying general cargo and sugar from Colombo to New York. Unfortunately the cargo, being American, was neutral. The ship could only be used as a "rag picker" to save the *Buresk* from overcrowding. The freighter received orders to fall in behind the *Buresk*.

Shortly after midnight more lights hove into view. While her retinue followed, the cruiser fell upon the new arrival and challenged her in the usual manner. She was the *Exford*, built in 1911, and owned by W. T. Tateen of Cardiff. This was now the second of the colliers chartered by the British Admiralty that the *Emden* had intercepted. With 4,542 tons' capacity, she was overflowing with 5,500 tons of the best Cardiff coal. The *Emden* could now stay afloat for at least a year.

The *Exford* squeezed herself between the *Emden* and *Troilus*. Once more the cruiser had collected a small squadron of ships that was difficult to keep in formation. The *Buresk* crowded the *Emden* on at least two occasions, and the *St. Egbert* displayed a tendency to take off on her own. Poor maneuverability on the part of the heavy steamers further complicated matters, and to top it all a cloudburst opened up. When it cleared the *St. Egbert* had vanished. This was most unfortunate, for she had no radio equipment. The *Emden* had to retake her at all costs, if only for the sake of the prize crew on board.

### 19 October 1914

For the time being the cruiser lay dead in the water, remaining close to the spot where the *St. Egbert* had disappeared. Lo and behold, after about two hours the runaway returned. Her British captain was less than pleased; he had hoped to escape the cruiser's reach. His good humor returned, however, when the crew of the *Troilus* was brought aboard. He knew from the newspapers that the *Emden* was regularly forced to release one ship out of a convoy to send back any prisoners she had taken.

The cruiser would replenish her provisions from the *Troilus*. Lieutenant von Mücke took over the operation on the Blue Funnel liner. By now the *Emden* was pretty well denuded of senior officers. Besides Müller, only two ensigns and the navigation, gunnery, and torpedo officers remained. With this sparse crew the cruiser had to hoist one of the cutters about an hour after the transfer started and take off after a smoke cloud receding in the direction of Aden. One of the last remaining naval officers climbed aboard the new captive with a tiny prize crew. It was a 5,220-ton British ship, the *Chilkana*, built in 1910 and belonging to British India Steam Navigation, of London. The *Emden* quickly hauled in her cutter and with this latest booty returned to the others.

For the rest of the day, traffic resembled that of a bustling port. Men scurried over the decks of the *Chilkana*, collecting provisions, pharmaceuticals, and radio equipment. Boats hurried back and forth laden with supplies and people. When it was the turn of the *Chilkana* crew to abandon ship, her captain stood with tears in his eyes. The Chinese crew, for their part, couldn't have cared less about departing, so long as they were paid. Like the Chinese in the *Troilus* before them, they willingly replaced the Arab stokers and firemen in the *Buresk*. The *Exford* too received a full share of Chinese. Eventually the crews of the *Clan Grant*, *Ponrabbel*, and *Benmohr*, all still in the *Buresk*, were transferred to the *St. Egbert*. By now, her decks were like those of a refugee ship, crawling with people.

Meanwhile, the *Emden* fired a few shells into the *Troilus*. The captive passengers in the *St. Egbert* watched the drama with fascination. For hours, uncounted cameras waited to record the sinking for posterity, but it was all in vain, for although the *Troilus* listed heavily to port she refused to go down. The *Emden* was in no hurry. She maneuvered away from the Blue Funnel liner, taking position amid the other ships. This provided an advantageous view of the traffic around her.

It was an unforgettable sight for the men of the *Emden*. Here, on a desolate stretch of the Indian Ocean, their cruiser was anything but alone: five seagoing vessels surrounded her, one sinking, the others loaded with five to six hundred people. All the while the little boats continually swarmed about. The cruiser would be well supplied. For the officers on watch the view was not so inspiring; they had to be devilishly careful to avoid collision between their ships and the boats. More often than not the ships overshot their targets because of troublesome engines. The *Exford* was particularly dangerous. At one point the officer in command, Lieutenant von Levetzow, avoided collision with the *Emden* by desperately shouting through the megaphone, "Damn it, sir, speed ahead. My engines can't back against the wind!"

Huge amounts of fresh meat, ice, flour, potatoes, and canned goods were loaded into the *Emden* and *Buresk*. There was even a live lamb or two. The *Exford* had a well-stocked larder from which flour could be spared. The *Emden*'s physician returned with instruments and medicine. The entire radio shack of the *Chilkana* was transferred to the *Exford*. As a future tender of the *Emden*, she had to have radio communication. There wasn't time to install the radio; that had to be postponed until later. For now, advantage was taken of the opportunity to transfer part of the oil from the *Buresk* to the *Exford*.

Meanwhile, Lieutenant Gaede hunted the huge sharks that swam the waters during the transfer operations. One particularly stately specimen, accompanied by several blue- and white-striped pilot fish, held steadily to the port side. He was tempting. Gaede took a rifle and shot from the bridge. Because of a smooth and transparent sea the shark could be seen about two meters below the surface, in line with the command bridge. But Gaede missed his mark and the shark shot out of sight. The rifle's recoil sent the lieutenant's tropical helmet flying overboard. This was to be the shark's undoing. He didn't waste a moment before rearing his head and snapping at the unappetizing object. In that instant Gaede hit his target. The shark thrashed about and slammed against the ship. Then he dropped back into the water, white belly up, and sank to the bottom, still escorted by the faithful pilot fish.

Now Gaede had to exchange his rifle for heavier artillery. The *Troilus* was still afloat and in need of a few shells. It was 1500. The work would not be complete until 1800, despite more than six shells that had opened her waterline and flooded her engine and boiler rooms. The seacocks had already been broken open. As this was going on the seacocks of the *Chilkana* were opened. At 1630 she sank, considerably faster than the *Troilus*.

Lieutenant Geerdes, in charge of the prize crew, delivered orders for port of destination to the captain of the departing *St. Egbert*. He could head to any Indian port except Bombay and Colombo, but, he was warned, if the *Emden* should run across her in either of these two harbors, she would be sunk immediately. Müller wanted the British captain to think that the *Emden* was prepared to inflict further damage on trade out of Bombay and Colombo. But communications somehow failed; the captain understood his orders to mean that he was to avoid all Indian ports. After hearty farewells, during which he expressed relief at not having lost his ship and wished the *Emden* men good luck, the prize party returned to the *Emden* and the *St. Egbert* got under way.

She headed for Aden, which surprised Müller. He had assumed that she would take up a course to the nearest port, as her food supplies were running short. Ensign Geerdes was ordered to the bridge and asked what he had recommended to the captain of the *St. Egbert*. Now the misunderstanding came to light. The *Emden* chased after the departing ship and set matters straight, whereupon the British ship changed course in the direction of Cochin, a short day's journey away. The *Emden*, accompanied by the *Buresk* and *Exford*, set course northeast and followed the freighter, then swung to the south. Still in sight of the *St. Egbert*, she turned north. Müller hoped to create the impression that he had made a mistake—thinking his ship to be out of sight of the freighter and having her unwittingly reveal her true course; for it was well known by now that on leaving a theater of operations the *Emden* usually followed a false course. Only when darkness descended completely did the *Emden* take up her intended course south.

With that, the German cruiser withdrew from the scene of her greatest series of triumphs.

For the first time, the men were able to relax. Duty, as it was known in peacetime, was of course impossible. At any given time a large section of the crew busied itself with watch duty and engine upkeep. The rest had to be prepared for unexpected combat, alert in body and spirit. For the most part they slept by the guns, at least in good weather. This was not only for reasons of vigilance; oppressive heat continued to dog them. Topside on a clear evening a regular army of snorers swayed in their hammocks. For those not fortunate enough to be off duty, it was a funny sight when a cloudburst emptied itself overhead, sending the lightly clothed sleepwalkers rushing for refuge in sheltered deck areas.

But the cruiser didn't avoid rain for the sake of the slumbering ranks. Fresh water was a precious blessing. Indeed, during the day if a cloud appeared on the horizon the cruiser often ran toward it without any regard for the planned course. "Cloudfinders" were constantly on watch. If the petty officer piped, "Cloud in sight, undress for showers," the deck became a sudden swarming mass of bodies shedding clothes. The men took position where they usually lined up for muster—the stokers and seamen on the forecastle and between decks, the officers on the poop deck. They stood as if on the edge of paradise, waiting anxiously for water to descend. As soon as the first drops of moisture landed, a brisk soaping began. The customary salt-water shower produced no foam, so the rinsing off of soap bubbles was one of life's undeniable pleasures. Woe to the duty officer on the bridge who let the cloud pass too quickly. Then the crew members would stand as nature had made them, soaped from head to foot with no relief. Of course, they could wash off with sea water, they had an ocean full of that; but it left itching traces of salt behind which could turn painful in the tropics. So if the longed-for rainwater didn't arrive the men literally had to shave soap off one other with a spatula-like device. They did it, spouting irreverent epithets intended for the duty officer. He couldn't help it, and always managed to shun responsibility by referring to "higher authority."

The five cats born in Langini Harbor, meanwhile, were thriving. To tell them apart, the men had given them collars, each a different color. And each cat had been given a distinctive identity. On christening day it had been decided to use the names of captured freighters. So there was a little Pontoporos, a small

Lovat-Indus, a miniature Kabinga, and a Lilliputian King Lud roaming the decks. For the last kitten they had had some difficulty finding a proper name. Her scrawny body wobbled on four spindle legs and was made top-heavy by an oversized head that carried a pair of dumb, protruding eyes. The name *Diplomat* didn't fit her at all, so the men decided to call her Little Idiot.

All the off-duty officers played nursemaid to prevent the cats from falling overboard, but one day Little Idiot managed to elude them despite their vigilance. She was nowhere to be found. Assurances from the "kitten watch" that she couldn't have fallen overboard met with disbelief. Deep sorrow pervaded the decks. But when it was time for the evening inspection, a sailor found Little Idiot aft, sleeping peacefully on a 10.5-cm ammunition box. She had made her way there by leaping from the poop through a munition shaft. The adventure didn't leave her badly hurt, though she did drag her hind leg for a few days.

The cats were not the only animals that war had bestowed on the *Emden*. The casual observer would have been astounded to see what the ship carried with her. On the bow, near the garbage bins, he would have happened upon two eternally grunting pigs, and next to them, several bleating ewes and rams. Continuing his walk aft, he would have had to shoo a flock of pigeons out of the way. They usually sat on the guide rail of the ammunition conveyor, occasionally scattering to a loft fastened to one of the funnels. Further aft he might have stumbled across a dozen chickens whose clucking was drowned out by a gaggle of geese swimming in a vat of salt water. As always, the *Emden* had her menagerie on board. For purely ornamental display the miniature antelope took the prize. She had been found in the *Clan Grant* and brought aboard by Lieutenant von Mücke. The crew cared for all the animals; whenever one was butchered it set off an abysmal fit of wailing.

If the shipboard menagerie provided entertainment of a sort, a more civilized variety came with the daily afternoon concert. There were old favorites such as "It Was in Schönberg" and the beloved "Snuten and Poten," a sea chantey. Some men danced the slide step to that. Others would sit on the forecastle, around the music makers, smoking and singing along. In the evening, after dark, they usually formed a good strong choir and sang German folk songs, which never failed to bring out the best in their voices. Then there were the risqué songs, the salty ones, stressing innuendo more than rhythm and rhyme. The concert always ended with everyone joining in to sing "The Watch on the Rhine."

# CHAPTER SEVEN

# THE UNBELIEVABLE
# RAID ON PENANG

*20 October 1914*

The *Emden* steamed on a southerly course through thc Indian Ocean; her target, however, lay to the east. Müller planned to launch his attack on the harbor of Penang and the enemy warships he hoped to find there. The cruiser had to steer far to the south, rounding Ceylon.

In the *Emden* they finally found some leisure time. Both commanding officer and crew could quietly reflect on the exploits of their commerce warfare. Since the departure from Tsingtao their cruiser had covered an impressive stretch of ocean, had captured no less than twenty-two enemy ships, over 100,000 tons, and sunk most of them. In the eyes of the world press the Swan of the East had become the Scourge of the Oceans and a huge pack of panting hounds constantly pursued her. The crew looked forward to an encounter with the enemy. After rather routine raiding operations, they wanted to smell real gun powder and meet the foe in true combat, man to man.

Once more the *Emden* ran into a steamer. But it stood far off and Müller let it go. His cruiser should remain undetected in view of the planned operation. Above all, he had to cross the sea lanes as quickly as was possible with the slower *Exford* in company.

During the night bad weather set in, tropical rain torrents that deluged the men. Visibility was zero. Contact between the ships of the little squadron was lost. One moment the *Buresk* was missing, the next the *Exford* disappeared. In the search for one another they constantly faced the danger of collision. The men on all three vessels were glad to see the night pass without a serious mishap.

## 21 October 1914

When the cruiser stopped at 1400 the sun was again shining brightly. The *Emden* could no longer escort both colliers, so Müller decided to detach the slower *Exford* for an extended period. Naval Engineer Haass tested the ship's engine and boilers. The *Exford* and the *Emden* exchanged provisions and personnel. Then came the farewells. The British ship received orders to hold a position thirty nautical miles north of North Keeling. There she was to remain and wait for the *Emden* until at least 15 November. The same order applied to the *Markomannia* and any other German supply ships in the area. In case the rendezvous was not kept, the *Exford* should, on depletion of her food supply, head for the Nusa-Besi Strait.

With the *Buresk* as her lone companion, then, the *Emden* steamed ahead. After crossing the sea lane between Colombo and Singapore, she stood on an easterly course in the southern sector of the Gulf of Bengal.

The bridge was unbearably hot these days, the narrow chart house even worse. In his impeccable white uniform, buttoned up, as always, the commanding officer sat before his manuals and charts, taking notes, thinking and planning. Most certainly they would search for him in his now well-known hunting reserve. No one would suppose that he was planning a strike against Penang.

There the island was on the map, showing the harbor with its dangerously shallow approaches. Between the Malacca Peninsula and Penang, where the port of Georgetown was located, lay a narrow sound, open to the north and south. For the German ship the only approach possible was from the north. But this, too, posed navigational problems, especially at night. If the suspected French armored cruiser and destroyer were really there, the *Emden* would have to run a fifteen-kilometer gauntlet in the bottleneck. Müller weighed every uncertainty and difficulty and concluded that they would have to mount a surprise attack on the enemy at dawn. It was the only way they could succeed. In the narrow harbor the cruiser would have to turn as if on a dime and escape through the bottleneck to the north. It could easily become a trap.

Would such an operation be in accordance with his mission, conducting cruiser warfare? With this daring surprise attack he wanted to destroy both war and merchant ships lying at Penang. The destruction of even larger enemy warships was possible. A successful undertaking would curtail the important trade coming through Singapore. Alongside the shelling of Madras, it would do real damage to England's prestige.

The crew, noticing that no steamers had been clipped the night before, knew their commander had something special in mind. All over the ship sailors and stokers put their heads together, trying to guess what the future might bring. The gun crew cleaned their weapons more carefully than usual. In the boiler and engine rooms there was lively activity: machine parts were thoroughly overhauled. A spit and polish spirit permeated the ship.

### 22 October 1914

Today was a holiday, the birthday of the empress. Every pennant in the ship flew high on the masts. At 1000 there was a formal muster. The officers presented themselves in dress uniform with every medal in place; the remainder of the crew turned out in parade dress. There had not been such a display of spotless uniforms in a long time. The picture might have been seen in peacetime. Müller delivered a short speech about the empress' devotion to her people and to the fatherland. An enthusiastic cheer broke over the middle deck, now bright with sun-shine. The band played the German national anthem, and in the empress' honor a twenty-one-gun salute was fired.

### 26 October 1914

Around 0100, after crossing the sea lane between Jalang and Colombo, they saw the silhouette of the Nicobar islands coming over the horizon. Under their shelter the *Emden* wanted to re-plenish her coal supply once more. The *Buresk* was anchored in False Bay and the *Emden* came alongside her. At 0700 the men began the tedious job of bunkering the coal. This time they fully recognized its necessity and therefore did it willingly. At 1600 the work was done.

Because of her slow speed, the *Buresk* could not be taken on to Penang. That day she was detached to a rendezvous forty nau-tical miles west of the north end of Simeulue. Like the *Exford*, she was to wait for the *Emden* and, in case of the cruiser's ex-tended absence or a shortage of food, run into the nearest neu-tral harbor. After the *Buresk* was camouflaged, her name and home port painted over, she departed, growing smaller and smaller until finally she was a tiny dot fading into the misty blue distance.

The *Emden* weighed anchor at 1800 and set course for Pe-nang, steaming at twelve knots. Soon she crossed the sea lane Calcutta-Singapore. Now she could stop for nothing, not even a fat freighter. The approach would have to be made undetected.

### 27 October 1914

The cruiser was steaming at fifteen knots. In late morning Müller held a briefing for the officers in his cabin. The ship, just as before the bombardment of Madras, was made thoroughly battle ready. Awnings were unrigged. The war log went under armor for safe keeping. Every gun emplacement received double ammunition and there was a vigorous scrubbing down of the decks. In the afternoon all the men bathed and were issued new uniforms.

At 1700 the long-awaited order sounded throughout the ship: "All hands aft!" There was a great scurrying everywhere, seaboots clattering on the worn steel decks. Everyone wanted to be the first topside. The men saw it in the faces of their officers: something big was about to take place. They waited in suspense on the quarterdeck. Then the captain spoke. While outlining his plans in a short address, he saw by looking at his men that he could totally depend on them. They had grown close in the long weeks, the cool, intelligent, chivalrous commanding officer and his men. The crew listened to Müller's clear and quiet words. No one doubted the success of his plan.

### 28 October 1914

Everyone was sure about one thing: the operation against Penang would be nothing like the one against Madras. There the *Emden* had been able to navigate from a safe open roadstead. She could shell the harbor installations and move about freely on all sides. In Penang's harbor, warships could maneuver only in the tightest of spots, as if in a tube. And there were further difficulties: should the *Emden* manage to penetrate within range of the enemy, a few salvos from her small-caliber 10.5-cm guns would not suffice to dispatch enemy warships quickly. Only a surprise torpedo hit could do that. The cruiser would have to come within a few hundred meters of the opponent, and no one knew how many ships lay in the harbor. So before them lay a challenging, audacious operation.

During the night they adjusted their speed so that the *Emden* would reach Penang exactly at daybreak. The course took her dead ahead. Meanwhile, final preparations were being made. At the guns machinists tested breeches, range finders, trigger mechanisms, and recoil and brake cylinders. Every boiler filled with steam, and the fourth funnel was put in place. "The smoking lamp is out. Stow hammocks," called the petty officer on watch. There being little danger of discovery on so dark a night, a normal war alert was carried on until midnight. One hour later the watch was doubled. At 0200 the white lights of the lighthouse of Pulau-Penang came into view. Now the standby watch was alerted.

The battle breakfast consisted of a hearty milk soup, a much-loved navy specialty. The first officer in his wisdom had discovered that men fought better on a full stomach.

Now came the dangerous part: the approach to Penang from the north. The southern approach was too shallow for the *Emden*. Lieutenant Lauterbach, who as a former merchant marine officer had often approached Pulau-Penang and knew the entrance well, took over the navigation. All around the ship a solid line of lookouts was posted.

Again the element of surprise proved to be the right approach, for the beacons were as bright as in peacetime. Shortly after sighting the lighthouse, the men in the *Emden* spied lights to the starboard. It was a freighter, also heading for Penang harbor. Sample soundings revealed that a swift-running current had carried the *Emden* farther than the time plan allowed. To evade detection by signal stations, the *Emden* came about for a short time and steamed away from the island. She also wanted to give the freighter a chance to enter the harbor, maintaining the picture of normalcy.

The cruiser turned and ran toward the harbor at a speed of eighteen knots, leveling off at seventeen an hour later. At high speed the engines made the ship vibrate. The time was 0300 hours. She aimed for the brightly lit navigational buoy just outside the inner harbor. At 0430 the men were called to attention. To port were a few small islets from which a patrolling torpedo boat or destroyer could break out only too easily. Double lookouts were essential. But they saw only shadowy fishing craft and loaded junks.

All was quiet in these moments of mounting tension. With the islets behind them, Müller had the standby watches relieved. Then on their starboard a rowboat appeared, surely the pilot boat. It came within twenty meters as the gray cruiser rushed by. The pilot certainly ought to have been wondering why a cruiser sped so close to the inner harbor at eighteen knots. Yet he could hardly have recognized the *Emden* as an enemy ship. She was

carefully blacked out, flew no flag, and, with her fourth funnel
in place, resembled a British cruiser of the *Yarmouth* class. At
any rate, an eye not familiar with cruiser types would find it
difficult to recognize her.

The cruiser stood directly off the navigational buoy, turning
slightly to starboard. The inner harbor spread out before the
watchful eyes of the crew, lit up like a railroad station during a
holiday. Not even the slightest precaution had been taken.

It was 0450. Any minute now, the first light of dawn would
break and the action begin. "Attention, stand by!" came the renewed order from the bridge. The ship steered with decreasing
speed into the beacon's path. All eyes were trained on the spot
where the charts had located the anchorage for warships.

Exactly what ships would they find at anchor? Would they be
the expected armored cruisers, *Montcalm* and *Dupleix*? That
was the crucial question. The kaleidoscopic effect of lights made
it hard to distinguish anything and the men saw only a web of
masts and funnels. Then the first glimmer of light filtered over
the hills above the harbor. Within seconds the lookouts spied
a black mass of warships lying in unsuspecting sleep. Were
the stern lights those of torpedo boats or destroyers? Only at
twelve hundred meters could they tell more: what they saw was
the quarterdeck light of a large warship with a mast between the
second and third funnel. At eight hundred meters they recognized the Russian light cruiser *Zhemtchug*. Nothing moved over
there. The crew was sound asleep. Even the men on watch were
unsuspecting; they did not recognize the *Emden*'s German pennants. A boat had just reached the Russian cruiser, dropping off
the messmen.

In the *Emden* the torpedo tubes were all clear. The enemy
ship came directly into their line of sight, a dark cutout against
the congealing light. At 0518 Müller gave the order to fire. Lieutenant Witthoeft, the torpedo officer, jerked the havoc-raising
lever. As soon as the weapon shot out of its tube the gunnery
officer was ordered to fire. Meanwhile the *Emden* reduced speed.

A telltale trail of bubbles traced the wake of the torpedo as it
rushed the short distance of three hundred meters toward the

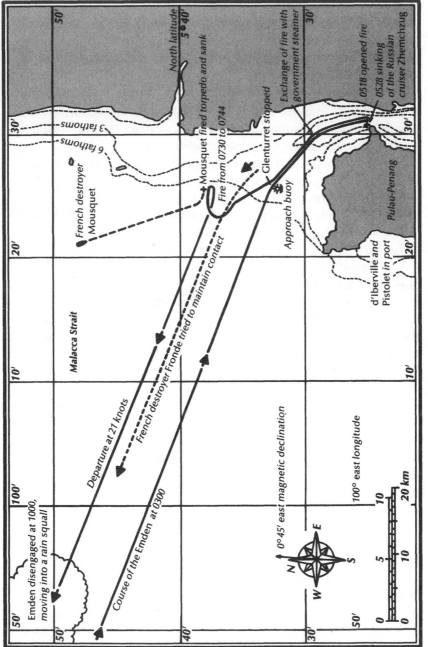

*Action Against Penang, 28 October 1914*

oblivious enemy. Eleven seconds later it penetrated the Russian cruiser in the vicinity of her after funnel. They heard a dull thud and water swirled around the maimed ship in a gigantic whirlpool. Because of its short run the torpedo had hit too deep to destroy its target. When it exploded the deck tilted high at the stern, then sank all the way down to the foot of the flagstaff. The gunnery officer, Lieutenant Gaede, ordered the five starboard guns into action. Shells pelted the sinking bow where crew's quarters were located. One shell after another struck the hull amidships, and soon it was riddled with holes. The sound of salvos in the narrow maze of harbor echoed with ear-shattering force. Drowsy morning had turned into hard, bloody day. The entire forward superstructure of the enemy ship had been blown away. Only a few of the sleeping crew escaped. Shortly the warship's belly looked like a blazing sieve of flames. Small explosions followed closely on each other.

Müller turned the *Emden* sharply to port, close to a freighter anchored in mid-harbor. The cruiser could not afford to become entangled in the merchant vessels lying all around. There were at least twenty of them, mostly English and Japanese. While the German ship swung around several shells whistled over her. A few sailors on the *Zhemtchug* had managed to reach their twelve-cm bow guns, but the only effect their action had was to damage several freighters. Then shots came from another direction. Deep behind a mole lurked several small warships, the French dispatch boat *d'Iberville* and two French destroyers, as they learned later. That cannonade resulted only in a hit on a British freighter.

Meanwhile, the *Emden* slid past the Russian cruiser and maneuvered among the merchant ships. Space was tight. If she did not move quickly more adversaries would descend on her, but there was only room to turn laboriously in place with the help of her two screws. The Russian ship would have to be destroyed before she could launch one of her torpedoes.

The *Emden*'s guns hammered the foe while the port torpedo tube was made ready for action. Again the lever was pulled, and the insidious whooshing stream of bubbles headed toward its target, no more than eight hundred meters away. The *Emden*'s port battery opened covering fire at point-blank range. "One . . . two . . . three . . . ," the German crew counted. At 0528 another heavy detonation drowned the deafening battle noises in the narrow harbor. The second torpedo had hit the *Zhemtchug* under the conning bridge. A white and yellow and black cloud engulfed the ship, a shaft of yellow-green lightning pierced the cloud. High over the masts a flame reared. The Russian cruiser had been torn in half. Huge chunks of iron catapulted into the air and whirled about before plunging into the water. When, after about two minutes, the thick cloud rose above the *Zhemtchug,* all that remained of her was a nest of straggly mastheads.

From the first to the second torpedo launch barely ten minutes had passed. One adversary was beaten. Boats swarmed in the vicinity of the sinking ship, and many warships were now visible in the harbor. It would be their turn next. Already the *Emden* was turning to starboard to take on the *d'Iberville* and as many freighters as possible. The latter would pose the greatest difficulty, as Müller wanted to be absolutely sure of their nationality. But a new dispatch boat, one that would save the *d'Iberville* and the still-unrecognized French torpedo destroyers *Fronde* and *Pistolet,* relieved him of that problem. From the outer harbor it bore down on the Germans, a gray-painted vessel enveloped in black smoke. Assuming the newcomer to be a torpedo-boat destroyer on patrol duty, Müller turned back to port and rushed toward it. A clash with a ship like that could be deadly. The *Emden* would have to escape from this mousetrap posthaste.

The men on the bridge maneuvered magnificently. At a distance of about six thousand meters the *Emden* opened fire. The first shots missed, owing to a strong refraction that distorted the measurements of the optical instruments. That proved fortuitous: the ship under attack, which swung to starboard and headed for land, turned out to be a harmless government schooner. Immediately the *Emden* ceased fire. One shell had hit the boat's funnel, but there were no dead or wounded.

By now the *Emden* was already out of the harbor. Reluctantly, Müller aborted the plan to destroy the *d'Iberville* and the freighters. Returning to the inner harbor would take time, during

which a stronger enemy might mobilize himself. The commanding officer consoled himself with his results so far.

The top flags were taken down and the cruiser ran by the
islets undisturbed. Once on the high seas again, the crew was
ordered to the quarterdeck. Lieutenant von Mücke gave a running account of the battle to the attentive assembly. Their adversary and victim had been the Russian light cruiser *Zhemtchug*,
equal to the *Emden* in tonnage, speed, and torpedo armament,
somewhat superior in gunnery. The battle had been the first
highly successful one in history involving surface ships with torpedoes. Pride reflected in the faces on deck.

No sooner had the men been dismissed to wash up than the
alarm sounded general quarters. It was 0700. Once more they
rushed to their battle stations. This time the encounter could be
more serious. The ship coming at them from the outside threatened to cut off their escape route. What's more, gauging by its
size, their foe was an auxiliary cruiser.

Quickly the distance between ships was measured, the guns
were readied, the standby order was given. Müller held the ship
somewhat to starboard so that he could use all of his portside
guns. At any moment the other ship would commence firing.
But it never did. As it approached, they saw that it was only a
British freighter carrying an explosives flag on her masthead.
From a distance it had appeared to be a larger ship. The refraction of the tropical rays had deceived the *Emden* a second time
that morning.

The crew stepped back from the guns, and the British ship
was challenged and stopped. For the first time in what seemed
like ages, Lieutenant Lauterbach and his prize detail were at
work again. He had orders from Müller to inform the captain of
the British ship that the *Emden* had not stopped to save survivors of the *Zhemtchug* only because plenty of boats had been in
the area. The government ship had been mistaken for a torpedo
boat and shelled for that reason. The captain of the *Emden* re-
gretted the incident.

The prize detail had just boarded the freighter, the *Glenturret*,
when it was hastily called back. To the north another vessel had
been sighted. This time, despite the optical confusion of the

windless sunny morning, they definitely recognized a warship. Apparently it had been patrolling the northern approach to the harbor when radioed for help. The *Emden* immediately set her fourth funnel back in place. The *Glenturret,* to the delight of her captain, was dismissed. Sounding the alarm for general quarters, the *Emden* steamed at high speed toward the new adventure. At about seven thousand meters the Germans realized that they would be taking on a torpedo-boat destroyer.

It headed for the *Emden* about two degrees to starboard, raising the tricolors of France. Did it take the *Emden* for the British cruiser *Yarmouth?* For the second time that day the German cruiser hoisted her topmast banners, at the same time swinging wide to port. At forty-three hundred meters she fired her first salvo from the 10.5-cm guns. At this point the French ship committed a tactical error. Instead of launching a follow-through torpedo attack, it turned hard to port and headed for the coast.

That move sealed its fate. The maneuver alone cost it precious time, which the cruiser's guns took advantage of by firing mercilessly. After the third salvo had wracked the destroyer from stem to stern, the *Emden* switched to rapid fire. The distance between ships narrowed. Boilers in the destroyer exploded and a steam cloud billowed into the air. The ship lost momentum, lay dead in the water. This notwithstanding, the French sailors bravely took up the uneven battle. Their port guns opened in rapid fire on the *Emden* but failed to hit. When the cruiser crossed the line of sight the French launched torpedoes, but they too missed their target. Now every German salvo connected, hacking the destroyer to pieces. Soon it disappeared behind a cloud of steam and smoke and several huge columns of water raised by the penetrating shells.

Sometime after the tenth salvo Müller ordered cease fire. He wanted to see if they would raise the white flag on the other ship. A moment before a warship had sat intact; now it was without mast or funnel. The bridge was totally crushed. But the white flag did not appear and that meant caution. Perhaps the enemy's torpedo tubes were still functioning. The *Emden* could not afford to be crippled by a defeated enemy at the last moment. A ship without port, she could undertake only minimal repairs. Heavier damages would be the end of her corsair action. So her guns took aim once more and fired an additional ten salvos. Now the fight was over for good. After a twenty-minute battle the opponent's bow had already sunk deep in the water. A few seconds later it disappeared entirely. The wreck dove head first into the ocean, lifting its stern straight into the air. Soon the quarterdeck slid under, sea closing over it in quiet riplets.

Presently the *Emden* smelled more danger. She was in shallow water and could become grounded any moment. With lowered top flags she maneuvered over the sternpost, close to the sunken ship, and as soon as she lay idling soundings were taken.

To rescue survivors Müller had the boats lowered, first the port cutter, under the command of Ensign Fikentscher, then the starboard cutter, which took longer since it had been filled with sea water to prevent fire. When the German boats approached, the French survivors tried to swim away. Apparently anti-German propaganda had convinced them that they would be killed on the spot. Only after seeing how carefully their wounded comrades were lifted into the boats did some of them let themselves be fished out of the water. One survivor who would not let a boat near him managed to swim to land. Of the seventy-six-man crew the *Emden* rescued only thirty-six, including one officer. Twelve were wounded, one severely.

When the cutters pulled alongside the *Emden* the non-wounded climbed on board. Then the boats were hoisted to the hammock crates, where the already-bandaged wounded were carefully passed over in hammocks and carried to the ship's infirmary and compartments nearby. Doctors Luther and Schwabe, who had been complaining about lack of work, had their hands full now. There were numerous amputations to perform.

The healthy survivors made themselves right at home. German sailors gave them new uniforms, food and drink, chocolate and cigarettes. By and by they overcame their reserve and began to talk.

Their ship, the torpedo-boat destroyer *Mousquet*, 310 tons, built in 1902 and armed with one 6.5-cm gun, six 4.7-cm guns, and two torpedo tubes, had been on patrol duty off the northern entrance to the harbor of Penang. At night she had sought shelter near the coast. Some of the French sailors reported they had seen the *Emden* on her approach but because of the fourth "funnel" had mistaken her for the English cruiser *Yarmouth*. On hearing explosions and gunfire in the harbor, they had scurried to find out what was going on and run straight into the arms of the *Emden*. The air pressure of the first salvo catapulted a lot of people overboard. Others leapt into the water in a hail of shells. Soon the commander, Lieutenant de Vaisseau Théroinne, who had stayed with his men on the bridge, was badly wounded. Both his legs had been shattered. The brave man, seeing that his ship was sinking, had himself tied to the command bridge so that he could go down with her.

When the rescue work ended it was high time for the *Emden* to disappear. The radio station at Penang had spread news of the attack to the entire world. Surely enemy forces would soon be in hot pursuit. A sister ship of the *Mousquet* had already left the inner harbor of Penang and was following the German cruiser doggedly, though at some distance, radioing the *Emden*'s position and course to enemy naval forces. The destroyer, which turned out to be the *Fronde,* must have been in port but without steam up. Sheltered by many freighters, she had been completely overlooked by the *Emden*. Fortunately the cruiser had not returned to finish off the *d'Iberville* and other ships, for the *Fronde* and her sister, the *Pistolet,* while they were getting up steam, would have found it easy to torpedo her.

The *Emden* increased speed to twenty-two knots and set out on a northwesterly course to confuse the *Fronde* and the northern signal station on Penang. Time passed but she failed to shake her clinging pursuer. The destroyer was equal to the cruiser in speed and nothing could be done about it. Müller only hoped that no enemy ships were lingering in the vicinity. The *Fronde,* with her lower coal capacity, could not stay on his track forever.

A solution to the problem came sooner than expected. The heavens, which up to now had safeguarded the *Emden*, came to her rescue once more in the form of a rain squall. The German cruiser disappeared into it, the turbulent sea leaving no telltale sign of her presence. Hours later, when the sun appeared, she was alone on the sea, her tracks covered. Now she could resume her old course, north-northwest.

Even in an undertaking as dangerous as this, the *Emden* had had luck on her side. Shelled by three enemy ships, she had not suffered a single hit and not a man had been wounded. Naturally, her crew would have liked to square off with the French armored cruiser *Montcalm* and *Dupleix* instead of the Russian *Zhemtchug,* but the unexpected sinking of the *Mousquet* made up for that. They were proud of their new triumph, particularly the torpedo gang, who had been able to launch two of their carefully nurtured eels with such success.

The *Emden* throttled back to seventeen knots to save coal. It was Müller's intention to find a freighter in the sea lane between Penang and Rangoon that could relieve him of his prisoners, particularly the wounded. Their suffering gave the German sailors, for the first time, a sense of the hard reality of war. Every effort was made to alleviate the plight of the victims, but after all, the cruiser was no hospital ship. Several of the Anamite stokers had been badly burned and sailors stationed on the destroyer's deck had wounds caused by shell fragments.

Until 1600 the *Emden* held her course on the sea lane between Singapore and Rangoon. She met with no ships. As Müller planned to push through to the Nicobar islands the next day, they steered toward the St. George Canal, at 2000 passing it. Now the ship was more or less safe. The port engine, whose ball bearings needed some work, was stopped for the time being. The *Emden* steamed slower, turned southwest, then west. After her bold move, described in the local press as an "unbelievable adventure," the *Emden* had escaped unscathed once more.

# CHAPTER EIGHT

# THE LAST REPRIEVE

*29 October 1914*

During the night two of the wounded French prisoners died. They were buried with honors the next morning, the tropical heat demanding quick action. The crew of the *Emden* assembled on deck, the enlisted ranks in Sunday uniform and the officers in decorated dress uniform. The prisoners gathered at the starboard gangway, where the two bodies lay in state, sewn into sailcloth which had been wrapped in the tricolors of the French Republic and weighted with irons. When the honor guard stepped on deck, all engines stopped. Commander von Müller gave a short address, first in German and then in French. He remembered the two who had passed away and how bravely they had fought for their country. Then, after the Lord's Prayer, the bodies were committed to the sea and three volleys were fired.

*30 October 1914*

Much to the regret of the *Emden* crew, another French sailor died of his wounds during the night. The doctors could not save him. He, too, was buried at sea with military honors. Müller's wish for a vessel that would take the remaining injured to a hospital on land grew desperate. His ship's limited facilities and the abominable heat would result in nothing but more deaths.

At 0400 the long-awaited smoke signal appeared and the cruiser set a direct course toward it. A handsome white ship was halted in the customary fashion. *Newburn* was her name, a 3,000-ton British vessel. According to the manifest for a German company, she was carrying a cargo of salt from England to Singapore. With these credentials the freighter seemed ideal for taking the French sailors off the *Emden*'s hands. And so the *Newburn* received orders to deliver the prisoners to Sabang, not more than twelve hours away. There she would find a well-equipped Dutch hospital. The captain, who wanted to save his ship from sinking, was only too happy to oblige.

Before they left, the prisoners had to submit a written declaration not to fight against Germany again in the war. The first officer of the *Mousquet* and some of his fellow officers thanked Müller for the humane treatment received aboard the German ship. Then the transfer took place. Dr. Schwabe saw to it that the patients were properly attended to and gave the *Newburn*'s captain instructions for their care. After that the British ship was allowed to depart. The French sailors crowded along the railing, waving their goodbyes.

The *Emden* headed on a westerly course, cutting through a smooth blue sea. When the *Newburn* was out of sight she turned south to rendezvous with the *Buresk*, forty nautical miles west of the northwestern tip of Simeulue.

### 31 October 1914

At 0300 hours the *Emden* reached her appointed destination. The *Buresk* hove into sight right on time. How easily she might have been seized by an enemy cruiser! There was great joy on both sides.

### 2 November 1914

On Sunday the ship continued southeast and Müller decorated about forty of his men for gallant service. In the early morning hours of the second, a Monday, the *Emden* came alongside the *Buresk* in a calm sea and replenished her coal supply. The place was North Pagai, near Padang. About 0900 the dirty

work began. The crew took on 500 tons, bringing their supply
up to about 950.

At noon a sailing cutter flying the Dutch flag approached
from land, laboriously running its heavy oil motor because of
the dead calm. The craft circled the *Emden* in a wide sweep and
then drew in at the port gangway. Fumes from the motor filled
the *Emden*'s wardroom with a heavy petroleum stench. Out of
the boat stepped a khaki-clad gentleman who identified himself
to the officer on watch as a captain in the Dutch Colonial Army
and the local government representative. He was directly taken
to Commander von Müller. At the moment he was on an inspection trip, he declared. He had come only to convince himself
that the German cruiser was lying outside the neutral three-mile
limit, for the *Emden* had taken on coal about a month before in
Dutch waters. Müller satisfied the Dutch officer on this count
and offered him a few whiskey and sodas, which loosened his
tongue. He said that Portugal had declared war on Germany,
a piece of news that did not particularly upset Müller or his
men. Meanwhile, unbeknownst to the Dutchman, the two ships
drifted closer and closer to the three-mile limit. Thanks to the
whiskey and sodas, the coaling would continue without interruption. About 1500 the Dutchman left the ship in high spirits,
wishing them smooth sailing and good health.

Two hours later, with the coaling finished, the *Emden* set out
on a westerly course. Once beyond sight of land she swung to
the southeast, toward that part of the Sunda Strait between Java
and Sumatra. There Müller planned to cross back and forth in
hopes of catching a few freighters. The crew would have loved to
corral a Japanese ship. For weeks Tsingtao had been under
heavy shelling from Japanese artillery; it could not hold out
much longer.

### 8 November 1914

A fruitless couple of days had passed; no victims had appeared off the Sunda Strait, and when the *Emden* had then gone
to the designated rendezvous with the *Exford,* that ship also
failed to show. Now it was Sunday, and services were under way.
There were no pastors assigned to light cruisers in the German

navy, and so the Protestant service was conducted by the senior Protestant officer, Commander von Müller. After Sunday muster the boatswain had piped church call, whereupon the entire Protestant off-duty crew had gathered amidships to worship. The band was playing hymns, which would be followed by a reading from the Bible, a sermon from Müller, and the Lord's Prayer. At the same time, on the forecastle, mass was led by the senior Catholic officer, Ensign von Guérard (when he was on duty responsibility fell to Ensign Prince von Hohenzollern) for the Catholics in the crew. This included the reading of the Epistles and the Gospel, general responses, and meditations. The Litany was recited at the close. Müller insisted that church services be held regularly, and despite little time for preparation they were as inspiring and ceremonious as possible. The moments of contemplation shared by this isolated crew on a small ship made Sunday a special event in the calendar of work-filled weeks.

When services were over the *Emden* found the *Exford*. It actually was poor navigation that had kept her from the rendezvous. During the last meeting of the two ships, in the heat of coaling, the synchronization of chronometers had been completely overlooked—a mistake that would later prove deadly to the *Emden*.

The crews threw themselves energetically into personnel transfers. Among other exchanges, Lieutenant Gropius, who had reluctantly had to give up his post as navigation officer to Lieutenant Lauterbach before the action at Penang, returned to the *Emden*, while Lauterbach assumed command of the *Exford*. At noon the chronometers on all three ships were synchronized. Lieutenant Lauterbach received a new rendezvous point near the island of Socotra, on the other side of the Indian Ocean. Müller wanted to shift their scene of operations completely. The *Emden* men watched the disappearing collier wallow through heavy swells in a northwesterly direction, little realizing it would be the last time they met.

There being a dearth of freighters at the time, Müller planned to pay a visit to the Cocos. There they would destroy a cable and radio-transmitting station on Direction Island and, Müller hoped, initiate a wave of panic in Australia that would draw part of the enemy fleet from Indian waters to follow a false trail around Australia and in the Pacific. With the enemy thus engaged, the *Emden* would be free to undertake a lightning strike on the sea lanes of the Red Sea, on the opposite end of the Indian Ocean. (The *Königsberg* could no longer be counted on. She lay blockaded in Rufiji Delta, if one could believe British reports.)

At 1900 the *Buresk* was dismissed with orders to steam to a point about thirty miles north of the Cocos and then, following radio directions, approach them for coaling. The *Emden* turned her bow toward Direction, where Müller wanted to be at daybreak. A landing party was to be sent ashore—an unprecedented mission for the *Emden*—to destroy the communications facility and, if possible, to cut the cable and tow it out to sea, thus making repairs more difficult. That was Müller's grand plan.

# Three

# The End
# of a
# Cruiser

# CHAPTER ONE

# THE ACTION NEAR THE COCOS

Was it wise to attack an island group equipped with a radio station? As far as can be judged, yes, for there seemed to be no enemy ships nearby.

The *Emden*'s radio room and its operators were excellent. In the constantly pursued cruiser, however, it could only serve as a listening post; any outgoing messages were immediately intercepted by an attentive fleet. Of course, all naval communications passed in secret code, but the signal itself betrayed a ship's presence, and varied methods of transmission gave away additional information. Experienced radiomen could differentiate between a Marconi and a Telefunken transmitter, and between the casual fingerprint of a merchant vessel and the disciplined, precise tapping of a navy ship. They could measure the distance to the signal and even determine the source and origin of the message. Since they knew where their own warships were located, any intercepted message far removed from the known sea lanes could only originate in an enemy cruiser. Thus a smart warship would arrange a rendezvous with a freighter using written orders. Communications with tenders were made by semaphore, signal flags, signal lamp, or searchlight.

On the Cocos the presence of the German cruiser became known when she called the *Buresk* with her strong Telefunken transmitter. The radioman on Direction Island asked her what ship she was. Receiving no answer, he resolved the question merely by looking out the window. An unidentified gray warship was anchored near the harbor. He sent an S.O.S. out.

The radio equipment used by the *Emden* so long and masterfully, now so carelessly, would precipitate her downfall. What would ultimately prove to be her nemesis was not the well-planned countermeasures of the British Admiralty nor the tracking experience of the warships of four great navies, but chance. It so happened that a large convoy of troop transports, escorted by an armada of warships to protect it from feared German cruisers, was steaming in the vicinity of the Cocos when the *Emden* arrived.

As always, the *Emden*'s radio operator had listened all day to crisscrossing messages. Enemy warships did not seem to be in the operational area. It was estimated that the warship answering the S.O.S. of the Cocos station was about 250 miles away. That meant, at highest speed, it would still take the ship ten hours to reach the islands. In ten hours the *Emden* would be miles away, her work done.

But in these days the methods for determining the bearing and distance of foreign radio signals were still in their infancy. Actually, the British convoy was only fifty miles away from the islands, a mere two hours at high speed. Coincidence, which had served the *Emden* so well, now turned against her. As an operational warship the German cruiser had only five hours to live.

### 9 November 1914

At 0600 the cruiser stood off the northernmost island. At 0630, daybreak, her anchor chains rattled down and sank into the hard coral bottom of Port Refuge, the anchorage of Direction Island. (A night attack had been ruled out because reefs crowded the island approaches. In the dark the ship would have had to operate with searchlights visible from land.) The landing party, commanded by the first officer, Lieutenant von Mücke, who was given Ensigns Schmidt and Gyssling for support, had assembled. With the approval of the commanding officer Mücke had picked thirty-two ordinary seamen and fifteen technical specialists, the best men on the ship, in particular the "nine-year men" who were fully committed to careers as noncommissioned officers. They were to be rewarded for their part in the success at Penang and offered a chance to exercise their land legs a bit. When the party of fifty men departed, the *Emden* would be left with a crew of 314, not counting the men dispersed in tenders.

The morning before the landing Ensign Fikentscher had learned that Mücke intended to take a hand-picked company including the gunners. As detailing officer he had pointed out to Müller that the *Emden,* by their absence, would be undermanned in strategic spots and certainly not battle ready. In reply the captain said that when the *Emden* entered the harbor the landing party would still be on board, the gunners in position to go into action if necessary. During their short absence, moreover, it was unlikely that an enemy ship would appear. Thus Commander von Müller had been warned.

At 0630 the small landing force debarked in the steam pinnace and the two cutters. The communications station was to be taken by surprise and destroyed quickly and quietly. The four heavy machine guns went along with them, protection against the possibility that the station would be guarded by troops. The pinnace took both cutters in tow and brought them at high speed through a passage in a lagoon to land. Those left behind looked after the boats in envy. Soon they saw them vanish.

Since the day before radio traffic had been heavy, but it was impossible to determine if any of it came from warships. Around the islands no vessels were visible. There appeared to be no imminent danger, though the British had noticed the approach of the *Emden*. "Unidentified ship at entrance," they radioed continuously. The radioman in the *Emden* jammed the message as much as he could. A few minutes later the landing party stormed the station. Now even a garbled call for help could direct attention to the *Emden*. Caution was the watchword.

The interior of the island was blocked to view. A woven belt of palm trees provided an impenetrable defense against prying eyes. Only the tips of the radio antenna with its Union Jack waving could be seen above the trees. Suddenly there was the sound of a strong crash. The radio tower had collapsed. This was received with great joy in the *Emden*.

Everything seemed to be going well. The weather was ideal, the sea smooth as a plain. Taking advantage of the opportunity, Müller had the radioman order the *Buresk* in for coaling. She was waiting nearby, and who knew when the *Emden* would have another such opportune moment? The command to prepare for coaling was issued. The band played spirited marches.

Still there were no enemy cruisers in sight. The only warship that had answered the S.O.S. from Direction stood, according to the measurements of the *Emden*, about 250 nautical miles away.

The good *Buresk* failed to answer the *Emden*'s call. It grew later and later. 0800 . . . 0830 . . . Where was she? Wasn't her radio working? If the order had been received, she would have been at the entrance no later than 1000. Her smoke plume would have been spotted by the lookout at 0900. The landing party too seemed to be taking its time, much longer than expected. Only a few minutes more and their deadline would be up. It passed. Perhaps the *Emden* would have to delay coaling. The danger of being surprised by enemy forces increased as the day wore on.

Soon the signalman in the crow's nest shouted, "Smoke cloud off the port bow in a northerly direction!" Finally, the *Buresk*. If she hurried, there would still be time to coal. But why was the cloud so thick? According to orders, the *Buresk* was supposed to sail almost smokeless. Then they remembered that a fire had been smoldering in her cargo hold. Could it have gotten worse? Maybe the *Buresk*, knowing that she was late, was trying to make up for lost time by running at full speed. They had to be positive. The adjutant climbed into the foremast and reported a ship with two masts and one funnel. For a while it looked as if the smoke cloud would disappear. Some of the men now thought that the vessel was an Australia-bound passenger steamer which, according to a radio report, was scheduled to pass the area about this time. That, however, turned out to be an illusion.

Presently the vessel turned toward the island again. Preparations for coaling had been completed on deck. Until the arrival of the *Buresk* nothing more could be done. Many of the men used the time to smoke a leisurely pipe of tobacco and listen to the lively marches of the band.

On the bridge the attitude was anything but relaxed. Heavy smoke poured from the approaching vessel. Something was wrong. But they were not ready to give voice to their suspicions. About five minutes later a new report came: "Smoke cloud approaching at high speed. Two tall masts and four funnels now visible. Apparently an enemy cruiser."

It was 0915. On the signal mast flags ordering the landing party back were hoisted. They should be easily spotted from land.

Now on the horizon slanted masts hove into view. Slanted masts and heavy smoke meant only one thing—an enemy warship. The *Emden* faced a battle. Sirens howled, alerting the landing party to approaching danger. Signal flags passed the message that the *Emden* would weigh anchor. Still no sign of the landing group.

The approaching ship carried the radio antennae typical of warships. The British battle flag was flying from her gaff. So now, after months of hunting, the enemy had finally cornered the *Emden*. Now it was a matter of survival. Every cruiser in these waters was more powerful than she.

Instantly Commander von Müller ordered steam up in every boiler. There had been only small fires under eight of them. Several more times he sounded the sirens for the return of the landing party, but soon it became clear that the *Emden* could no longer wait. The enemy was moving in too rapidly. His ship, it seemed, was a modern light cruiser of the *Newcastle* class, with four funnels and a speed and fire power that surpassed the *Emden*'s.

"Clear for action!" The orders reverberated through the ship. Alarm bells clanked, battle sirens howled. Shell hoists squeaked and groaned. The *Emden*'s drums and bugles called her men to their last battle. Finally they slipped anchor, wavering only a moment to give the landing party one last chance. But they could linger no more; as it was, the *Emden* would find it impossible to maneuver in the narrow, reef-studded roadstead. She turned around, facing the enemy. "All ahead full! Hoist the battle flags!" Müller ordered.

The commanding officer, along with the first gunnery officer, the torpedo officer, a combat helmsman, an ordnance petty officer, and a few seamen, manned the speaking tubes in the conning tower and the battle stations in the armored observation post. The forward crow's nest was occupied by the adjutant, who would observe hits on the enemy cruiser, note their effect, and inform the command bridge through a speaking tube.

On a northwesterly course, with battle flags flying, SMS *Emden* left the lagoon entrance at 0917. Her engines raced at top speed, the stokers feeding the boilers furiously. She held toward the harbor entrance, then turned abruptly to starboard to position herself for a running battle.

There was tension in the ship but everything seemed to proceed routinely. The electric conveyor brought an uninterrupted supply of shell cases from the bowels of the ship. Topside, the cases were hurriedly dragged to the guns and opened. The crew removed the shells, screwed on the fuzes, and piled them neatly on deck. A bright, metallic clanking accompanied the insertion of ammunition into the gun barrels. "Loaded!" the number-two man in the starboard gun crew bellowed, loud enough to be heard in the conning tower. The gun barrels rose as if they were to shoot at the heavens. The correct range was determined, and soon the eyes of the gun crew had the enemy in their telescope sights.

The two ships approached each other at high speed. Water sprayed high over the *Emden*'s bow. "Eleven thousand meters, 10,500 meters, 9,500 meters," the man at the range finder called in quick succession.

Müller gave his gunnery officer permission to fire. "Salvos . . . fire!" In a loud, steady voice the talker repeated the order, which echoed down the line of guns. The salvo bells pierced the air with their shrill sound, followed by a sharp *crack!* Five shells leapt from the guns and raced hissing toward the enemy ship. All eyes followed their paths. They landed close to the enemy ship.

From the beginning of the battle the *Emden* suffered under the handicap of slower speed. Her adversary not only was quicker but had been running with steam up for many hours, traveling at almost twenty-six knots. The *Emden,* having been at rest, could not possibly get up the necessary steam for top speed.

A second German salvo was fired. It too missed its mark. The third scored several hits, but still the *Emden* with her 10.5-cm guns was too far away to achieve results. So Müller decided to close the distance with a turn of two degrees to starboard.

Meanwhile the other ship flashed, unleashing its first salvo. Water columns raised by the impact were of uniform height, and tall enough to indicate that they had been produced by guns not of 10 but of 15 centimeters. Thus their opponent could not be, as they had hoped, the *Newcastle;* he was a more powerful adversary. Fate was against them.

Outclassed in speed, fire power, and armor, the *Emden* was struck again and again by 15.2-cm shells. She could only hope to win by scoring a few strategically placed hits.

For a few moments it had seemed as if her lucky star had not deserted her. Her salvos were well placed, the hits not widely dispersed. The third salvo had blasted the other ship's range-finding apparatus and its operator off the signal deck, right in front of the captain and his navigation officer. And a German shell had splintered the enemy's wooden after mast, though without toppling it entirely. After firing their eighth salvo, the men of the *Emden* saw the first large fire on board the British ship. The hit, made in the standby ammunition room near the lee guns, had put the nearest gun crew out of action. Part of the brightly burning ammunition had been caught by a cabin boy who carried it on deck and extinguished it in a washtub. Later he would receive the Victoria Cross for his brave action. Other shells, landing on armor plate, made no great impact, at most popping some rivets.

At this point time seemed to have run out for the German cruiser. She was still being harassed by enemy fire. Huge water columns obscured the gun sights and her gunners could not aim correctly.

Twenty minutes into the battle the *Emden* suffered her first heavy hit. A shell landed on the radio room. The bursting impact sounded like a giant boulder slamming into the ship. When the smoke lifted, there was nothing left of the radio room but a few glowing, battered sheets of steel. All the radiomen were dead or seriously wounded. Some had been thrown overboard by the force of the detonation. They were the *Emden*'s first casualties.

With a rolling salvo the enemy fired one gun after another. His superiority in guns and speed was taking its toll on the *Emden*. But he was not emerging from the battle unscathed. His ship's stern was on fire and he turned to draw out of range of the *Emden*'s shells. When Müller saw this he attempted to close the gap between them, but it was no use. The other ship was much faster. The British, aware that the dreaded German torpedo had a range of thirty-five hundred meters, never let the distance fall below seven thousand.

At the same time the radio room had been hit, a shell had landed near the foremast of the quarterdeck. Splintering wood flew far and wide. Quartermaster Mönckedick was in the process of getting a closer look at the enemy during a lull in the firing when the explosion shattered his lower left arm. Another shell burst on deck near the conning tower. For a second there was dead silence. Then, gradually discernible, came the moans of wounded and dying gunners and signalmen. Well-aimed enemy fire soon destroyed the electrical fire-control system. An announcement from the conning tower informed them that both main fuses were broken. Then rudder commands from the conning tower ceased. Shortly a direct hit blasted the foremost funnel, which fell to the port side as if blown over by a breath of wind. Early that morning, in preparation for coaling, support braces for the funnels had been unshackled. The pressure of exploding shells toppled one of the large funnels easily, as if it had been a house of cards. Speed and maneuverability decreased by the minute. Smoke billowed out of the funnel stumps, soot covered the gun sights.

Despite heavy casualties, and facing a stampede of shells, the *Emden*'s sailors continued to fire their guns. Slowly they were being beaten down on all sides. The huge gaps the enemy's fire had torn in their ranks could no longer be filled. Many of the ammunition bearers had fallen. The electric hoists had ceased to function long ago.

Commander von Müller knew that the end was near. Lack of ammunition was the decisive factor. Shells had to be manually conveyed now, a slow and painstaking job. Still the dying cruiser would not let up fire. Whoever was capable of movement stood at his post or hauled ammunition. Müller observed countless examples of courage and perseverance. Some guns were manned by a single wounded sailor.

Additional damage to the steering gear had made the *Emden* almost unmaneuverable. The enemy managed to come about to the port side again, planting three more devastating hits in the German cruiser. The first put the range finder and most of the personnel on the conning bridge out of action. Ensign Zimmerman, his duty thus terminated, headed for the guns. There, while tending the second port gun, he met his death. The second hit exploded on the bow, again near the conning tower. Shrapnel finished off the rest of the crew serving the guns in that section of the ship. The third and fiercest hit came at the stern, between storage bins servicing the after guns. About thirty shells detonated, killing everyone in the vicinity, including battery commander Lieutenant von Levetzow. Presently the entire stern was wrapped in a shroud of flames.

Scorching heat attacked the inner spaces and blistered the paint on the bulkheads. Fire spread with unbelievable speed. The navigation officer, Lieutenant Gropius, and his men, in the process of operating the manual rudder, were cut off by flames. So were a few of the survivors manning guns. Another shell

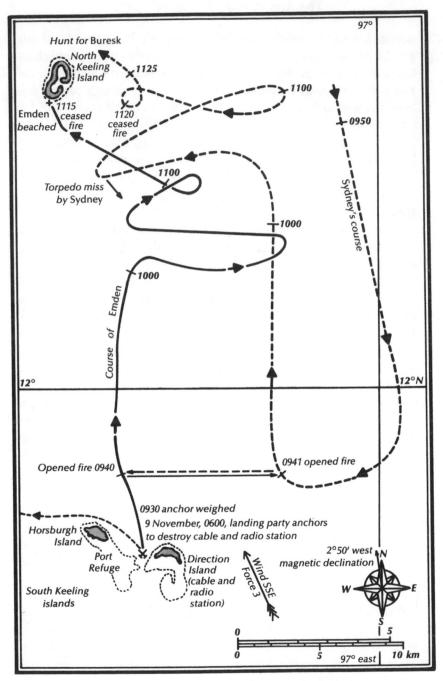

*Battle off the Cocos Islands, 9 November 1914*

scored a direct hit on the captain's cabin, sweeping almost all the men aft overboard; out of eighteen men only two, a first-class signalman and the signals' chief petty officer, managed to escape. A new barrage felled them near the conning tower. By now the port guns had fallen silent. Only now and then would a gunshot echo across the waters.

Müller decided, without great hope of success, to maneuver his badly wounded cruiser into position to launch torpedoes. This, given the superior speed of his opponent, was almost pointless. With her defective engines and boilers the *Emden* could hardly close the distance between them. She was slow in turning, and once again the enemy managed to catch her on the starboard side. A running battle now developed, one-sided to be sure. A direct hit caused the *Emden*'s foremast to topple over the port side. The cruiser dragged her rigging and mast alongside. In the crow's nest, Ensign von Guérard and a signalman gallantly met their death. The command bridge was destroyed and the two remaining funnels came crashing down. There would be no opportunity to launch a torpedo. The agile and mostly intact opponent would not let the *Emden* near. New hits continued to pound the cruiser mercilessly.

The *Emden*'s fire slackened, marking the end of her lucky and successful operations. She had no more gun crews, no guns, no opportunity to launch torpedoes, no avenue for escape. The ultimate decision of the captain was to beach his ship on the uninhabited coral reef of North Keeling Island, which had reared from the horizon during the battle. He was determined to keep his ship from falling into enemy hands and to save the wounded below deck from a horrible death in shark-infested waters. There were no longer any usable boats on board. The three largest had gone with the landing party, the others had burned on deck.

So once more the *Emden* turned to starboard, in which direction the island lay. The enemy turned starboard on the same course, following the crippled ship and lobbing shell after shell into her, hoping she would sink before reaching the reef. It was to no avail. The *Emden* held course. Müller stood by the skylight over the engine room and "steered" the ship, whose rudders were jammed, by operating both engines manually. At 1115 she stopped engines and ran aground in a gap between two coral reefs, which softened the impact. They were on the north coast of the island. Once more Müller ordered full speed ahead, for he wanted the wreck to sit as high as possible on the reef. Then they opened the seacocks.

Either the enemy was not certain he'd reduced the ship to a wreck or he wanted to use her for target practice, because he continued firing. To avoid further bloodshed, Müller gave those remaining on deck permission to jump overboard and swim one hundred meters or so to the island. Of those who did, some managed to reach shore. Others, not as lucky, drowned in the roaring surf. About five long minutes after the *Emden* beached, her opponent ceased fire. Miraculously, the *Buresk* appeared, luring him away. Now Commander von Müller could order all hands on deck. He counted 133 dead, 49 seriously injured. Three-fifths of his 314-man crew were dead or wounded, and his ship was a burning heap of crushed metal. Below the armored deck everything was a shambles. The upper bunker had taken a direct hit through the engine-room skylight. Lighting equipment was shattered. Corpses lay everywhere, flung amid machine parts and crushed oilcans.

In the boiler rooms the stokers had had an impossible task. There had been no ventilation in the suffocating heat of almost 140° Fahrenheit, and detonating shells had torn off the boiler jackets. But the intrepid stokers proved themselves no less dedicated than their comrades manning the guns above. Only one boiler room, where a hit threatened the men with exploding live steam, had had to be evacuated.

In the auxiliary engine rooms a portside condenser had been hit; steam was rerouted to starboard. The electrical circuit on the port side had given out, the switchboard burning like a bonfire. Only one circuit remained intact.

In the starboard auxiliary engine room the crew had suffered from heat, smoke, and fire. Constantly putting out flames, they had only been able to withstand the heat by holding their faces next to the fire hoses, where the cool spray gave momentary relief. Despite their agony, they had persevered under the leadership of their chief engineer, Petty Officer Aden, until the end. Once aground, they emerged from their hole covered with severe burns.

In the ship's stern, a hit had put both the automatic and manual rudder out of commission. Noxious choking gases had forced the evacuation of all personnel in the steering flat and in spaces nearby, including the infirmary. Most personnel on the middle deck had been killed. Exploding shells had barred their escape.

Considering the circumstances, loss of life beneath the armored deck was relatively light. How many courageous stokers would have drowned had the ship been sunk? One look at the twisted, riddled, jammed ladders and hatches answered that question. Later accounts from engine and torpedo personnel described the laborious, time-consuming efforts of men working their way out of blocked and sealed spaces. The crew in the control station had also been denied escape, and after the battle special care was given to freeing them. Most of the technical specialists were freed with sledgehammers and axes from twisted passageways. How lucky that the island had been close by . . .

And what had the men below deck experienced? Here is an account from Torpedo Petty Officer Püschel:

> We had never manned our stations so fast. All preparations were made with utmost speed—emergency lights lit, damage control timber cleared, that sort of thing. With torpedoes ready for launching, we waited for further orders during the long, agonizing minutes. Through the speaking tube I gathered from Lieutenant Witthoeft that the foreign ship was an English cruiser. By the *Emden*'s strong vibrations and the water rushing alongside her, I could tell we were speeding toward the enemy.
>
> Fifteen minutes later our guns unleashed their first salvos. We looked at each other speechless; the dance had begun. Ensign Prince Franz Joseph, the second torpedo officer, was on the ladder of the torpedo room companionway. My twelve men and I stood ready at his command. Again a salvo boomed, and then another. Our ears became ac-

customed to it. We hadn't received a hit. "First score on the enemy ship," Witthoeft announced from the bridge to the torpedo room. Our joy didn't last long. Fifteen minutes later there was a loud explosion and a sound like rolling thunder. Another huge explosion and then a creaking, splintering, bursting of iron and steel, followed by a hard metallic thud. The entire ship vibrated. I leaped to the speaking tube. "What's happening? What's going on?" I shouted, and a voice answered, "The foremast took a direct hit and the lookout and Ensign von Guérard were thrown overboard. Mast and rigging are dragging in the water alongside the ship."

Fresh explosions, louder and longer lasting than before, shook the ship. The riveted portside seams had been torn apart by the pressure of an incoming shell. We could see daylight. Water poured into our small compartment as if from an open sluice. What could we do? We picked up the hammocks and pressed them with all our might against the split bulkheads. Everyone labored with their last ounce of strength to contain the water. It was no use. Our flood-control timbers were broken like matches. We tried everything and still the water kept coming in. I contacted the neighboring fourth boiler room through the speaking tube to find out how things were with them. They'd been heavy hit in the starboard bunker. "On the double, man the bilge pump in the torpedo room, we're shipping water," I yelled back. Right away the pump started up. At first it seemed to be working well, but then it began to grind and hiss because part of a cotton rag had got caught in the suction mechanism, which could no longer pump fast enough. Now we couldn't get to the bilge where the mouth of the pump was. The water kept pouring in, our room was twenty-five centimeters under water. Again and again we heard the roar of guns. Could we possibly be the underdog in this fight? I jumped back to the speaking tube: "Bridge, ahoy there, bridge hello, bridge . . ." There was no answer. In the background I could hear loud voices and the rhythmic command of the gunnery officer: "Fire salvo! Distance nine thousand meters, distance ten thousand meters." No one heard my call. How did it look topside? The firing from our guns became fainter and fainter. Water was rising. The pumps couldn't drain it off. It had already reached our knees.

Another deafening explosion, then a blinding light like a fireball shot through the hatch. Automatically we ducked our heads. But nothing happened.

Again, through the speaking tube to the bridge: "What's going on? The torpedo room is flooding. Water now stands at forty centimeters." "Starboard amidships tube stand by to launch," the bridge returned. So there was still hope for a shot! Our torpedoes had functioned so well at Penang. "Torpedo ready," we reported, and the bridge came back with "Stand by!" I could feel my heart beat in my throat. My hands waited impatiently on the lever. Then a renewed explosion, followed by deep, deep darkness. A hissing surge of water and screaming filled the room. "Help! Open up," somebody called out. What had happened?

In a few moments the water was up to our noses. Now the thirteen of us had to swim, but where to? It was pitch black. We could see nothing. We could only hear and touch. Was the ship sinking? My hands groped for the pipes that ran overhead.

Someone heard our shouts, for suddenly the armor plate over the hatch lifted. A few shipmates nearby had been able to open it from the middle deck. That was what saved us. We have an oversight to thank for that: in battle, the turn-buckles of the armor plates should be dogged tight, but because the *Sydney* had taken us by surprise, this was forgotten. It would have been impossible for us swimming in the dark to open the catches from below.

Now air and light penetrated the gas-filled darkness. We were seized by the collar and hauled onto the solid deck. No one was left behind, no one was sacrificed.

Between decks was a horrible sight of wounded men crying out for help. We clambered over the smoldering wreckage to the stoker's showers, for we were plagued by a terrible thirst. Luckily we found some dirty bath water and slurped it greedily. I pushed my head through a porthole and saw the destroyed foremast dragging in the water. Leeward, I saw huge water spouts raised by enemy shells. How would we have looked if every enemy shell had found its mark? We were already devastated. Our guns only fired spasmodically, then fell off altogether. Was our opponent going to administer a coup de grâce?

Topside, at the guns, almost all our comrades had fallen. A deathly silence was also noticeable below. Only the whispers of the small group in the torpedo room could be heard. We were lucky to have escaped from the lower deck, but now we were imprisoned on the middle. We wanted to get topside to help at the guns; after all, we were trained gunners. The thought that we had to stand by helplessly and listen while our comrades were picked off one by one became unbearable.

Acrid smoke and poisonous gases had drifted into the room and made breathing difficult. A raging fire nearby turned the air into a breathing hell. Should we now perish? I tried to force my way through a porthole without luck. In doing so, I saw that the *Emden* was still traveling at a good clip. So the engines had not been damaged. For a time I hung halfway out of the porthole. I had lost all concept of time. How long had the battle been going on?

I saw how the cruiser turned and made for the island. "Land in sight," I called to my comrades. A few more hits, then a tremendous bump, a strong vibration throughout the ship, and we had run aground. "All hands on deck," we heard from topside. How could we get out of this heap of rubble? Very carefully we stretched our necks through the shot-riddled bulkheads. Astern I saw the enemy cruiser, a smoke cloud overhead, hurry away. Finally, after a long search, we found a crack in the bulkhead large enough so that, with some effort, we could escape through it.

Off the stern we saw the enemy cruiser grow smaller as it sped away. Standing beside the guns and over our fallen comrades, we cursed the fleeing ship in anger and frustration. Was he going to leave us to our fate? It seemed that way, for he knew the *Emden* was a helpless wreck.

In the meantime, the survivors on deck had not been idle. Engine rooms, boiler rooms, ammunition holds were flooded. Breech blocks, sighting apparatus, torpedo launchers, some unused shells, all had been thrown overboard. Nothing was to fall into enemy hands. What was left of unused hospital supplies was being administered to the wounded by the staff physician, Dr. Luther.

The *Emden* sat tight on the coral reef. A heavy surf washed over her. The cawing cries of a thousand birds, seagulls of a size never seen before, filled the air. Like carrion kites they shrieked and swooped down on the wreck. Would the men now be torn apart by scavenging birds? The healthy ones could defend themselves, but the wounded? With heavy flapping of wings the birds attacked, long curved beaks going for faces and eyes. Their loud cawing could be heard above the moans of wounded and dying men. Those men sandwiched in the wreckage, soaking in their own blood, had to be borne to safety gently and painstakingly. The deck was a chaotic heap of twisted metal, and moving over it with the wounded, men had to climb shapeless masses of steel. It was not possible to ease the pain of the dying; doctors could not be everywhere at once. Bandages and medicine had been destroyed by fire. There was nothing to eat, and worse, nothing to drink. Glowing heat from the burning stern barred passage to the ship's interior. Yet, at great risk to themselves, men dragged many of their comrades from nearly inaccessible compartments.

Badly wounded sailors were brought to the forecastle and bow, where they were given morphine to ease their suffering. They were all plagued by thirst. All that could be found in the wardroom was a little milk. The tanks containing drinking water had been shot to pieces.

Lack of water and the strong surf, which it was feared would break up the craft, made it advisable to abandon ship. Surely on the island they would find water and coconuts.

Only one hundred meters away the luscious shore of palm-dotted North Keeling beckoned them. But how could they get there without boats? The men had to thread a line through the surf and then form a type of breeches buoy that would carry the crew to the island. They tied rope to hammocks and empty ammunition crates. But all their attempts were frustrated. The current flowed laterally, and sharp coral reefs shredded the ropes. Only once did the men on land manage to catch one of the lines thrown them, but presently it was too shredded.

They tried to shoot lines with the line-throwing gun. Then they tied the lines to volunteer swimmers and finally to captured birds, the very ones that had been on the attack earlier. Those that hadn't been clubbed to death were captured, then attached to a thin line with which they were to fly to the island. This too was destined to fail. The birds lost their equilibrium during flight and drowned.

Again and again tireless swimmers headed for the island. Only a few managed to battle through the high surf. Others, observed helplessly from ship deck, were tossed on the razor-sharp reefs and there hacked to death.

Attempts to reach the island occupied them for hours. About 1600, contrary to expectation, the enemy cruiser returned. It had two rowboats in tow identified as coming from the *Buresk*. Survivors in the *Emden* believed they would be rescued now.

Surprisingly, the ship turned out to be Australian. Was it the *Sydney* or the *Melbourne?* It wouldn't be long before the truth was known, for she released the two boats and closed to about four thousand meters. Then she signaled something. Since there was neither signalman nor code handbook in the *Emden*, they couldn't answer. By semaphore Müller sent the message, "No signalbook."

But what was that! Suddenly the other ship flashed brightly. "They're firing again," the men shouted, and already shells crashed on board. Rage is all the men could feel. To shell a helpless wreck hours after a battle was disgraceful, abominable. At least four to six salvos hit, killing or wounding twenty-five more men. For a second time Müller announced, "Those who can swim, save yourselves and jump."

It seemed like the last chance and so many jumped. Of them, only a few managed to reach shore. Others lowered themselves down the hull leeside and dangled between sea and sky. Had the enemy reopened fire because the battle flag was still flying from the mainmast? The ensign so many men had given their lives for had never been hit.

In deference to the seriously wounded men, Müller sent the international sign of surrender. After all, the *Emden* was no longer a fighting ship. On her bow they hoisted a white sheet. After running through a thick patch of flames, Ordinary Seaman Werner risked his life climbing the mainmast to haul down the flag. His action saved many a life that day. The enemy cruiser finally ceased fire.

Still the enemy made no move to rescue survivors. He merely sent a boat from the *Buresk* with the prize crew's commander, Ensign Fikentscher, on board informing them that the Australians would have to check out Direction Island the following morning to determine what had occurred there; before that, rescue of the *Emden* crew was unthinkable.

Once more the enemy cruiser steamed away, leaving the survivors to their precarious fate. Those on deck hauled exhausted men hanging from ropes back on deck. Others were still calling for help in the violent surf. Men on board had to watch as one after the other was swallowed up by waves, never to appear again.

The sun was going down. Suddenly a tropical rain burst over them, extinguishing lingering fires that threatened to blow up the ammunition room and bringing much-needed drinking water for the wounded. The prospects of getting them off the wreck alive had sunk to zero. If the *Sydney* should attempt to land at Direction, Lieutenant von Mücke, his men, and their trusty machine guns would give her a bloody welcome. The survivors could count on their five fingers the reasons the enemy ship would abandon them if she had to withdraw with losses. It looked bad. Still, not a few wished for such a turn of events on Direction. In any case, some no longer believed that the ship would return for them. Müller ordered the international distress signal hoisted. Sooner or later a freighter had to come by.

Meanwhile, what had happened to the *Buresk?* The collier had appeared on the scene some time before the battle. During the night, following orders, she had waited off the island for a radio message to come to the Cocos for coaling. The call actually came at 0730 on 9 November, after Mücke's landing party had been put ashore. The *Emden* did not seem to be receiving the *Buresk*'s signals. At about 0920, the men in the *Buresk* spotted the thick smoke of a warship heading south; suddenly, it turned north off the starboard side. As it executed this maneuver, the officers with binoculars recognized the foreign ship and knew immediately: today would be a trying one for the *Emden*. Before them they had the newest type of British cruiser, much more sophisticated than the *Emden,* with five 15.2-cm guns broadside and a speed of twenty-six knots. It also had a water-line armor over seven centimeters thick; it would hardly be scratched by the *Emden*'s 10.5-cm shells, and certainly not at a great distance.

The *Emden* did not reply to the radio alert the *Buresk* sent regarding the enemy. Around 0930 the men in the collier saw the *Emden* race out of the inlet at high speed with flags flying. Then they heard the thunder of guns from the southwest. The *Emden,* running out of the harbor, must have opened fire at a distance of about 9,400 meters. The first salvo landed wide, a fact that the *Buresk* reported to the *Emden* immediately. The next salvo was still short by 300 meters.

During the opening part of the battle, the collier steamed directly off the bow of the enemy, reducing speed to observe the salvos of the *Emden* and report their fall. When the radio room on the *Emden* was destroyed and the *Buresk* could no longer be of use, she left the scene to await the outcome of the battle. When it drew to a close she tried to break away, but the hunter was quicker. The *Sydney* chased the collier and with a few shots across the bow brought her to heel. At a top speed of only nine knots, there was no chance for the *Buresk*.

Being a far-sighted commander, Lieutenant Klöpper, the *Buresk*'s skipper, had made advance preparations so that his ship and her precious cargo of five thousand tons of coal would not fall into enemy hands. The seacocks were opened and the valves in the engine rooms removed. Then the radio equipment was destroyed. Small arms and secret papers flew overboard. When the cruiser ordered the *Buresk* to stop, the Australian captain was looking at a sinking ship. He sent a boarding party over, only to find that water spouts were already forcing their way into the ship's interior.

But what should happen now? Nothing could be saved. Klöpper's men had done their work efficiently, and the *Sydney* had to take on all hands. Klöpper had prepared the two cutters with water and provisions in plenty of time. The *Sydney* lobbed a few more shells into the sinking ship and then proceeded toward the *Emden* at low speed, towing the cutters along with her.

The time-consuming chase had given Lieutenant von Mücke and his fifty-man landing party an excellent advantage.

After the *Sydney* had cast off the cutters and sent two full broadsides into the iron derelict that was now the *Emden,* her captain instructed Ensign Fikentscher, in one of the cutters, to inform Müller that the Australian cruiser was heading for the Cocos "to check on conditions there," since the ship's radio was out of order. Any rescue attempt in the high surf with night approaching was impossible. With great difficulty they maneuvered toward the beached ship, in the process rescuing a German sailor who had jumped overboard. Fikentscher cautiously brought the cutter to the stranded *Emden.* Incoming waves seized the boat, pushing it haphazardly alongside the wreck. The danger of being shattered on sudden impact was real, but they managed to catch hold of a chain hanging from the broken railing and thus secured the boat alongside.

Ensign Schall begged for medicine, bandages and drinking water and received them. The greatest gift for the wounded was water.

When the survivors found out their opponent had been the *Sydney,* they were not surprised that their ship had been defeated. This turbine cruiser, launched early in 1914, had a displacement of 5,700 tons, a top speed of almost twenty-seven knots, an armament of eight 15.2-cm guns and four 4.7-cm guns, and a crew of about four hundred men. She had deck armor of 26 millimeters and waterline armor of 76 millimeters.

Commander von Müller, covered in smoke and soot, approached Ensign Fikentscher and greeted him warmly. He wanted him to take on the job of adjutant in place of the officer thrown overboard when the foremast toppled. There was a lot of work ahead. The ship was a dreadful sight. Grounding on the coral reef had shattered the steering flat. All shafts and munitions hoists were riddled with shell holes. As a result of a direct hit on the after deck, all the reserve ammunition had blown up. The foremast and two funnels were gone. The heat caused by the fires had melted small iron parts, bottles, portholes, and panes of glass until they were unrecognizable. Of the gun crew, only two men survived without injury.

The *Buresk* men were badly shaken. Together with the uninjured, they searched every part of the wreck for more wounded. That was not as simple as it sounds. Because of crushed ladders and hoists they could only penetrate the ship's interior through cracks and portholes. More than once rescuers were seized by the surf and almost swept into the sea. A bucket brigade extinguished the last smoldering fires on the after deck with sea water. Among the volunteer workers was Commander von Müller, his face and hands yellow with gun powder. Quietly and firmly he directed the rescue work. The bow, where most of the casualties lay, could only be reached with wooden planks. Doctors Luther and Schwabe helped with the medicine sent along by the *Sydney*. The injured were wrapped in wool blankets and placed on the relatively sheltered foredeck. The stern of the wrecked ship was being flooded by the turbulent sea.

To meet the further demand for drinking water, Dr. Schwabe and four volunteers dove overboard, hoping to make it to land. Schwabe was overcome by weakness owing to all the strenuous work he had done and the mighty surf slammed him against the coral reef. During the night he died of his wounds on the sands of North Keeling Island.

By 0200 everything humanly possible had been done. Together, amid the wounded, Commander von Müller and Ensign Fikentscher climbed under a dirty, singed wool blanket and tried to get some sleep. Neither was successful. The drinking water had long been consumed and the moans of thirsty, injured men were almost unbearable.

### 10 November 1914

Time crawled by like a slow, troublesome stream on the shattered wreck. While the Germans rested, weary, hungry, and thirsty under the tropic sky, the *Sydney* steamed slowly toward Direction, which she could approach only the following morning. All night long she cruised back and forth in front of the island.

In the morning, the commanding officer of the *Sydney* wanted to land several boats. He suggested to Ensign Schall of the *Buresk* that he go along as an intermediary with a flag of truce. Schall declined, and an English-speaking German sailor from the collier went instead. The armed landing party was set afloat, loaded guns cocked, a white flag fluttering off the bow of their boats. With breathless suspense the undertaking was observed. The *Sydney's* crew stormed on land with weapons cocked and ready. But nothing happened. No shot was fired. Then came the hushed moment when the boats returned and the first officer made his report to the commander: "Sir, no Germans are to be found on the island."

Where were the fifty Germans?

At the gray of dawn the enemy cruiser once more approached the *Emden*. What did she want this time? Would she fire at the wreck again? The men searched for new cover. For more than an hour the ship lurked around her derelict victim, then disappeared again.

On board the wreck, the contents of the ship's treasury went to the survivors. Each man took as much as he could stuff in his pockets. In this way the money became the property of the individual and could not be seized as spoils of war. Much later, during captivity, the men returned every dime, nickel, and penny to their captain.

For the third time the *Sydney* returned. After noontime, about 1300, she appeared. The boats swung away from her; finally, rescue was near. Two cutters drew alongside. With them came Lieutenant Garcia, who boarded the *Emden* with a letter for the commanding officer. Müller approached in his flame-blackened uniform spotted with the blood of his wounded men, with the mutilated and dead around him and the moans of the dying in his ear. He had difficulty understanding the language and contents of the message that his opponent, Captain Glossop, had sent. Was it possible? Did this letter not have the polite, proper, almost sportsmanlike tone of the captain of a winning cricket side consoling the loser?

Royal Australian Navy
HMAS *Sydney*
At sea
9 November 1914

Subject:

DEAR SIR!
I have the honor, in the name of humanity, to request that
you surrender your ship. As a sign of my admiration for
your bravery, may I sum up the situation as follows:
  1. Your ship is grounded.
     Three funnels and one mast have toppled.
     Most guns are unserviceable.
  2. You can no longer leave this island.
     My ship, on the other hand, is intact.
If you surrender, which, if I may point this out, would be
no dishonor but merely a misfortune, I will attempt to do
all I can for your sick and wounded and turn them over to
the nearest hospital.

I have the honor, dear sir,
of being your obedient servant,
JOHN A. GLOSSOP, Captain

To the Commanding Officer
of His Imperial
German Majesty's
Ship *Emden*

He had to pledge, this commanding officer of the beaten *Emden,*
that none of his men would stir up trouble aboard the *Sydney.*
His opponent gave a return guarantee that he would shelter and
care for the survivors. Therewith began the transfer of the remaining crew. The English cutter had brought no litters for the
wounded, and so first only slightly injured men were placed in
the boats and returned to the *Sydney,* where the necessary litters
were loaded. Now it was time for the seriously wounded, a difficult task carefully performed by the English crew with seaman-
like skill and over many hours. The next to the last boat left
carrying Witthoeft, Prince von Hohenzollern, and Schall, along
with three uninjured engineers. Müller, still aboard the *Emden,*
remarked to Ensign Fikentscher that it was time to set fire to the
bow. Under the forecastle, where personal lockers had blown

open, was a mass of clothing. Müller, however, could not get enough of a fire going with matches. Then Fikentscher remembered that on departing from Tsingtao he had ordered three cans of gasoline hung over the stern to avoid fire danger. During the fire aft, they had miraculously escaped igniting. Clambering over the now cooled port cabin deck, he fetched two of the canisters and carried them to the bow, where Müller emptied them and lit the saturated debris.

The last to leave the *Emden* was Commander von Müller, escorted to the enemy captain's launch by a group of English officers, even though he had requested no honors. Upon arrival, he was saluted by an honor guard and piped aboard. Captain Glossop, standing by the gangway, escorted him to his own cabin and gave him new clothing. For the *Emden* men, a large room was readied on the forecastle. There, too, a meal was waiting for them. Hungrily, the German sailors fell upon it—boiled potatoes, herring, canned meat, tea, bread, and tobacco.

There was hardly a sign that the Australian cruiser had been in battle. She had kept at a great distance, virtually immune from the small shells of the German cruiser. Had both cruisers been equally modern and powerful, the outcome might have been quite different. So thought the men of the *Emden*.

They learned how and why the *Sydney* had appeared so suddenly and unexpectedly at Direction Island. She belonged to the escort of a troop convoy headed from Australia to Europe, a convoy that had been in the vicinity by coincidence.

Their treatment on the Australian cruiser was judged good by the *Emden*'s men. The enemy was polite and obliging, and the English doctors and their staff outdid themselves in the care of the wounded. Tirelessly they worked. Many of the seriously wounded owed them their lives.

Meanwhile it grew dark. The *Sydney* could not think about rescuing *Emden* people still stranded on North Keeling that night. Her anchorage unsuitable, she steamed along the leeside of the island and sent a boat with Ensign Schall and some *Emden* seamen ashore to gather up men there. They were to stand by for transfer the next morning. During the night the

*Sydney* steamed back and forth in the waters off the island while the rescue party proceeded with their task. It was most difficult to gather people dispersed in the impenetrable underbrush and assemble them at a designated spot. The injured, without water for two days and exhausted, had to be cared for. Aside from their wounds, they were tormented by insects and beach worms, all this under the merciless, parching sun. Several of the dead had to be buried, Dr. Schwabe among them. The able-bodied could do very little for their wounded comrades. Despite a desperate search, they could find no water. A few coconuts and bird's eggs were all they could offer. Drifting hammocks reached the shore, providing skimpy bedding for the seriously wounded. It was high time help arrived. Even the uninjured, scantily clothed, had suffered severely under the broiling tropical sun. Lack of water had driven everyone to the breaking point.

*11 November 1914*

Early in the morning the embarkation took place, running smoothly and quickly. The *Sydney* steamed back to Direction, put the station doctor ashore, and set course for Colombo. But where were the forty-nine men of the landing party? It was said that, under Lieutenant von Mücke, they had escaped in an old schooner lying in the harbor.

# CHAPTER TWO

# THE ADVERSARY

According to Lieutenant C. R. Garcia, RAN, 9 November 1914 passed as follows on board the *Sydney:*

> We steamed about fifty nautical miles east of the Cocos, southwest of Java, and set course for Colombo. About 0700 hours we received a garbled radio call from the Cocos station: "Strange ship off entrance." The *Melbourne,* whose captain was senior officer on the convoy, ordered us to get up steam for full speed and to check out the situation on the Cocos.
>
> I was just taking a bath when my shipmate, Bell-Salter, barged in with the news that the enemy was only forty nautical miles away. At first I regarded the whole thing as one of his jokes, but soon he convinced me that this time he was serious. The noise of the turbines accelerating to high speed added to the mounting excitement.
>
> At 0915 we saw the tops of the coconut palms on Keeling Island appear over the horizon. By 0920 the *Emden* was visible—or more accurately, the rims of her funnels were about twelve to fifteen nautical miles away. At 0940 she opened fire from a great distance. Shortly thereafter, we began our artillery exchange.
>
> During the entire battle I was busy running between the

ammunition hoists on bow guns or those on forward starboard and port side.

The most intense part of the battle was the first half hour. We opened fire with our portside battery. I stood close to portside gun number one. The directional guide asked me if he should load. I answered no, not until he got the order. Then he reported that the *Emden* had fired. So I said, "All right, load up, but hold your fire." Later on I found out that the order to load had been passed to the other guns a good ten minutes before that.

A little later I heard a crash. I looked aft and saw that an enemy shell had hit in the vicinity of the number-two starboard gun. Because of the protective armor plate around the guns I couldn't see that the hit had put the entire service crew out of commission. I saw no flames or smoke. (On board, small fires could be extinguished immediately.) I stayed at my post. It was a spot that demanded constant attention. The men performed superbly, just as on maneuvers. Keeping an adequate supply of reserve ammunition topside is dangerous in battle, and there has to be an even distribution of shells, cartridge cases, and so forth between the two guns on starboard and port side. The safety caps had to be removed with small pins that were hard to handle. We stood by to help with duds and shells that misfired. On top of this, we had to rouse one or two men who weren't doing their jobs. That left little time to gaze at the *Emden* and wonder about her condition. On my way to the starboard side I looked once or twice at the portside guns, which seemed to be in the midst of a raging battle. It was deafening—*whee-oo, whee-oo, whee-oo* echoing all over the ship, mingled with the roar of guns and the *bat-bat-bat* of shells hitting water on the other side of our ship. Since the distance was considerable, the impact angle was steep.

On the way aft I heard a loud crash. A shell had hit the upper edge of the protective shield on the number-one starboard gun. A petty officer came limping toward me and told me he had just carried an officer below. Apart from that, the fire control station was totally out of order, all its occupants wounded. I told the petty officer, if he could, to go to starboard gun number two and see if a fire had broken out there. If he saw any cartridge cases lying about, he should toss them overboard immediately. The man bravely gathered himself together and limped toward the stern. There he found the beginning of a dangerous cordite fire. Later I saw smoke rising from the stern. I ran to it immediately but found only the glowing remains of the fire and two men with bad foot injuries sitting on a platform.

During that entire time our cruiser ran at a speed of twenty-five knots, sometimes twenty-six. Being faster than the *Emden,* we could dictate the nature of the battle. We now shifted fire to the starboard battery. I was quite deaf by now. In my haste, I had neglected to stuff my ears with cotton. It was something I wouldn't forget the next time.

As I left my position on the bow guns and stepped aft, I met a group of men shouting "Hurray!" and waving their hats in the air. "What happened?" I asked. "She sank, sir, she sank," was their reply. I ran to shipside and, finding no trace of the enemy cruiser, I ordered all men to stand by lifeboats, for there would surely be survivors swimming about. Just as my men were ready to lower the boats, somebody called, "Look, sir, they're still firing!" Quickly we all returned to the guns. A cloud of thick yellow smoke had covered the enemy ship and given the impression that she had disappeared. Later, our cruiser put about again and renewed the battle with another broadside.

By now, the enemy's three funnels and foremast had been shot away. A raging fire was burning astern. We turned again and fired one or two salvos with our starboard guns. Then we noticed that the cruiser had run aground on North Keeling. So we discontinued firing at about 1120. The battle, all told, lasted an hour and forty minutes.

The hits on our ship were not serious. We received three hull shots. The shell that exploded near the cabin boy on the mess deck only destroyed his personal effects. Two or three days later cabin boys were still finding splinters from the shell. The only real damage was at the after fire control station. It was now a mass of twisted, riddled iron. Other hits were of no consequence.

Next I chased down the coal ship seen lingering about the *Emden.* As we boarded her, we noticed that her seacocks had been opened and that she was sinking fast. We took on all the men and returned to the *Emden* at about 1600.

On the *Emden* someone climbed the mainmast and cut down the still fluttering flag. On the bow, someone waved a white sheet. Slowly it grew dark. Not knowing if the cruiser *Königsberg* was near by, we could not initiate rescue measures and had to steam off. Suddenly, we heard a sharp cry in the darkness and came to a stop. Lifeboats were lowered and we saved an exhausted but happy German sailor. He was the fourth man that we fished out of the water that day.

Early in the morning of 10 November we sailed to the cable station, where we planned to capture the group landed there by the German ship for the purpose of destroying it. There we learned that the German crew had requisitioned a schooner and disappeared. The poor devils wouldn't get very far, for the ship was leaky and unseaworthy. Besides that, leather washers had been removed from the pumps, leaving them exposed. The German landing party had destroyed all radio equipment, but the station personnel dug up buried spare parts and soon had the installation going again.

At 1100 we arrived back at the *Emden*. I was sent over in a cutter. Luckily the ship's stern loomed above the surf breakers, and with the help of a hanging rat line I could get close to it, pointing my bow seaward. Then I was received by the captain of the *Emden*. I explained the offer of our captain: If he would give his word of honor (*parole*), we would be ready to take his crew on board the *Sydney* and bring them directly to Colombo. At the word *parole* he hesitated, but agreed readily once I explained its exact meaning. Then came the terrible task of transferring the seriously wounded to the boats.

I took the opportunity of congratulating the commanding officer of the *Emden*. I told him he had fought very well. He stopped short and said brusquely, "No I didn't." I left his side abruptly. Soon he approached and said, "I thank you for your kind words, but I am not satisfied. We should have done better. You had a lot of luck on your side since my whole command system was destroyed at the beginning."

When all the boats had left, I wandered about the enemy ship. I can't describe the horror. Aside from the bow, which from the edge of the bridge to the stern looked untouched, everything was a ghastly, twisted heap of rubble. The German doctor begged me to signal the *Sydney* for morphine, so I went aft and didn't return to the bow of the German ship.

The Germans were touched and most grateful to learn that, by order of the captain, on our arrival in Colombo there were to be no cheers or other signs of victory. No one wanted it anyway, in view of the long rows of seriously wounded men on the after deck.

Commander von Müller is a noble, distinguished, and remarkable man.

In Colombo we turned over all the wounded, both English and German. By counting the number of men we rescued, 150, we determined the German losses. We knew the number that had landed on the island and escaped, the number in the boarding party on the coaler. The German ship must have lost at least 180 men; 20 were seriously wounded and about the same number were slightly injured.

Later on, I had conversations with several of the German officers. The first day on board our ship one of them said, "You shot at our white flag." I looked into the situation immediately. But then a German torpedo lieutenant and a naval engineer emphatically stated that no, they hadn't shot at the white flag. Even with that, the officers of the *Sydney* could not let it rest. One of us went to the captain. We also received Commander von Müller's assurance that this had not occurred and that he intended to meet with his officers and set the record straight.

Before Commander von Müller left our ship at Colombo, he came to the after deck and thanked me for the rescue and considerate treatment of his wounded. He shook my hand and saluted. This was both generous and courteous. Ensign Prince Hohenzollern also proved to be a gentleman on that trip. We both agreed it was our duty to eliminate each other from the theater of war, but in that there was nothing vindictive or hostile.

How could the *Sydney* have taken the *Emden* so by surprise? Had the German cruiser fallen into a well-laid trap? No, a coincidence had ended her career. How different it would have been if Müller had had the information that a few hours before the operation against the Cocos, the first section of the Australian escort accompanying the troop convoy overseas had skirted them, and that the convoy was still near by, heading toward the Middle East. Commander von Müller explained on board the *Sydney* that he would have attacked the convoy during the night.

Commander C. W. Stevens of the Australian navy, who witnessed the action on board the *Melbourne,* remembered how the convoy came to be created and ran so close to the *Emden*'s area of operation:

On 3 August 1914 the Australian government made an offer to Whitehall to raise a contingent of twenty thousand men for duty overseas. They had to find the means of transporting so large a number of soldiers and a secure convoy to deliver them. After all, Graf Spee's powerful East Asian Squadron was still in Pacific waters.

The government of New Zealand also offered a contingent but worried about the safety of the expeditionary force since the German East Asian Squadron had shown up at Samoa on 14 September. There were many hesitations regarding the assembly of the transport ships at Albany.

After long discussions between the Australian and New Zealand governments and in the British Admiralty, the convoy was finally formed in Albany on 27 October. The small convoy from New Zealand joined it on 28 October.

No one in the cruiser *Melbourne* could forget the stately picture as the New Zealand transport of ten ships in two divisions linked up with the Australian convoy. They were all painted in war gray, the best ships on the Australian coast. All were under the command of naval reserve officers. The ships, which had assigned positions in the convoy, were the best in these waters, from the *Euripides,* 15,000 tons, with 2,340 men on board, down to the little *Saldanha,* 4,600 tons, which only carried 50 soldiers and 200 horses. Their rates of speed were as varied as their sizes, ranging from the eighteen knots of the large liners down to the ten and a half knots of the old *Southern.*

On 1 November 1914 this large and impressive convoy left Australia. It included thirty-eight ships and carried more than twenty-eight thousand officers and men, the most massive convoy ever assembled in the annals of British naval history. Ships that had once been dispersed over the globe came together, the yellow funnels of the Orient Line, the famous blue of the Alfred Holt Line, the Shires, the liners of the White Star, of the P & O, and the ships of the

Clan Line. Among other variously colored funnels could be seen the dull gray of the escorting warships. The convoy commander, Captain A. G. Smith, RN, aboard the *Orvieto,* set the course and speed, the latter according to the highest speed of the slowest ship, namely, the poor old *Southern.*

The exact course of the convoy was held in absolute secrecy, the route being announced on the high seas, at a meeting with the commodore in the armored cruiser *Minotaur.* All mail and telegrams were held back during the run out of Albany. Not one word of information about the convoy leaked.

The commanding officer of the German cruiser *Emden* later declared that had he known about the convoy, he would have launched a night attack. That was simpler to say than it would have been to execute, for we had distinct orders regarding an attack by an enemy ship.

The convoy ran in three sections. The first or middle part was led by the *Orvieto.* The second, portside column was headed by the *Wiltshire,* and the third, starboard, was led by the *Euripides.* The New Zealand ships followed astern in two squadrons. First came the *Maunganul* and then the *Arawa.* The convoy's escorting forces were arranged as follows: five nautical miles in front of the middle section steamed the armored cruiser *Minotaur* with the commodore of the convoy, Captain E. B. Kiddle, RN. Four miles to starboard came the Japanese armored cruiser *Ibuki,* and four miles to port, the Australian light cruiser *Sydney.* Both cruisers were abeam the leading transport ships. The light cruiser *Melbourne* was stationed five nautical miles behind the middle squadron. As the transport column was seven nautical miles long, it was more than practical to have the *Melbourne* five miles behind the convoy. During the first days of our trip, daybreak would find a disarray of ships alongside us or aft, even though the *Melbourne* was supposed to be the tail end of the convoy.

One can imagine the tension of captains and officers of the watch who, in the black of night, had to depend on the taillight of the preceding ship for navigational help. Changes of speed and position rippled like a moving wave through the column. Sometimes running slower, sometimes faster, navigators could only hope that those aft of them would react to changes the same way. At first daylight, it was amusing to watch everyone jockeying for their old positions; no one wanted to face a reprimand from the convoy commander. You could see the improvement with a few day's experience; the ships eventually held their position, an example of the high caliber of the seamanship demonstrated by captains, deck crews, and engine personnel. The great assemblage steamed close together, squadrons no farther apart than one nautical mile. Between individual ships the distance was no more than four cable lengths, six hundred feet.

The convoy sailed northwest until 8 November. On that day the *Minotaur* left our convoy, turning over to the *Melbourne* a black Japanese box with important orders and notifications. The *Melbourne* was now our command ship. The escort for the convoy changed when the *Melbourne* took over. There was now an empty space aft—not exactly desirable, but the convoy continued. The Japanese armored cruiser *Ibuki* made us angry. Despite numerous warnings to steam smokeless, heavy black clouds continued to pour from her funnels.

Around 0640 on 9 November 1914 the following radio message was received from the Cocos: "Strange warship at the entrance." The entire convoy immediately reacted and black smoke rose from every funnel—despite strict orders to avoid this. The Japanese cruiser *Ibuki* even raised her battle flag.

The intercepted radio message was whisked to the commanding officer and a brief, intense conference of staff officers took place. Then our commanding officer appeared on the bridge of the *Melbourne* and addressed the officers standing by: "For forty long years I've served the Royal Navy faithfully with the high hope of meeting such a day. But now I have to send another warship against the enemy." He called for the signal petty officer and had an order passed on for the *Sydney* to detach for the Cocos and clarify the situation.

The *Sydney* shot forward at high speed and disappeared over the horizon. The *Ibuki* was hardly pleased at not being permitted to join in the action against the foreign ship. Quickly the escort for the convoy changed again: the *Melbourne* now replaced the *Sydney* and the *Ibuki* was ordered to lead. She hesitated to follow the order and it took several signal exchanges to straighten the situation out. As the Japanese commander later explained, "We were of the opinion that the battle should be carried out by daylight and that we should lead the attack forces." We in the *Melbourne,* too, had no more fervent a wish than to fight, but the safety of the convoy was the commanding officer's first duty.

On board the *Melbourne* tension was high. The Cocos lay only about sixty nautical miles away. The *Sydney* had left the convoy at about 0600. We received the following radio messages from her:

0920: Enemy in sight.

0923: What is identification signal of unknown ship?

0958: Opened fire on adversary, following him north.

1048: Battling opponent with effective hits.

1120: Opponent beached. Now tracking supply ship.

1140: *Emden* beached and totally out of commission.

Thus only with the 1140 report did we learn it was the famous raider *Emden* that had run aground.

At the time it was rumored that the *Königsberg* was operating in these waters, so around noon when our ship sounded the clear for action alarm we rushed to our battle stations. On the horizon we recognized a three-funnel ship that seemed to be approaching our port side. Our range-finding gear was operating, our guns were aimed. Changes in distance were constantly being measured. We intended to open fire at fourteen thousand yards. Shortly before that our code request was answered. The ship so slow in answering the recognition signal turned out to be the British auxiliary cruiser *Empress of Asia.*

A terrible task awaited the crew of another British ship after 19 November 1914. The cruiser *Sydney* had sped away, leaving behind a torn wreck with its bloody, shredded corpses. After every battle the dead had to be buried—a ritual of war observed at every battlefield in the world. At sea the men were generally spared this gruesome task by the sinking of the defeated ship. But the *Emden* had not sunk. She hung on a coral reef off an uninhabited island in the middle of the Indian Ocean. A week after the bloody battle there was little left that could command a dignified burial. The lot for this macabre work fell to the crew of the old British gunboat *Cadmus.* She had been on Yangtze River patrol and, after the confusion at the outbreak of war, been ordered to the waters north of Borneo in search of the German cruiser squadron. This creaking, expendable ship was closest to the wreck of the *Emden.*

Bert Keil, at that time the British ship's chief petty officer and gunner, remembered the terrible work on the *Emden:*

> We got orders to go to sea, course Singapore. We were only a small gunboat with six antiquated ten-centimeter guns, a kind of dispensable tracker whose mission was to search little bays and inlets that were too narrow and shallow for the German armored cruisers to anchor. Any useful information obtained we were to forward to other warships. We discovered nothing, but we stayed at the job until we heard the electrifying news about the *Emden*'s destruction. Our old *Cadmus* was ordered to the Cocos to bury the dead on the *Emden* as expeditiously as possible. Our boat was not equipped to approach a ship in the heavy surf. Off the Cocos we met the cable ship of a telegraph company and she led us to the *Emden.* It was indescribably difficult to board her.
>
> The *Sydney* had lobbed Lyddite broadsides into her. Lyddite is poisonous. We saw all those lifeless, poisoned corpses stretched out next to each other on deck, over two hundred of them. Others before us had brought blankets from below deck and tied them around the necks of the bodies. We saw yellow everywhere, the yellow color of the Lyddite powder.
>
> Some of the shells had entered the *Emden*'s starboard side and come right out again on the port side. We were surprised at the sharp-edged, pointed exit holes. It looked as if a hand had punched through a newspaper several times.
>
> The officers told us it would be impossible to bring the corpses on land for burial, for there were over two hundred. We tried grabbing one corpse by its feet. Other men packed corpses underarm and tried to drag them to the gangplank, but limbs suddenly gave way and tore off. After all, the ship and her dead crew had been lying in the grueling sun for nine days. You can imagine the horrible stench that hung in the air. After the first try we didn't want to touch another body; in those days, there were no gas masks on board, and we were already faint from the decomposing odor. Many of them had bloated to almost double their size; throats had closed up and locked all the gases inside. Motion released them.

We didn't accomplish much that day and had to return the next. The ship's doctor gave us gauze saturated with chloroform. Thus masked, we decided to conclude our work as cleanly and efficiently as possible. We searched the engine and boiler rooms for shovels and similar equipment. Using them, we brought the cadavers to the gangway. We built a type of chute over which we dragged them. All this work was done with our faces averted. When we started to throw the bodies overboard the sharks were right there. Some of them must have weighed ten tons, the largest sharks I had ever seen. They would grab a corpse, turn like lightning on their own axis, and dive. Two men were in boats below, bobbing up and down, surrounded by those murderous, thrashing fish. They swore at us with every known curse a seaman can muster. They were so close to the sharks that the roiled water splashed into their boats. This ghastly work lasted three to four days.

The next thing asked of us was to salvage one of the cruiser's torpedoes. The water was clear. We could see the trapdoors of the torpedo tubes and they were open. With great precaution our diver went below. The master gunner ordered him to unscrew the fuse from the torpedo head. First we had to fetch the winding tackle and pull the torpedo forward so he could get at it. With the fuse removed, the torpedo was pulled from the tube. Laboriously we brought it aboard and ultimately sent it to the Vernon Torpedo Works in England. On top of that, we had to salvage one of the guns. We noticed something curious. The shell cases used for the German 10-cm guns were as large as those used for the 10.5-cm guns on our ship.

In his diaries, which later became *The World Crisis,* Winston Churchill, then First Lord of the Admiralty, wrote as follows about the actions of the German cruiser:

Meanwhile the depredations of the *Emden* in the Bay of Bengal continued. On the 22nd she appeared off Madras, bombarded the Burma Company's oil tanks, and threw a few shells into the town before she was driven off by the batteries. This episode, following on the disturbance of the Calcutta-Colombo trade route and the numerous and almost daily sinkings of merchant ships in the Bay of Bengal, created widespread alarm, and on October 1 I sent the following minute to the First Sea Lord, proposing, *inter alia,* a concentration on a large scale in Indian waters against the *Emden*. This concentration would comprise *Hampshire, Yarmouth, Sydney, Melbourne, Chikuma* (Japan), *Zhemtchug* and *Askold* (Russian), *Psyche, Pyramus* and *Philomel*—a total of ten—and was capable of being fully effective in about a month. . . .

The strain upon British naval resources in the outer seas, apart from the main theatre of naval operations, was now at its maximum and may be partially appreciated from the following approximate enumerations:—

Combination against von Spee, 30 ships.

In search of the *Emden* and *Königsberg,* 8 ships.

General protection of trade by vessels other than the above, 40 ships.

Convoy duty in the Indian Ocean, 8 ships.

Blockade of the Turco-German fleet at the Dardanelles, 3 ships.

Defence of Egypt, 2 ships.

Miscellaneous minor tasks, 11 ships.

Total, 102 ships of all classes.

We literally could not lay our hands on another vessel of any sort or kind which could be made to play any useful part. But we were soon to have relief.

Already on October 30 news had reached us that the *Königsberg* had been discovered hiding in the Rufigi River in German East Africa, and it was instantly possible to mark her down with two ships of equal value and liberate the others. On November 9 far finer news arrived. The reader will remember for what purposes the *Sydney* and *Melbourne* had been attached to the great Australian convoy which was now crossing the Indian Ocean. On the 8th, the *Sydney*, cruising ahead of the convoy, took in a message from the wireless station at Cocos Island that a strange ship was entering the Bay. Thereafter, silence from Cocos Island. Thereupon the large cruiser *Ibuki* increased her speed, displayed the war flag of Japan and demanded permission from the British Officer in command of the convoy to pursue and attack the enemy. But the convoy could not divest itself of this powerful protection and the coveted task was accorded to the *Sydney*. At 9 o'clock she sighted the *Emden* and the first sea fight in the history of the Australian Navy began. It could have only one ending. In a hundred minutes the *Emden* was stranded, a flaming mass of twisted metal, and the whole of the Indian Ocean was absolutely safe and free.

The clearance of the Indian Ocean liberated all those vessels which had been searching for the *Emden* and the *Königsberg*. Nothing could now harm the Australian convoy. Most of its escort vanished. The *Emden* and the *Königsberg* were accounted for. . . .

. . . The discovery and blocking in of the *Königsberg* on 31st October liberated two out of the three vessels searching for her. But this was not enough. The destruction of the *Emden* on the 9th of November was an event of a very different order. It afforded us immediate relief, and relief exactly where we required it. The Indian Ocean was now clear.

# CHAPTER THREE

# THE PRISONERS

Conditions on board the *Sydney*, with an increase in personnel that included about eighty wounded, were cramped. Captain Glossop and his crew did everything to make life as comfortable as possible in the temporary quarters. The slightly injured were housed on the open middle deck, there being no room below. Glossop ordered awnings and tarpaulin partitions erected. Still the men were soaked through and through by heavy seas and monsoon rains, and so he radioed the auxiliary cruiser *Empress of Russia* for help. On 12 November, in a calm sea, all the lightly injured and part of the uninjured *Emden* crew were transferred to that ship, where more space and better medical facilities could be offered. Officers and seriously wounded men remained in the *Sydney*.

On Sunday, 15 November, at about 1000, the *Sydney* arrived in Colombo. The harbor was swarming with warships, including the British cruisers *Hampshire*, *Melbourne*, and *Newcastle*, the Russian cruiser *Askold*, and the Japanese cruiser *Ibuki*. There were also over forty transports, among them the Australian–New Zealand troop convoy that the *Sydney* had originally escorted. It all made a tremendous impression on the German prisoners—the number of ships and the fact that the victorious

*Sydney* sailed in with hardly a sound from any of them. Captain Glossop explained to the German officers, "In honor of our gallant and famous adversary, we have forbidden any ship to break out in the usual three cheers." Only one steamer had apparently not received this order, and to the embarrassment of the officers of the *Sydney,* its crew broke out in hearty cheers as the cruiser slid by.

In Colombo Captain Glossop gave the officers of the *Emden* a radio message from Winston Churchill. In it, Churchill acknowledged that the successes of the *Emden* had always been achieved according to the rules of humanity and British laws of the sea. On 11 November he had transmitted the following message to the British naval commander in China: "The captain, officers, and crew of the *Emden* have earned the most honorable treatment possible under the rules of war. If there are no incidents that would preclude otherwise, the captain and his officers may retain their daggers." The *Emden*'s officers treasured this gesture of military courtesy. But the daggers were no longer in their possession; destroyed by shell and fire, they rested on the wreck of their cruiser, beached on a coral reef in the middle of the Indian Ocean.

Captain Grant of the *Hampshire* would not be denied the opportunity to call on the commanding officer of the *Emden,* congratulate him on his courageous fight and survival, and console him over the loss of so many brave men.

The *Sydney* had anchored in the harbor between two buoys. Soon many boats came alongside to remove the wounded German and English sailors and take them to a hospital. After their recovery the forty-nine wounded *Emden* men, among them Lieutenant Geerdes, would be shipped to Australia to prisoner-of-war camps. The uninjured would be taken to the *Empress of Russia* and one day later distributed among several transports. Commander von Müller, Dr. Luther, Ensigns Prince von Hohenzollern and Fikentscher as well as thirty-two petty officers and ratings were taken to the Orient liner *Orvieto.* Chief Engineer Ellerbroek, Torpedo Officer Witthoeft, and forty others were placed in the *Omrah,* also an Orient liner. The remaining officers were distributed singly, with about twenty men among other Australian and New Zealand ships.

After the dispersal of the convoy on 17 November, its continuing voyage to Aden en route to Europe proceeded in relative comfort for the prisoners. On 28 November 1914, upon their arrival in Suez, all *Emden* personnel except for those in the *Orvieto* were collected and quartered in the armored cruiser *Hampshire*. Those in the *Orvieto* were to remain on that transport as far as Port Said.

Soon they received a less than welcome message: they were to be brought not to England but to Malta.

During the hot Suez Canal trip the *Emden*'s prisoners were kept below deck in steamy quarters. Only occasionally did they catch a glimpse of the surrounding desert and the strong guard on both sides of this important waterway. On 2 December the *Orvieto* reached Port Said, where the *Hampshire* was already anchored at a buoy. The harbor was crowded with warships, among them old acquaintances from the Far East like the French armored cruisers *Montcalm* and *Dupleix* and a string of troop transports. There were also torpedo boats, weather ships, mine sweepers, hospital ships, and a few German freighters interned at the outbreak of war.

At this time, Commander von Müller and his men were transferred from the *Orvieto* to the *Hampshire*. In the surrounding ships passengers and crew crowded the railings, hoping to catch a glimpse of the famous prisoners and photograph them. In the *Hampshire*, meanwhile, Captain Grant greeted his prisoners in a friendly, hospitable manner—particularly noteworthy since the English ship had been in constant pursuit of the *Emden*. As luck would have it, the victor's laurel wreath had fallen to the Australian cruiser *Sydney*, not to the *Hampshire*. The *Emden* officers got the impression that Grant and his officers were relieved at this turn of events. After all, only a year before they had met in Nanking under friendly circumstances. Thus fate had spared them the painful experience of battling their German comrades at sea. At any rate, Grant graciously offered his cabin and wardroom to the officers of the *Emden* and moved to a sofa in the chart house. In Port Said he ordered civilian clothes for the officers and new British naval uniforms for the men. Before leaving he went ashore to fetch English and German reading materials with which the *Emden* people could relieve the monotonous lot of prisoners of war.

The *Hampshire* received daily radio messages about the war. Thus the *Emden* crew learned of the victory of Admiral Graf Spee's cruiser squadron over Admiral Sir Christopher Cradock's squadron near Coronel.

Sunday, 6 December, the *Hampshire* steamed into the harbor of La Valetta on Malta. With best wishes Captain Grant and his officers said goodbye. The *Emden* men viewed the event with mixed feelings. They were leaving the hospitality of the Royal Navy for the uncertain care of the British army. The petty officers and the crew were taken to Camp St. Clements and later to Fort Salvatore, while Commander von Müller and his officers were transported to Camp Verdala.

When the doors of the prisoner camp finally closed behind the *Emden*'s officers they received a jubilant welcome from the civilian prisoners, mostly merchants and employees of hotels and companies in Egypt and Malta. There were also captains and officers of German and Austrian ships and citizens of all nations enjoying friendly relations with Germany. The very first day the camp's glee club came to serenade Commander von Müller in his cell with the national anthem.

Considering the times, the officers' accommodations were quite adequate. But the crew, lodged in Camp St. Clements, lived in a makeshift tent city. During frequent rainstorms they had to dash outside and refasten torn tent flaps. Many of the tents were flooded, which endangered health and destroyed clothing. Communication between the captain and officers of the *Emden* and her petty officers and ratings was strictly forbidden at first. Later on it was allowed, but infrequently and under heavy guard.

Müller immediately joined the camp committee and was elected to its executive council. Untiring, he shared in all the inconveniences of prison life, hoping through petitions, grievances, and complaints to improve the lot of his subordinates. When he wasn't attending to documents in his cell, reconstructing the final battle of his cruiser in a war diary or writing the relatives of his fallen crewmen, he paced solemn and brooding about the small yard of the camp. He and his men faced many years in prison. There they sat, condemned to inactivity while around them the world was aflame and their own country was fighting desperately for survival.

They were delighted and proud to learn, at last, that the first officer of their cruiser and his landing party had managed to escape British capture. Where might these brave men be now?

*The light cruiser Emden on a trial run, summer 1909. Built at the Imperial Shipyard in Danzig, she was the last light cruiser of the Imperial Navy fitted with expansion engines.*

*SMS* Emden *in harbor at Kiel in April 1910. She was never to visit her sponsor city Emden.*

*Cruisers of the world powers on the Yangtze off Nanking, August 1912. Far right:* the Emden *moored by the German consulate. A few days before she had silenced a rebel fort that had been firing on her.*

*The* Emden *at the mole in Tsingtao. The cruiser has rigged awnings and dressed ship for a holiday.*

*Officers and sailors of the* Emden *coaling in Tsingtao. For loading, every type of clothing was permitted. After every "coalfest" there was a thorough scrubbing down of the ship. Resupply of coal was a raiding cruiser's greatest problem.*

*The* Emden *taking on coal at Tsingtao. Chinese coolies were still willing to work. During the war, this difficult task would be carried out by the crew no less than eleven times in three months, in hidden coves or on the high seas.*

Left: *The British armored cruiser* Minotaur *on a visit to Tsingtao, June 1914. Center: SMS* Scharnhorst, *flagship of the German East Asia Squadron of Admiral Graf Spee.*

*The skipper of SMS Emden, Commander Karl von Müller (1873–1923). He received the Order Pour le Mérite for his successful conduct of cruiser warfare. One of the most popular commanding officers in the Imperial Navy, he possessed ability, courage, and chivalry that made him world famous. The sponsor city Emden bestowed honorary citizenship on him.*

Right to left: *The armored cruisers* Scharnhorst *and* Gneisenau *and the light cruiser* Emden *in Chinese waters off Tsingtao, June 1914.*

*One of the first successes of the German Navy in World War I: The seizure of the Russian passenger ship* Rjäsan *by SMS* Emden. *After the* Rjäsan's *conversion to the German auxiliary cruiser* Cormoran, *she joined the cruiser squadron and tried her hand at commerce raiding. She was interned by the United States at Guam on 14 December 1914 and, subsequent to the U.S. declaration of war in April 1917 was sunk by her crew.*

*SMS* Emden *shortly before leaving Tsingtao on the eve of war.*

*Loyal companion and collier of the cruiser* Emden: *the HAPAG steamer* Markomannia.

*The* Emden *shelled the Indian port of Madras on 22 September 1914. Most of the 130 shells fired hit vital military targets. Oil tanks erupted in flames. During her withdrawal, the* Emden *could see the thick smoke cloud hanging over Madras from a distance of eighty nautical miles.*

*The French torpedo-boat destroyer* Mousquet *at Pulau-Penang. On 28 October 1914, fooled by the* Emden's *false funnel, she was sunk with heavy loss of life after a short gunnery action.*

*Taken by surprise, the Russian cruiser* Zhemtchug *was sunk by SMS* Emden *at dawn on 28 October 1914.*

*Salvage companies in Pulau-Penang attempt to raise the wreckage of the* Zhemtchug.

*Lieutenant Hellmuth von Mücke, first officer of the light cruiser* Emden *and commander of the landing party. The daring and adventurous odyssey of the* Ayesha, *the voyage to the Red Sea, landing in southern Arabia, trek and battle in the desert, and return to Germany via Constantinople proved his outstanding abilities as an inventive corsair, a bold "sea devil," and a skilled military leader.*

*The radio station on Direction Island whose call, "Strange ship at entrance," brought the* Sydney, *which had been escorting a troop transport nearby.*

*The pier on Direction Island, 0920, 9 November 1914. The sirens of the Emden, which has been taken by surprise, are recalling the landing party. In the roadstead lies the as-yet-overlooked Ayesha. British radio and cable personnel watch with great interest.*

*Early morning, 9 November 1914, in the Cocos. In front of the British radio and cable station is a group from the Emden's landing party; they have just finished destroying the communications installations. A German officer (center) is gathering information from the island's inhabitants.*

British settlers on Direction Island allow themselves to be photo-
graphed as German prisoners, beneath the imperial war flag and
watched by guards from the Emden, in commemoration of a dramatic
day in the island's history.

When the landing party realized they would not reach the fast-
disappearing Emden, *they returned to Direction and took up defensive
positions. The small detachment had brought four machine guns and
plenty of ammunition with them, which would prove most useful in
the deserts of Arabia.*

Emden *sailors loading the cutter and steam pinnace with supplies. In the distance lies the Ayesha, where the rest of the men are setting sails.*

*Sailors of the* Emden *landing party with loaded lorries, normally used to carry copra, will furnish the Ayesha with provisions.*

*Burned out and totally disabled, the wreck of the light cruiser* Emden
*lies off North Keeling Island.*

*The Australian ship* Sydney, *a modern light cruiser far superior to the*
Emden *in speed and size, armor and armament.*

*After the battle, crew members of the Sydney pose happily on the forecastle of their cruiser. The wing of the bridge and splinter protection mats show damage sustained during the action. The cruiser had taken a hit on her forward control station.*

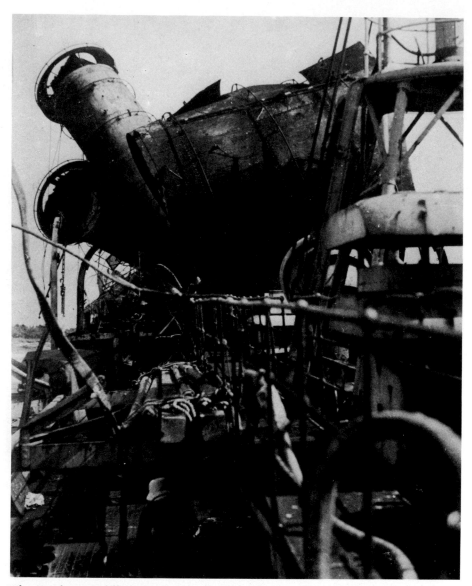

*The* Emden's *riddled waist. The funnels, from which the stays had been removed for coaling, had fallen in battle like a house of cards.*

*The first boat from the* Sydney *approaching the beached* Emden *one day after the battle. Survivors gathered on the blackened, smoldering after deck.*

*The burned-out stern of the* Emden. *Her guns are in their last firing position. All rescue boats had to pull alongside the stern, as the bow lay in the surf high on the reef.*

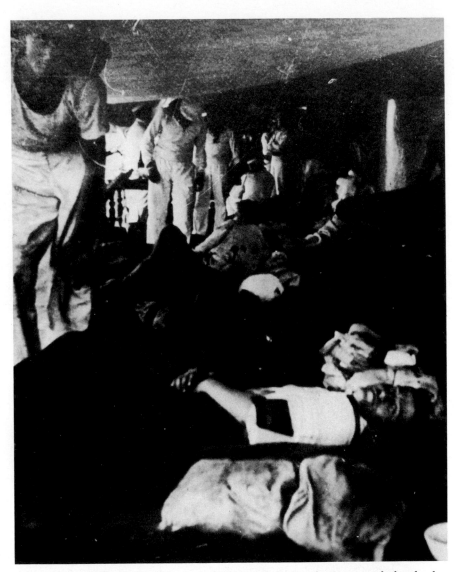

*The middle deck of the* Sydney *housed the* Emden's *wounded, who lay under a hastily rigged awning, attended by their comrades and Australian sailors.*

The Sydney *returning to Direction Island to capture the* Emden *landing party. The fifty* Emden *men, however, had disappeared in the old schooner* Ayesha.

*An armed landing party from the* Sydney *unloading guns on Direction Island.*

*Again and again the* Sydney's *boats had to return to the wrecked* Emden *to rescue survivors.*

At Padang the Ayesha *was only allowed to take on limited provisions and water. Dutch warships isolated her from other German ships, though some anchored merchant vessels managed to slip her provisions.*

The schooner Ayesha *lying in the Dutch harbor of Padang.*

*The small North German Loyd freighter* Choising *had to maintain strict neutrality under the watchful eye of Dutch authorities. She managed, however, to deceive them, and under the pretext of proceeding to Laurenzo Marques met the* Ayesha *at sea.*

*Arriving by Turkish torpedo boat at the Golden Horn in Constantinople, Lieutenant von Mücke and his freshly uniformed landing party present themselves to Admiral Souchon. After months of hair-raising adventures, Mücke reported laconically, "Landing party of SMS* Emden *reporting for duty."*

*Surf and weather have taken a further toll on the* Emden *off North Keeling in this photograph from the early 30s. What remained of her was broken up by a Japanese salvage company in 1950.*

In 1916 the Imperial Navy commissioned another Emden. This one carried the Iron Cross, awarded by the kaiser, on her bow. She participated in the operation against the Baltic islands in 1917. After the German fleet had been delivered to Scapa Flow, she became flagship of the internment group under Rear Admiral von Reuter. Scuttled by her crew in 1919, she was salvaged by the French and used in demolitions experiments.

The first postwar cruiser of the republic's navy was christened Emden. The third cruiser of this name, which also carried the Iron Cross on her bow, participated in many operations in World War II. She burned after a British air attack on Kiel in April 1945 and was sunk in Heikendorfer Bay. After the war the wreck was broken up.

The modern West German navy has not forgotten the Emden, bestowing her world-famous name on a fast escort ship launched on 21 March 1959 at Stülcken Yards in Hamburg. The fourth Emden assumed duty on 24 October 1961.

Four


The
Landing
Party

# CHAPTER ONE

# THE LANDING

*9 November 1914*

It was 0630. Lieutenant Hellmuth von Mücke reported to Commander von Müller on the quarterdeck of the *Emden:* "Reporting landing party consisting of three officers, six petty officers, and forty-one men, ready to leave ship, sir." The *Emden* was lying at anchor at Port Refuge, a harbor formed by the Keeling reefs. Alongside her were two cutters with the officers and men of the landing party. A steam pinnace was ready for lowering and towing. Their orders were to destroy the radio and cable station on Direction, the northerly island of the Cocos. If at all possible, they were to bring back signal books, code books, secret papers, and the like.

From Direction three important cable links ran out: one to Mauritius, one to Perth, Australia, and a third to Batavia. This station was the last purely English connection between Australia and the mother country; the remaining cables had been destroyed by other ships of the German cruiser squadron. The landing party, which fully expected to be met by force on shore, took four shipboard machine guns along. Two were carried in the steam pinnace, the other two in the cutters. The crews were armed with rifles, bayonets, and pistols. With the pinnace taking the cutters in tow, they departed for Direction and an uncertain future.

The island lay about three thousand meters away. It was a flat place with tall palms through whose crowns the roofs of European-style houses and the radio tower were visible. They steered toward the latter. Right below the landing platform a small white sailing ship was at anchor.

"Shall we destroy that, too?" one lieutenant (j.g.) asked the commanding officer.

"Naturally. She's sailed for the last time. Detail a man to stand by with an explosive charge," Mücke said.

With machine guns and small arms ready, the landing party tied up at a little bridge on a beach in the inner lagoon. Meeting no opposition, they double-timed towards the radio tower. Demolition of the white sailing ship was postponed. Their primary purpose was to scout the area and maintain signal communication with the *Emden*. Quickly they found the telegraph building and signal station, took them over, and halted all communications. Mücke got hold of one of the surprised English civilians and ordered him to call the station director, whereupon a Mr. Farrant appeared posthaste. He turned out to be an easygoing, humorous man.

Mücke explained himself: "I've been ordered to destroy your radio telegraph station. I warn you, don't offer resistance. You would also be wise to give me the keys to the individual houses so we don't have to break down the doors. All arms in your possession are to be turned over immediately and all Europeans are to gather in front of the telegraph building."

The director accepted his plight with composure. He wouldn't think of resisting, he assured them. He pulled a large ring of keys from his pocket and pointed to the shacks where the radio transmitters, not yet installed, were to be found. Then he said, "By the way, congratulations are in order!"

"What for?" the surprised Mücke said.

"For the Iron Cross. Reuter telegraphed the news only a few moments ago."

But the German seamen had other things to think of. The radio tower had to be demolished as soon as possible. Torpedo specialists attached cartridges to the structure's supports and then blasted them away, bringing the tower down. Everything that seemed important was smashed to smithereens.

In the telegraph building the Morse transmitters were still frantically busy. What they were telegraphing could not be ascertained by the *Emden*'s sailors since it was in code. A few strong ax chops and Morse machine, inkwells, table legs, and cable terminals were flying around the room. Orders were to do a thorough job. The men searched everywhere for spare equipment. Anything that looked as if it contributed to the operation of the station was destroyed, even a seismograph. The simple sailors mistook it for an important telegraph apparatus.

Most difficult was the work of finding and cutting submarine cables. A diagram of their location could not be found at the station, but on the beach there were several tablets with the heading "Cables." Obviously these marked spots where the cables came ashore. With the steam pinnace and a few grapnels, they were fished out of the water. The work was not easy, the cables being very heavy. It was impossible to bring them directly to the surface. When the bight of the cable was elevated, sailors had to dive under and attach winding tackle to it. Then, with great difficulty, they managed to drag the strands into the boat. Explosives were not used to destroy them; the *Emden* still needed those for scuttling ships. Instead the thick cables were attacked with crowbars, axes, and chisels. After laborious effort they cut two cables and dragged the ends away with the steam pinnace. The third cable, despite frantic searching, could not be located.

A small corrugated iron shack loaded with spare parts and reserve equipment was blasted open with percussion caps and then set on fire. All newspapers, books, Morse ciphers, and the like were put in sacks to be taken away.

Presently the *Emden* flashed a message in Morse: "Speed up the work." Mücke gathered his men and abandoned the idea of destroying the little schooner that lay in the harbor. It was immaterial now. The *Emden*'s sirens wailed and blasted away, signaling an immediate return to ship. As the landing party reached their embarkation point, the *Emden* was hoisting a flag indicating that she had weighed anchor already. The reason was unknown and puzzling to the landing party. At top speed the little convoy navigated the shortest distance over the reefs and toward the ship. Meanwhile the *Emden* had turned her bow seaward and run out at high speed. Mücke assumed she was off to meet the coal ship *Buresk,* to pilot her through the reefs. The pinnace continued to put-put behind the *Emden,* the distance between them growing ever greater. The cruiser ran at sixteen or seventeen knots, while the pinnace, with its heavily loaded cutters in tow, could only make four at best.

Suddenly a battle flag unfurled on the *Emden.* Cannon thunder rolled—the cruiser had fired her starboard broadside. Still the landing party didn't know what was going on. It was assumed that the *Emden* wanted to capture a freighter in the vicinity. But why fire the whole battery?

Astern of the *Emden* a salvo of five heavy shells hit the water, sending huge water columns shooting into the air. Now it was clear: their cruiser was engaged in a serious battle. The enemy could not be seen by the landing party; Direction Island and its thicket of palms obstructed the view. The *Emden,* meanwhile, was several nautical miles away, still widening the gap between herself and her boats. It was impossible for them to catch up. They turned around. The *Emden* had left her landing party behind.

The boats returned to Direction and tied up at the same spot. The landing party gathered the Englishmen again and confiscated their arms, then hoisted the German flag over the island. A state of emergency was declared and communication with enemy ships or other islands was strictly forbidden. The landing party received orders to prepare the beachhead for defense, mount the machine guns, and dig trenches. The Cocos were now German territory. Should the *Emden* be chased away or even destroyed, the enemy cruiser would surely run into the harbor to check on the radio transmitter. Mücke had no intention of surrendering the island, now flying the German flag, without a fight.

The English were little cheered by this prospect. They begged for permission to get out of the way, go to another island, should it really come to a fight. Their request was granted.

Mücke made all necessary preparations for the defense and then hurried to the northern beach to observe the battle. He did not recognize the enemy ship; it had four funnels and two masts, all angled to the stern. In armament she seemed much stronger than the *Emden*. She appeared to be of the *Yarmouth* or *Sydney* class, and she ran under a thick smoke screen, burning either Indian or Japanese coal. The *Emden* held the lee, later the weather side. The opponent fired rapidly but inaccurately, shells landing many hundreds of meters apart. It took a long time for her to get on target. According to the Englishmen who witnessed the beginning of the battle from land, the *Emden* found the range early and grouped her shots well.

When Mücke first caught sight of the battle, the *Emden* had already lost her forward funnel. She turned at high speed toward the enemy and prepared for a circling battle. Apparently a torpedo had been launched. At the beginning of her run she was already burning fiercely aft, and in the vicinity of the mainmast several shells had already found their target. She burned with high, bright flames and was engulfed in heavy white smoke clouds. Perhaps it was only steam escaping. After the torpedo launch she turned sharply to port, as did the enemy ship. So it was possible that instead of a running battle, it had come to a fight in the round.

Reluctantly Mücke left his post to look after the work his landing party was doing. Then he chose a higher observation post on a roof and followed the remainder of the battle. By 1100 the German ship had suffered so greatly at the hands of her superior enemy that any return to the island, even under favorable circumstances, seemed unlikely. At best she could try to reach a harbor to repair her hull, bury her dead, and land her wounded.

During the long months and years of overseas service, SMS *Emden* had become country and home to her men. How often on their return from work or leave had the familiar silhouette of three funnels and two masts amidst strange ships, bizarre structures, and exotic trees given them a feeling of security? Now that silhouette was no longer there; a mast had fallen, the funnel was crushed, the ship was burning. For the men on the small coral island, it was as if they were civilians watching their homes, their farms, their villages go up in smoke. Tight bands clamped around their hearts, overwhelming anger gave way to an almost debilitating sorrow and bewilderment, a feeling of unreality. It couldn't be true, it was a horrible dream.

But it was reality, and now their mutilated, dying homeland was disappearing on the dark horizon. For the length of a heartbeat the men felt like orphans, totally deserted. As an organized, efficient, pulsating weapons system, SMS *Emden* had ceased to exist. Now they had to think ahead. What should they do next? According to the Englishmen, there were several Royal Navy cruisers, among them the *Minotaur,* in the vicinity of the island. In the absence of radio traffic they would conclude that a German landing had been made. It was to be expected, therefore, that they would appear sooner or later. They might also put in to undergo repairs in Port Refuge or drop off wounded, there being doctors on the island. Another possibility: a British warship could run in to check the radio and cable station, since transmission to Australian ports and to Batavia and Mauritius had been disrupted. Any small British detachment Mücke could oppose with his four machine guns of two thousand rounds each, twenty-nine rifles of sixty rounds each, and ten pistols of twenty-four rounds each. On the other hand, he would be utterly helpless in the face of gunfire from the English cruiser. A hero's death or British internment lay before them. Or? Mücke glanced at the little white schooner in the harbor. The *Ayesha,* named after the favorite wife of the prophet Mohammed, had served to haul copra two or three times a year from Direction to Batavia; each time she returned loaded with provisions. Since the introduction of a regular freighter route, she lay without a mission, without tackle, rotting in the harbor. She could help them out of this trap. Mücke decided instantaneously that they would sail her away from the island.

He took the steam pinnace by himself to the schooner to see if she was still seaworthy. On board, he found the captain and a sailor. First he asked about munitions, disguising the real reason for his inspection. A short walk about the deck assured him that she was indeed seaworthy. Officers and men arrived to ready her. There was a lot to do. Everything had been stowed away, and the first task was to reset sails and tackle.

When the English inhabitants realized what the German landing party was up to, they warned that the *Ayesha* was old and rotten and would not survive a journey at sea. Besides that, the English armored cruiser *Minotaur* and a Japanese cruiser were close by and would surely capture the schooner. Even the captain, who left the ship along with his one-member crew, spoke these hardly reassuring words, "I wish you a safe journey, but the ship's hull is rotten."

As the German sailors, despite all, continued to ready the *Ayesha,* the Englishmen developed a spirit of cooperative sportsmanship. They did everything they could to help. Was it gratitude for the considerate behavior shown them, or the wish to be rid of these foreign invaders as soon as possible that moved them? Some were delighted that their strenuous communications duties were, for now, a thing of the past. They showed the Germans where provisions and water were to be found, urging them to take the freshest supplies. They brought pots and pans, water, oil lamps, old clothing, and blankets to the schooner. They provided pipes and tobacco. They were also generous with advice, particularly concerning the course to follow. Later on, it would be revealed that their comments on the wind, weather, and current were actually sound. They wished the Germans smooth sailing and thanked them for being considerate in the accomplishment of their difficult mission—a mission in which all the *Emden*'s men had acted in fairness. Then the English swarmed over the *Ayesha* taking photographs.

Presently a lookout on one of the roofs announced a smoke cloud appearing from the north. They saw a black puff drift toward the island, apparently from an enemy cruiser burning Indian coal. The ship was still below the horizon. Masts appeared, as did those of the *Emden*. They were off to the east and moving slowly in that direction. Suddenly the enemy shot toward the *Emden* and their masts became indistinguishable. It was then that a high white column rose through the black smoke of the enemy ship. Had there been a torpedo hit? The opponent broke off the battle and resumed a northwesterly course, while the *Emden* continued eastward. The distance between the two ships seemed to grow until at dusk both disappeared below the horizon again.

Because of so many coral reefs, sailing out in total darkness was impossible. Thus Lieutenant von Mücke halted the loading operation to get ready to sail. They had water for four weeks and provisions for eight. Gaff sails were hauled down and foresails rigged. Descending night forced them to leave the harbor in haste. When the last boat shoved off the Englishmen broke forth in loud hurrahs. Mücke gave a short address and, amid three cheers for the kaiser, hoisted the battle flag and ensign of the newest ship in His Majesty's Navy, the schooner *Ayesha*. The flags fluttered high on her mast in the evening light. Slowly the steam pinnace dragged her out to sea. The new commander climbed to the top of his foremast to locate reefs and shallows lying ahead; he had no accurate charts. With a sharp boat whistle he directed the steam pinnace to port or starboard, depending on the outlook. The two cutters remained in tow.

The sun disappeared completely, for near the equator there are no lasting hours of twilight, and Mücke could no longer see the ocean's bottom from his perch on the foremast. He had to mount the fore channels, portside, and give his orders from there. Just before passing the last dangerous reef they had a few anxious moments. In spite of the darkness, they saw every stone, every pebble, every tuft of sea grass on the sea floor, a sign that the schooner was in very shallow water. But they managed to glide by without touching bottom.

Meanwhile some of the sails were set, easing the pinnace's tow work. Soon the ship was sailing free of the sheltering islands. Long, heavy ocean swells now rocked her. Far enough at sea to cruise clear of the swells to lee, the steam pinnace was called in so that the rest of the crew could be taken on. High swells made the maneuver difficult; the little boat slammed the port side of the *Ayesha*. Even if the fate of the pinnace was at the moment of no consequence, there was great concern about the aged sail-boat. The last man on board the pinnace restarted its motor with what steam remained in the boiler, and with hooks the rudder was manipulated to port side. In an elegant curve the boat struck out, vanishing at about 2030 in the darkness. Perhaps it foundered a few hundred meters away in the crashing surf; perhaps it floated like a ghost ship over the wide Indian Ocean.

The schooner still had the two cutters in tow. For the time being they held to a westerly course to avoid falling into the hands of an enemy cruiser and to fool any observers following their progress from land. Lieutenant von Mücke did not want to head to a neutral harbor but rather, ultimately, to German East Africa. Moreover, the *Buresk* was probably standing off the western part of the island; perhaps she had not fallen into enemy hands.

During the night they tacked and continued in a northeasterly direction. There was no sign of the *Buresk*. The *Emden* would have to run into a harbor soon, if not for the dead and wounded then certainly to repair damages and take on provisions and coal. Mücke thought of Batavia and Padang, both equally distant. He was without navigational aids, without the chronometer journal. Even the chronometer's registered standings were dated. His only guidelines were the measurements of the noon meridian. He had to get farther north to reach the area of the northwest monsoon, which blew in November about eight degrees latitude south. Thus, they closely held the course north by northeast with the wind hard over the port bow.

The cutters were a danger to the ship, smashing into her square stern despite a long tow line. Her port tow roller and part of her railing tore away. Two cutters were too many. During the night the *Ayesha* made little headway with her small sails. Eventually one cutter drifted away. It was leaky and, in the swells and rising sea, had been colliding with the other.

The great adventures of the *Emden*'s landing party, in a sailboat bearing the name of Mohammed's favorite wife, had just begun.

# CHAPTER TWO

# SMS *AYESHA*

The journey of the small, decaying schooner *Ayesha* is best described in the original logbook, from which the information in the following pages is taken.

*10 November 1914*

On this first morning at sea the new commanding officer pondered the uncertain fate of his comrades in the *Emden* and held a short devotional service. Then more sails were made ready and run up. By noon all gaff sails, foresails, and main and mizzen topsails had been rigged. The ship ran at a tolerable speed in a light to moderate east-southeast breeze.

Explosives went overboard, as there was not room to stow them and, in any case, the temperature was too high for safety. Other provisions were carefully stored. Crew members and petty officers split into two watch details. Enlisted men slept in the crew space—it was equipped for five men—and in the hold, while petty officers took the chart room aft and officers, two small cabins in the deckhouse. The chart room served as a mess. The use of water and provisions was strictly supervised. Water tanks remained under lock and key, and everyone received his carefully measured ration from the supply officer.

A careful inspection of the ship's keel brought reassuring news. The vessel, contrary to the opinion of her erstwhile captain, seemed to be sound down to her bottom hold. She wasn't taking on much water, and by pumping twice a day the crew kept her good and dry. The tackle was in good shape, mainsails good, side sails for the most part well worn. Charts were scarce and limited to the Batavia-Cocos run. Most of the time they had to navigate by means of a general map. They found an old sailing manual, but the information in it was badly dated, going back to the period from 1824 to 1845. On hand also were a protractor, a nautical yearbook in decent shape, and a patent log that was put to good use. They tried to determine their east-west deviation from course by observing the sun, calculating longitude, and establishing an exact chronometric reading. Meanwhile they found a navigational book only two months old with a chronometer control; it also contained the daily deviation. An instrument reading tallied with the calculated course and position and thus could be considered approximately correct. With that, they learned a great deal for the purposes of navigation.

### 11 November 1914

Before noon, in addition to repetitive work like cleaning ship, the rigging was tested, the bilge pumps were operated, and the lower topsail was set. In an east-southeast wind of force three to four, the jib topsail, flying jib, jib, inner jib, foresail, lower topsail, upper topsail, mainsail, main topsail, mizzen, and topsail were set. The ship was making 3.8 to 5.1 nautical miles. At 2335 the cutter tow line broke and the boat was left adrift.

### 12 November 1914

During the day the wind picked up and turned south. At night the sails had to be secured. The ship steamed for an hour at 8.2 knots, at 5.5 to 6 miles over the day. The foresail stays started to give way.

### 13 November 1914

At 0500 a heavy squall bore down. In boats hanging from davits plugs were inserted and scuppers were tightly set; all containers available were readied to catch rainwater. Even a large sail and cabin roof were pressed into service. The entire crew stood naked on deck, using the opportunity to bathe in fresh water and rinse out their underwear. They gathered a barrel of drinking water.

### 14 November 1914

At 1330 they changed course, heading closer to land to avoid the zone of unpredictable calms and squalls that forms when the monsoon changes from southeast to northwest. At 1700, a thunderstorm. Afterwards the wind was still and the ship, with loose sails, wallowed heavily in rolling cross-swells.

### 16 November 1914

The long-awaited northwest monsoon had not yet begun. Light winds blew, bringing isolated squalls, and so the sails were secured several times. With heavy weather threatening at night, light sails were set at twilight. In the evening a short church service marked the week that had passed since the battle and departure from Port Refuge.

### 17 November 1914

In a dead calm the ship's bow was swept in a northwesterly direction. They tried to tack while the wind blew more and more to the north. Two swells rolled across each other. Low in the northwest hung heavy dark clouds that slowly rose on the horizon. Could it be the hoped-for monsoon?

The water situation was improving. What had been gathered in lifeboats was brackish but could be used for bathing and washing clothes. Rainwater collected in barrels was potable; everybody took a shot of lime juice with it. Potatoes could be boiled in salt water, which saved drinking water.

At 1500 the barometer stood at its lowest so far, 729.78. Up to now the day's curve had been rising steadily, but now it sank. Apparently more wind was in store. At 1600 a light northwester came through. Course was north by northeast. In the evening the wind died entirely. Top and gaffsails were furled and tied down. The ship rolled heavily in the swells.

*18 November 1914*

By 0900 another whiff blew in from north-northeast. Course was east-southeast and they were steering on even keel. There was almost no movement forward; sails continually lurched to windward. To keep the men occupied, lessons were given in compass reading and rigging identification. The swells grew and the current sent the ship southeast. By noon she had returned to her position of 16 November, and the wind did not look as though it would pick up during the day.

A measuring of the water supply showed that in one week they had used half a tank. There still remained three-quarters of a tank of fresh water, enough for six weeks, plus a reserve of a tank-and-a-half of rainwater. As for the food reserve, it would carry them through eight weeks.

During the night they set all sails except the square and foresail.

*19 November 1914*

Still there was no sign of wind. The current continually bore the ship back to the southeast. It was hot and the skies remained cloudless. The awnings were set.

*21 November 1914*

Hope that the northwest monsoon would finally break through had still not been fulfilled. What the ship accomplished in the squalls was canceled in the calms. At 1000 a smoke cloud was sighted in the northwest drifting eastward. Even from the top platform only smoke was visible, no ship. By noon a slight breeze arrived from the northwest. The ship, now steerable, proceeded on course northeast-north. The freighter had vanished. The breeze increased, coming from a northwesterly direction. It seemed they had reached the outer edges of the monsoon. At 2100 a thunder squall swept in. Because of an operating error the mizzen topsail landed on the gaff arm and tore; now it hung useless. Salvage was impossible in the squall. One by one sails, all except the fore stay sail, lower topsail, and mizzen, were stowed. The ship rode well, made good headway. Saint Elmo's fire burned bright on the mast heads. Lightning and thunder were extraordinarily heavy. At 2100 the storm had passed, the wind died down.

*22 November 1914*

Lieutenant von Mücke decided to head for Padang, not Batavia. An intermediate port such as Benkulu, Enggano, or Pagai Island should be approached only in the doubtful event of an emergency. Mücke chose Padang for several reasons: that was where they were most likely find the *Emden*, a German consul was stationed there, one of the ensigns on board had served in the *Gneisenau* and was familiar with the place, and the *Ayesha* was not known there. Surely there were German merchant ships in the area, possibly the *Kleist*, which could do seventeen knots top speed. Moreover, at Padang they could anchor far enough out from the docks not to call attention to themselves but still close enough to allow boat traffic to the shore. Finally, now that the northwest monsoon checked in at four degrees latitude south instead of eight, Padang looked much more favorable than Batavia. The ship had taken seven days to traverse the belt of calm. That was a lot longer than they had figured, believing the monsoon's southward thrust would push the ship rapidly through it. To set course for Batavia would mean riding out the calm zone once more. Considering their limited water and provisions, that simply was not feasible.

The difficulty would be the navigation. A map of the northern portion of the Indian Ocean was available, but there was no chart or map of the west coast of Sumatra. For the time being, it looked as though the schooner would have to sail through the Seaflower Channel. An observation at 1430 revealed her position to be seventy nautical miles southwest of the channel. The chronometer, though, was not totally reliable; positions on chronometers were known to have errors of margin of over a minute, and thus it was not certain if any of the positions were correct.

For the crew it would be most advantageous to reach port soon. There they could replenish clothing, toilet articles, and other necessities. Everything was falling apart, particularly the clothes brought along from the Cocos; they had turned to rags. Toothbrushes were nonexistent and the ship held only one comb. Salt water served as hair lotion and one shaving kit made the rounds.

At 2000 the wind sloughed off. At midnight it shifted to the northeast and increased to force five. Course: northwest to north.

### 23 *November 1914*

Machine guns, rifles, and sidearms were readied for use. Lieutenant von Mücke had decided that, should they find an enemy destroyer at anchor or coaling, they would go alongside and board her.

At 1010 a lookout on the upper topsail yelled, "Land ho!" Four degrees to port they could see land, apparently Siberut and the islands of the Seaflower Channel. So the longitude was correct. By 1600 the shoreline was distinct. It was Siberut. With allowances for a lee drift and a southerly current, all sails were set for an approach to the channel, course northeast at four to five knots in a northwest wind of force three to four.

At 1840 the *Ayesha* stood close by the channel. Moonlight straggled through a cloudy sky. To the east, lightning flashed. The possibility of crossing the channel by night was questionable. Mücke wanted to try, but at 1940, because of darkness and lack of wind, the project was abandoned. They reversed course and headed out to sea. Light sails were set.

### 24 *November 1914*

During the night the *Ayesha* had drifted south. Now she stood in mid-strait. To port lay Siberut, to starboard, Sipora. In the course of the day the ship sailed with a slight breeze out of the northwest through the Seaflower Channel. Even without charts they had no navigational difficulty. A squall brought more water for washing, and each man received an extra bottle of soda water.

Shortly before 1900 the patent log showed that they had covered eight hundred miles in their journey from Direction Island.

*25 November 1914*

At daybreak Sumatra appeared clearly on the horizon. The wind blowing from land was weak and from sunrise on there was dead calm. The *Ayesha* drifted with the current, southeast by east-southeast. For lack of tobacco the men were smoking tea leaves. At noon, with all sails set, their course followed the coast northeast. In case of a calm during the night they would anchor near land, provided the schooner could get close enough. Perhaps there they would meet a countercurrent.

An enlarged pencil drawing was made of the entrance of Padang according to information found in a sailing handbook. This incomplete map showed numerous reefs and islands that would have to be circumvented. The island to port, apparently Mosquito, had a beacon not shown in the book.

At night a thunderstorm struck and they saw the flashing lights of Padang.

*26 November 1914*

The *Ayesha* had been driven five nautical miles from land overnight. With the current she drifted farther to the southeast. At 0830 the large boat was lowered for towing, at 0900, the small one. Both boats towed the schooner and the men aboard her pulled on cutter oars that had been lashed together. Not much headway was made. At noon she was becalmed.

A steamer with flags in her tops hove into sight at 1500. When she approached, the Germans identified her as the Dutch destroyer *Lynx*. She drew close and inspected the schooner, searching for the name on her stern, but it had been painted over. Appearing to resume course, the Dutchman turned about five thousand meters away and followed the *Ayesha*. Evidently the schooner had been expected.

The battle flag·was made ready to hoist, but after a while the *Lynx* headed for port. The *Ayesha* followed course northnorthwest for approximately four miles. A blacked-out steamer approached to the starboard, out of Padang. Through an exchange of signals with another ship she gave her name away—

the *Lynx*. The destroyer turned, showing red and green lights, and again followed the *Ayesha*. With that, the Germans were convinced their identity had been discovered.

They steered northerly all night, position uncertain because soundings could not be taken. The *Lynx* tenaciously remained in their wake. About 2100 the Germans improvised a signal lamp with a white light and a plank held in front of it; twice, once in English, once in German, they asked why the *Lynx* was following. Both times the signal was received but not answered. Then the Dutchman drew out of their wake and proceeded alongside and ahead of the *Ayesha*.

*27 November 1914*

At dawn, rain and calm. The *Lynx*, which had disappeared in a rain squall, now hove into view again, flags flying in her tops. Because of that, and because the schooner was without a doubt in the Dutch islands, perhaps even in territorial waters, the Germans hoisted their ensign and battle flag.

The *Ayesha* drifted with the current to the southeast. Mosquito Island was first far to the starboard, then dead astern, finally to port. They set a southerly course and at about 1000 had slowly pushed past Mara Island. At 1130 several small Malaysian boats came alongside with pilots. They took one aboard who told them the pilot fee was twenty-five guilders. This was more than fair, as they were in water with dangerous invisible reefs. With the pilot on board, the *Lynx* pulled close at high speed, reason unknown. The *Ayesha*'s battle flag was set. When the *Lynx* passed, Lieutenant von Mücke ordered double to port side piped. Officers and men saluted and the salute was returned. With flagging, shifting winds, the schooner pushed on to Padang. From deck, the Germans could already see the installations and freighters, various Lloyd steamships among them. At 1510, close to Padang, the schooner signaled the *Lynx* that she was sending a boat. In uniform Mücke went on board the destroyer to explain his situation to the Dutch captain. He revealed his intention to enter Padang. The Dutch officer de-

clared that he had orders to escort the schooner but that everything else was in the hands of the civil authorities. Nothing
stood in the way of *Ayesha*'s entry; he did not think, however,
that she would be allowed to leave. Mücke replied that the
*Ayesha* was a warship, adding in jest that he hoped their two
ships would not have to battle it out if he should depart Padang.
After being informed of the fate of the *Emden,* he returned to
the *Ayesha.*

Soon the harbormaster came on board the schooner and anchored her, according to Mücke's wishes, quite close to Padang.
Mücke told him that the *Ayesha* had run into port for repairs
and provisions; as soon as everything necessary had been done,
she would depart. Meanwhile, he wanted to see the German
consul. Later he explained to questioning Dutch officials that,
without the agreement of the German government, no one could
board or leave the ship. In the evening he accepted an invitation
from the captain of the Dutch gunboat *Assahan.* There was no
further news. German ships lying in the harbor expressed delight when they learned that the *Ayesha* had arrived. At once the
schooner was surrounded by German dories bringing welcome
gifts of cigars, cigarettes, tobacco, wine, fruit, clothing—even
sewing and shoe-polishing kits, lighters, eggs, tea, and pipes.

### 28 November 1914

Toward 0900 Lieutenant von Mücke was told that his schooner
would be considered a prize of war, as he had no written orders
from the captain of SMS *Emden* making him the legitimate
commander of the *Ayesha.* Mücke immediately launched a protest through the German consul. It read:

> This morning I was informed by the official representative
> of the Royal Dutch government in the presence of the Ger-
> man consul on board SMS *Ayesha* that the Royal Dutch
> government is determined to designate the *Ayesha* a prize
> of war. I am submitting a protest against this designation
> and demand that the ship be treated as a warship. All con-
> ditions of a warship are met by her. There are only mem-
> bers of the Imperial German Navy on board; the crew is

therefore militarily organized. The officers on board are all in the active Imperial Navy and are in the Imperial Navy's official list. The *Ayesha* flies the pennant of a German naval commander and the battle flag of the German empire. The question of how I came into possession of the ship and by what right I am its commanding officer are matters of German domestic concern, and in explaining this turn of events I am responsible only to my superior officer. In resupplying the *Ayesha*, I refer to the proclamation of Dutch neutrality regarding the war waged between Russia, France, and Serbia on one side, and Germany and Austria-Hungary on the other. I entered Padang as an emergency measure, that is to say, because of the unseaworthy condition of the ship and for lack of provisions and water. Immediately upon correcting these deficiencies, I intend to put to sea again.

It appeared that the Dutch would attempt at all costs to keep the *Ayesha* in confinement for fear of the Japanese. However, the schooner had made an emergency entry, and so they could not deny her provisions in the face of Mücke's protest. A list of necessities was drawn up, and the consul took charge of the procurement. Mücke also requested a doctor from one of the anchored German ships. Although the health of his crew had up to now been excellent, inadequate living quarters, monotonous meals, bad drinking water, and the tropical climate posed the danger of spreading illness. Additional crew members were denied. The "neutrality officer" got on the line to Batavia and asked if soap, toothbrushes, hairbrushes, and the like could be delivered with the rest of the goods. He took great pains to help them, promising his utmost, but the principal figure with whom decisions rested was the harbormaster, a native Belgian. They did not expect much from him. A whole day passed without the arrival of awaited goods. Meanwhile the German ships continued to send all sorts of provisions, including newspapers. Finally, they could read German newspapers instead of the propaganda reports of the English.

At 1900 some of the provisions came alongside. Water had already been taken on board. The neutrality officer still made every attempt to persuade Mücke to allow his officers and men to be interned, drawing a picture, prompted by directions from Batavia, of the impossibility of putting out to sea. Hydrographic charts could not be delivered, nor could nautical books. Clothing, moreover, was not available. It appeared that nondelivery of these needed articles was intentional. When von Mücke replied that he would sail even without charts, the neutrality officer handed him a telegram from the Dutch admiral declaring that a run out of Padang would be hopeless, that several Japanese cruisers were lurking in the area. A Japanese ship had been observed off Padang a day before the arrival of the German schooner; the *Ayesha* had been able to enter port only by luck. The *Emden* had achieved enough success, no one would think badly of them if they gave up this misadventure. Mücke asked for permission to contact Berlin secretly by telegraph for guidance. The decision should come from there. It became obvious to the neutrality officer that his arguments were futile, and he abandoned his attempt to keep the ship in port.

The German consul, a man named Schild, secretly supplied Mücke with funds amounting to 190 marks, 7 pounds, and 200 francs. He also smuggled a note on board designating a rendezvous with a freighter. The same message had earlier that day managed to reach one of the German ships, even though the Dutch were keeping a sharp lookout when German boats transferred cargo. The text of the note read, "I will cruise until 20 December at 3°20′S, 99°20′E. The rendezvous will be within a 20-mile radius, depending on wind and current."

At 2000 hours they weighed anchor. The freighter that had brought provisions pulled the *Ayesha* out of the harbor. Then she cast off. Mücke lined up his crew aft and ordered three cheers for the German consul, then they sang "The Watch on the Rhine." Soon the schooner, all sails set to a light north-northeast wind, disappeared quickly and smoothly into the darkness. No Dutchman followed her. Mücke had begged the consul days before to inform the Dutch government that an obvious escort such as they had received upon arrival would appear unfriendly.

*29 November 1914*

At 0135 Padang was about two nautical miles away, to starboard. At 1430 a rowboat drew up alongside. It came from the North German Loyd freighter *Rheinland* and brought Ensign R. Willmann and Machinist's Mate First Class R. Schwaneberger on board. They volunteered for duty and were taken on.

*30 November 1914*

At night the *Ayesha* stood off the Seaflower Channel again. At 0230, to port, they sighted a steamer heading east. The schooner turned hard with the wind to reach neutral waters. The steamer slowly approached, a warship. Suddenly it exchanged light signals with another, as yet unnoticed warship. Meanwhile the *Ayesha* had come close to Siberut. The surf was already visible. One warship took off to the south, the other remained in the channel. As dawn arrived, the ship veered sharply and headed for the schooner. It was a Dutch flagship, *The Seven Provinces*. The *Ayesha* was escorted, but at a considerable distance, until Dutch territorial waters had been left behind.

*4 December 1914*

At 1010 a smoke cloud could be seen to the south, but there was no ship visible. The *Ayesha* now stood at the rendezvous designated in the smuggled note at Padang. The German freighter, unhindered by the Dutch, could run out and take on the *Emden*'s landing party.

*7 December 1914*

The air was still. The *Ayesha* tacked, dead in the current. At night, squalls swept in and light sails and upper topsail were fastened. There was nothing in sight.

*9 December 1914*

At the gray of day a freighter appeared, without flag. The *Ayesha* steered toward it. When the freighter sighted a schooner approaching, it veered sharply and ran in a wide, puzzling arc around her. The vessel had machine guns and rifles arrayed along its deck. It signaled a request for longitude. The *Ayesha* answered: 99°22'. Thereupon the steamer requested an identity signal. The schooner hoisted a random signal, HBCZ, with unidentifiable flags. Whence the steamer came was a mystery. It drew out of sight.

*14 December 1914*

Four days had passed and no sight of another vessel. Light winds blew at night. At 0340 the wind came about, and at 0900 wind force was six to seven. A steamer hove into sight at 1340. By 1440 it had disappeared. For fifty minutes nothing but squalls and haze and then the vessel reappeared, six degrees to port, steering east. With battle flag hoisted and all the sails that could be set, the *Ayesha* headed for it. The steamer approached, showing its German flag. It was the *Choising*.

So the first goal of the *Emden* landing party had been reached. The rendezvous was 3°23'S, 99°28'E. Because of wind and sea conditions, transfer was impossible. The two ships proceeded on course southwest, the *Choising* following. In the evening fresh gusts of wind came in from the west. Topsail and light sails were set, lower sails, reefed.

*15 December 1914*

The weather continued to deteriorate. Lower sails were tightly furled. At dawn the *Choising* signaled that because of high seas she could not continue on course. Thus both ships tacked. A rendezvous south of Pagai was agreed on. The *Choising* steamed away to the northwest.

*16 December 1914*

In heavy afternoon squalls the jib and tightly reefed foresail flew off their leeches. The fore stay sail tore. Goodbyes to the old schooner would be easy. At dawn she headed toward land, all sails set in a dying wind. At 0840 the *Choising* showed up off the port side. At 1030 they were leeward of Pagai. Presently all worthwhile possessions were transferred to the *Choising* and the *Ayesha* was prepared for sinking by drilling holes. At 1648 she sank.

The log showed that they had covered 1,709.6 miles under sail since departing the Cocos.

Thus the *Emden* landing party survived the first leg of its odyssey.

CHAPTER THREE

# THE NORTH GERMAN LOYD FREIGHTER *CHOISING*

The freighter *Choising* was a small ship belonging to North German Loyd. Built in 1901 at Rickmers Shipyards in Geestemünde and christened *Madeleine Rickmers,* she displaced 1,657 Brutto register tons and had a speed of 10.5 knots. In November 1906 North German Loyd bought her from Rickmers and placed her in service on the east Asian run. On 30 July 1914 the *Choising,* under Captain F. Minkwitz and sailing from Swatow, arrived in Singapore. With war imminent, her cargo was quickly unloaded, and on 1 August 1914 she departed Singapore, destination Batavia. The captain, however, had orders to cruise off the Strait of Singapore on 2 August and warn approaching German ships of danger—specifically, to order the Singapore-bound freighter *Chowfa* to Riouw, in the Dutch Indies. They never sighted the *Chowfa* but met up with the *Sandakan,* which, on the same mission as the *Choising,* had been ordered to Rio. In the evening the two ships continued the trip to Batavia together and arrived there on 5 August, anchoring within the three-mile limit but outside the harbor moles to save port and pilot fees.

On 25 September the *Choising* was requisitioned by the German East Asian Station to service the *Emden*. She left for Laurenzo Marques, clearing Batavia on 27 September at 0400 for a rendezvous with the cruiser. During the trip, the coal fire in hold one got out of hand. The crew fought it with every means available. Eventually, thick heavy smoke poured out of the hold and their only resort was to flood the entire space. In hold two the same situation was threatening. The captain decided to pump the foreship full of water, so that the vessel was seven to eight feet down by the bow but kept her specified position. Day and night without interruption the pumping continued, for fear that the water would not be cleared when the *Emden* appeared.

When the fire spread to hold three, Captain Minkwitz decided to run into Padang as an emergency measure. Apparently the *Emden* was much farther west and, for the time being, did not lack for coal and provisions. In the afternoon of 11 October the *Choising* anchored off Padang. On 27 November the *Ayesha* sailed into port. The next evening she departed after having replenished her supplies.

Early in the morning of the twenty-ninth Captain Minkwitz received a note written by the commanding officer of the *Ayesha*. Immediately he contacted the German consul, who had received the same message. It read, "Until 20 December I will cruise to 3°20'S, 99°20'E. Rendezvous will be kept within a 20-mile radius."

All this was reported to the German consulate general in Batavia. On 7 December Minkwitz received a message from Batavia in a code known only to him and two commissioners. They notified the Dutch authorities that the freighter *Choising* wished to continue passage to Laurenzo Marques. This caused great consternation among official ranks. Higher authorities in Batavia were notified. The *Choising* was watched day and night.

On 9 December she steamed into harbor, filled her freshwater tanks and false bottom, and returned to her anchorage. Dutch government officials now informed Minkwitz that he could take on provisions only for his own crew, and nothing that might resupply another ship. Every item coming on board was carefully inspected. But the Dutch weren't vigilant enough. The previous night the *Choising* had received all sorts of supplies ranging from mattresses to dinnerware from the freighters *Kleist* and *Rhineland;* they had even purchased items for the ship's pharmacy.

The *Choising* continued her trip to Laurenzo Marques escorted by the Royal Dutch coast defense ship *Koningin Regentes.* On 11 December, at 0600, North Pagai Island came into view, two nautical miles off at 180 degrees. After passage through the Strait of Sipora, the Dutch ship slowly fell back. The *Choising* now steered directly toward the designated rendezvous, arriving there at 1430. From 1500 to 1800 she proceeded east. During the night her course slowly shifted 80 degrees northwest.

Three days later, on 14 December, the *Choising* spotted the schooner to port, position 3°23′S, 99°28′E. Rain was continual, and the ships agreed to lay course southwest to reach better weather. The *Ayesha* sailed ahead. During the night seas grew rough and the *Choising* labored hard, taking on a lot of water even though she was riding high. Almost every fixture threatened to tear loose. On the morning of 15 December she signaled the *Ayesha:* "Cannot hold course any farther." They agreed to head for the southern tip of South Pagai Island to conduct the transfer in its lee. The *Choising* followed a roundabout course, avoiding further bad weather. The *Ayesha* sailed directly to the rendezvous.

On 16 December the *Choising* sighted the schooner south of Pagai. The waters were turning more and more calm. She drew closer. Lieutenant von Mücke begged to be taken in tow because his vessel was rolling heavily. The freighter maneuvered carefully, tossing over two lines that took the schooner in tow. At 1200 the transfer began, of men, guns, ammunition, sails, and the like. At 1630 the stripped *Ayesha* was cast off. Several holes had been smashed in her hull and she sank slowly, the *Choising* standing close by. At 1700 she had disappeared, laid to rest with a somber, short address by her commanding officer. This was followed by three hearty cheers and a flag salute from the *Choising.* On board the steamer at last, Lieutenant von Mücke and his officers went into conference with Captain Minkwitz to plan their future moves.

The *Choising* continued her voyage west. In the beginning they steered southwest to get out of the major sea lanes and stay clear of typhoons. Because the ship had taken on ballast, it was essential that she avoid all adverse weather. That meant they could not steer in a southerly direction. They stayed out of the way of every smoke cloud appearing on the horizon. On 5 January they searched for the western side of the Strait of Perim, which they found.

During the night of 7–8 January Lieutenant von Mücke hoped to push on. Wind and weather permitting, he would reach Hodeida with the four largest dories in order to get news about the war. According to an ensign formerly of the *Kleist*, the railroad now ran to Hodeida. Mücke did not believe the English had sabotaged the railroad; that would not only be malicious, it would threaten the pilgrimage to Mecca and cause an Islamic uprising. England would want to avoid that at all costs. Should the railroad not run to Hodeida, Mücke was prepared to proceed to Jidda by boat and from there continue the journey on land.

Destruction of the Perim cable station was also contemplated, though Mücke did not expect much from that, as there were other connections nearby that he could not touch. So depending on weather conditions, he would dismiss the *Choising* either at Perim or later on. The freighter should then try to contact the *Königsberg*. Captain Minkwitz received orders to that effect. From the *Choising* the ship's surgeon, Dr. Lang, and Ensign Geerdts would join in the further adventures of the landing party. The mood among the *Emden* crew was confident.

At dawn on 8 January the *Choising* steamed south and west of Hanich Island to avoid being sighted along the sea lanes. In the evening the freighter approached Hodeida from a westerly direction. On 9 January, between 0300 and 0400, they took soundings all the way northeast of Ras Mujamela where, in quiet waters four fathoms deep, they anchored.

The four largest dories had already been swung out and lowered to the railing. Everything necessary for a landing had been stowed aboard. Shortly before 0500 hours the landing party, now consisting of fifty-one men, cast off. The *Choising* had weighed anchor and was steaming away. Around 0600 she was followed out of Hodeida by a warship recognized as the French armored cruiser *Desaix*. The Frenchmen cruised up and down in the vicinity of the landing spot. Captain Minkwitz steadily continued on course until she was out of sight. To alter course suddenly would have aroused suspicion. So the *Choising* steamed before the wind, across the sea lane and to the west. In the settling darkness she came about and, according to instructions, headed back to Hodeida. It had been agreed that she would search out the landing site between 9 and 10 January and, if no danger was present, try to reestablish contact with the landing party. If need be, the *Emden* crew would reembark and continue their journey to Jidda, finally landing somewhat south of there.

At 0100 on 10 January the *Choising* stood off the rendezvous. The *Desaix* was anchored far to the south, in the same position as the night before. The *Choising* could not afford to remain past the appointed time because moonlight became much too bright after that. First slowly and cautiously, then at full speed, she steamed toward the west. In case she was no longer needed and continuing the journey to Jidda appeared dangerous, three signal lights were to be fired. From the bridge of the *Choising* they could make out only one such signal. To be doubly sure, Captain Minkwitz cautiously returned to the rendezvous in the evening, stealing carefully to the landing site. The wind was almost still. To avoid unnecessary noise they turned off the bilge pumps and covered the engine exhaust with thick sailcloth, which was also placed over the stern to muffle the beat of the screw. No light showed other than the compass lamps.

From 2235 until 0030 the *Choising* remained off the landing site. There was no sign of boats and no movement on land. The *Desaix*, meanwhile, seemed to have come closer; smoke clouds from her four funnels were quite distinct to the naked eye. Slowly the *Choising* came about. A longer stay was impossible. She steamed in a straight line toward the coast of French Somaliland.

On 11 January she anchored near Daramsas Island. Further progress was not possible according to the available charts. No one among the crew had knowledge of the area, so there they remained until 12 January. Continuing slowly, the *Choising* then anchored without further incident at the harbor entrance of Massawa in neutral Somaliland. On 13 January she entered the harbor. There, according to reliable sources from the other side of the Red Sea, Captain Minkwitz learned that the landing party had made it ashore, reached Hodeida, and received a friendly welcome from the Turks. Would the men of the *Emden* reach their goal, their distant homeland? Minkwitz and his crew fervently wished it.

The *Choising*'s mission, to resupply the German light cruiser *Königsberg* with coal and provisions off the east coast of Africa, could no longer be accomplished. The cruiser, without a coal supply on hand, had been overwhelmed by British naval forces and finally blockaded in the bottleneck of the Rufiji Delta.

In the summer of 1916, after a year of unbearable privation in the murderous climate of this port on the Red Sea, the *Choising* was confiscated by the Italian government. Although it had had a binding alliance with Germany and Austria, in a surprise move it had declared war on both. The North German Loyd crew had been interned and the confiscated freighter placed in Italian service under a new name. On 15 May 1917 a small Italian convoy consisting of a destroyer and three freighters encountered Austrian naval forces under Admiral von Horthy in the Adriatic Sea. In the ensuing battle only the freighter *Bersagliere* escaped. The destroyer *Borea* and the freighter *Verita* were destroyed by the gunfire of the Austro-Hungarian torpedo-boat destroyers *Csepel* and *Balaton*. Another victim was a small, slow freighter, the *Carroccio,* erstwhile the *Choising,* which had proudly carried the men of the *Emden* landing party clear across the Indian Ocean from Sumatra to the Red Sea.

CHAPTER FOUR

# THROUGH THE DESERT

What a high-spirited, adventurous, and providential story: after a month-long odyssey covering half the world, from the China Sea to the Indian Ocean, a handful of German sailors had arrived by way of "moveable platform" to a coast in the Middle East. Now the young seamen were prepared to take on all comers—English and French, xenophobic Mohammedans, thieving Bedouins, weak and corrupt officials, and proud sheiks. They were ready to face the vagaries of a land as inhuman in its heat as the frozen wastes of the polar region; a land that, at least on paper, was part of the Turkish empire now allied with imperial Germany. This had been the case since the coup de main of Admiral Souchon in the summer of 1914.

In 1914 the empire still included Asia Minor, Mesopotamia, Palestine, all of Arabia. But what an empire! A loose union bound by vassal rule and the obligation of tribute, without infrastructure, full of corruption. It catered to oriental lassitude, effeminacy, and luxurious decadence at the highest level; bitterest deprivation was reality for the greater part of the population. Tribal chiefs and satraps ruled autonomously and autocratically. Arabs had became fed up with their Turkish overloads and too often Turkish garrisons were prisoners in their own

land. Local squabbles were the order of the day, and only too
often revolutionaries allied themselves with the enemies of their
country. Flattery and bribery bought almost anything a person
could desire.

The young leader of the *Emden*'s landing party learned quickly.
Soon he caught on to the "you see how it is" attitude. Clearly,
here one could not operate as in an imperial shipyard. Neither
navy regulations nor the international code of conduct for navy
officers overseas helped here. Bartering and making deals were
the rules of thumb. No wonder the active young naval officer
had to acclimate himself. After three months of successfully waging war on two of the world's oceans, he had landed in Turkish-
occupied Hodeida, a city of shimmering heat surrounded by
blinding, limitless, invading sands, a parched hell. There he had
to deal with an alien tongue, words that never meant what they
said, men whose sentences were delivered in a language unknown to him, whose thinking and dealing followed unknown
and improbable reasoning. Europeans living in Hodeida had become accustomed to the mentality. Shrugging their shoulders,
they observed philosophically, "That's the way it is."

The impatient lieutenant with his fifty *Emden* cohorts seized
the initiative to get home, back to defend their fatherland. These
raiding cruiser corsairs believed they could accomplish anything. Although Lieutenant von Mücke, the first officer of the
most famous cruiser of all times, couldn't speak Arabic, it didn't
take him long to find his way about, to discover that flattery,
bribery, shiftiness, and threats delivered at the right moment,
worked every time. This swashbuckling man of the sea spoke
the one universal language. His arguments, even when money
couldn't talk, convinced sheiks, Turkish commanders, high officials, and noble emirs, for behind him stood fifty sturdy, determined seamen and the tapered black mouthpieces of four machine guns from the cruiser *Emden*. The guns had been used on
the Yangtze River against rebels, had hunted the Ponape mur-
derers, and had traveled two oceans. For one day they had herded
the occupants of an entire Indian Ocean archipelago island under the German flag. They had commandeered a rotting copra

schooner and turned an old east Asian freighter into a warship. They had been lovingly preserved against salty seawater and desert sands alike. These four machine guns were the talisman to whom the *Emden* men owned their safe return home. This spiderweb of lazy, nebulous enchantment, this Fata Morgana of great hopes and promises, this honey-sweet, intoxicating miasma of luxurious bribery could only be cut through by the lightning strokes of broad axes and navy swords.

Thus landed fifty seamen, without ship, without homeland, without allies ashore. Fifty sailors and stokers from a burned-out, broken German cruiser, out of China long ago, now lying wrecked high on a coral reef in the South Seas. Difficulties, diplomatic complications, plots, sand, heat, robbers, delays, problems. . . "We'll laugh at them!" Attention Bedouins and sheiks. Be on your guard, allied Turkish empire. The landing party of SMS *Emden* has entered Arabia!

*9 January 1915*

At sunrise on 9 January the steamer *Choising,* camouflaged as an Italian ship, stood off Hodeida. Because they lacked charts their exact location was unknown. Where, presumably, Hodeida was located, a row of dimmed lights was visible. Were they part of the harbor installations? The only available book describing coastal conditions was Meyer's *World Cruise Handbook.* It listed Hodeida as a major port. Lieutenant von Mücke had second thoughts. At three thousand meters from the lights the water still measured forty meters. The *Choising* changed course south. Mücke wanted to land near Khor Ghuleifaka and there put ashore with the dinghies. About six to seven miles south of the lights the ship dropped anchor. The boats were lowered, equipped with water for several days and provisions for several weeks. Weapons, ammunition, and baggage were also placed aboard. The freighter was dismissed with orders to stand outside the sea lanes. For the next two nights she should return to the point of debarkation after dark and, if necessary, pick up the *Emden* party. Otherwise they were to leave for Massawa after the second night.

The *Choising* disappeared from sight before daylight. The four boats were now rowed in the direction of the alien coast. Above all, they had to be kept buoyant. On board the *Choising* they had been freshly painted for water tightness. Still they drew heavily with their full loads. There were quite a few rolling swells in the prevailing southeast winds and the men had to bail water. After daylight Mücke ordered the sails set and the dinghies pulled far apart.

As it became light they strained their eyes to see what was ahead of them. The anticipated landing pier of Hodeida had put out its lights. When the sun rose it revealed itself to have two masts and four funnels and to be guarded by four guns. It was the French armored cruiser *Desaix*. Another part of the anticipated landing pier turned out to be the Italian freighter *Juliana*. The German boats turned out to sea and then headed for the beach under full sail. It was imperative that they draw out of sight of the enemy cruiser as quickly as possible. The lead boat anchored beyond the surf; the others joined it.

Mücke's last information on the situation in Arabia came from a three-month-old newspaper that had reported fights between Turks and English troops near Sheikh Said, but not their outcome. The presence of the *Desaix* suggested that Hodeida was in French hands. They made inquiries abut the situation of some Arabs in a nearby fishing boat. Yes, they said, Hodeida was full of Frenchmen. The *Emden* crew spoke German, the fishermen chattered away in Arabic, and so the message may have been garbled. Mücke decided that with all their supplies and weapons they would head east, toward the desert, and there go into hiding. At night one of the officers and a few men would slip into Hodeida for further information. If the area was really full of Frenchmen, Mücke and his men would head back to the *Choising* the following night.

About eight hundred meters off the beach, but far enough beyond the surf, the boats hit sand. All supplies had to be carried the distance to solid ground. First came the machine guns. One group set them up immediately. An attempt to converse with two young Arabs who were bathing did not succeed. When they

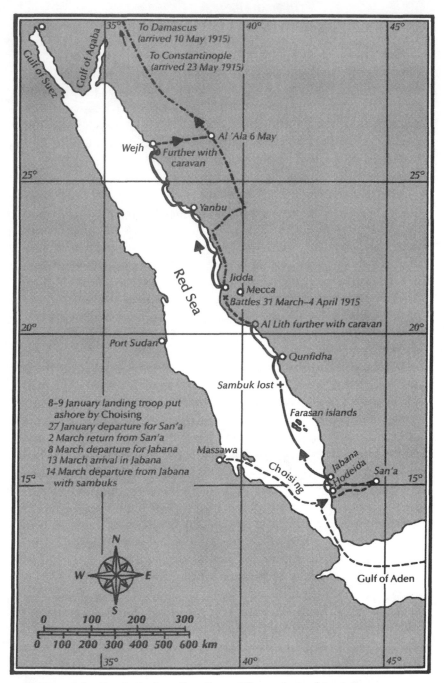

Route of the Emden's Landing Party Through Arabia, 8 January—24
May 1915

saw the armed landing party they took off like the wind. After some time a camel rider showed up. He wore a blue and red uniform and a turban wound around his head. What kind of uniform it was nobody knew. It might easily have been French. The man was armed. When he was within six hundred meters he halted, took hold of his rifle, and watched the ongoing work. Mücke approached, waving and calling, attempting in every way to let him know he wanted to talk. The stranger allowed him to approach to within two hundred meters, then quietly aimed his gun. Mücke remained motionless. The man lowered his weapon. Mücke proceeded a few steps farther and the man raised it again. Once more the German stopped. This nerve-wracking game was repeated until Mücke stood about fifty meters away. This time the stranger did not lower his gun, and Mücke stayed dead on the spot. He didn't want to shoot until he knew whom he was facing; the stranger was probably thinking the same thing. Mücke addressed him in French, English, Malay, and German, but nothing came of it, he didn't understand. Then the stranger gave a sign that could mean nothing else but for Mücke to stay where he was. He got back on his camel and disappeared in the direction of Hodeida, where white houses were barely visible in the distance.

That was a good beginning! In a few short hours the greater part of the French garrison of Hodeida would be down on their heads. Until then their tracks in the desert could be well covered. The departure was rushed along, but work proceeded slowly. To carry equipment through the water they had to build floating rafts out of masts, oars, wood, ropes, and life jackets. The men were dead tired. They had towed and tugged, worked like demons for hours. Besides that, it was oppressively hot and they were surrounded by unfamiliar desert terrain.

Before the work was finished a great number of armed Bedouins appeared over the sand dunes and came within four hundred meters of the landing party. They dispersed and then formed an extended line opposite the German sailors, taking full cover and remaining out of sight. Mücke too formed a skirmish line, gathering his men and preparing for his first land battle. He did, however, wait for the first shot to be fired by the other side. Perhaps they could still reach an understanding. The Bedouins did not appear to be regular troops.

Suddenly from their ranks a dozen or so men approached without weapons. Mücke unbelted his pistol and saber and walked toward them waving his free hands. He tried to make them understand his situation by showing the German battle flag, then the merchant flag, by gestures and words in German, French, English, and Malay, but without success. The animated sign language of the Arabs left him bewildered. Presently a knowledgeable smile appeared on the face of one of the strangers: he had recognized the face of the kaiser on a gold piece handed him. "Aleman," he cried, "Aleman," meaning German. The Bedouins fell into enthusiastic shrieks and laughingly surrounded the small group. They helped carry the heavy load and led the way to Hodeida. Then it was discovered that one Bedouin spoke English; he assured the *Emden* men that Hodeida was in Turkish hands. This came as a great relief to the Germans.

The march to the city attracted additional Arabs, until the German column was being escorted by hundreds of excited men. Mücke took it as a sign that, at least this side of Yemen, they were anti-English, anti-French, and pro-German. Their enthusiasm was spontaneous. They all knew of the "Emperor Aleman" and the "*Emden* croiseur."

The Yemenites were no more friendly toward the Turks than they were toward the English or French. For the landing party, everything would depend on how carefully they could balance their interactions with Arabs and Turks until the situation was clarified. During the march the escort continued to engage in intense yelling, firing of guns, and raucous singing. By and by they attracted Turkish troops to the procession, which continued to grow. Among the Turks were a good many German and French-speaking officers. Communication grew easier. At noon the *Emden*'s entourage entered Hodeida to lively cheers and salutes from the population. Quarters for the crew had been arranged in Turkish barracks. The officers were to be hosted by one of the best families in Hodeida, a rich Arab family named Shassili.

Turkish officials supplied fresh underwear, socks, and water for bathing. A meal was provided immediately.

That afternoon Mücke held long conferences with both civil and military officials. He spoke with the governor of Hodeida, the military commander, a colonel, his chief of staff, and many other officers of the garrison. Apparently near Kamaran an English blockade line was shutting off the entire Red Sea. There the English were searching every sambuk individually. Moreover, Hodeida was crawling with spies who would immediately contact the French cruiser about the Germans' arrival. Mücke was disappointed to learn that the railroad had not been extended to Hodeida, as he had been led to believe. Could he continue by camel caravan, he wanted to know? The governor and the colonel both confirmed that, even in the face of clamorous objections from other officers. The trip would be a long one, but it would be preferable to proceeding by sea. At any rate, they were unlikely to meet any enemy opposition. Mücke might be able to reach the terminal of the railroad in two months' time. Given such strong assurances, Mücke finally decided to dismiss the *Choising*. That evening they fired the signal rocket. Now the *Emden* crew was land-bound in Hodeida.

The advice of the Turkish officials, of course, proved unreliable. It could not have escaped them that continuing the journey by land was almost impossible. As every child in Hodeida knew, not even strong Turkish forces would venture into nearby areas in revolt. The reason for advising Mücke's group to push on will always remain a mystery. Perhaps it was to save face; the Turks could not tolerate exposing the tragic condition of their country to a stranger. Perhaps they were swayed by the vision of the little German group making an unmolested passage through the area, thereby opening it up for others; Mücke's disciplined and well-armed troops might be a warning to Arabs in revolt. Modern machine guns were impressive; the German sailors had four of them with two thousand rounds of ammunition each. In any event, the sailors had to get used to this totally alien form of diplomacy. What danger this handful of Germans posed to the government, should they turn out to be the enemy after all, is most puzzling. The regular Turkish garrison in Hodeida consisted of roughly three hundred men with artillery and cavalry. The German detachment would have faced hundreds of armed men. But guessing back and forth was exhausting. Mücke learned later that a few officials had concocted a plan to have the Germans camp at an oasis near Hodeida and there, in the middle of the night, to attack them. Only because most of the Turkish officers spoke German and were convinced that they were indeed dealing with German seamen was this plan abandoned. Still, they continued to delay Mücke's departure.

*19 January 1915*

The landing party had been in Hodeida ten days already. Mücke was continually pressing for permission to push on. The Turks, however, had begun to erect special barracks for the *Emden* men in preparation for a lengthy stay. Mücke had cornered the governor several times, never receiving definite permission to leave. Now he was asking for a definite departure date by which the preparations should be completed. The officials avoided commitment. Meanwhile, the German officers, thanks to a few under-the-table coins, found out something more. Mücke and his crew were being watched day and night. Was it out of curiosity? One of their Turkish "honor guards" was in reality a spy. He was to prevent any Greek or Armenian contact with the Germans. Mücke, outraged, complained of isolation from the outside world. As a result, the guard received other instructions: he was only to protect them from "foreign harassment."

The Turks tried to treat the German lieutenant as a subordinate. They requested detailed reports of his activities since leaving the *Emden,* which Mücke sharply refused to supply. He alone was in charge of his German troops, he explained, and he would follow orders only from superiors back home. Since such orders were not forthcoming, he would be responsible for his own actions. With a bombastic spate of words and abject apology, this point was quickly passed over. The Turks insisted that it was only the spirit of Turkish-German cooperation that moved them to these requests. After all, Germany and Turkey were allied, their armies as good as one. So far so good! But Constantinople and its central authorities were far away.

They requested Mücke to state the monthly pay of his men, as they now were to be paid by the Turks. Mücke again declined, with thanks, so as not to be put under obligation. He would, however, appreciate an advance, later to be paid back by his government, naturally. Thereupon he received 150 pounds of Turkish gold against a voucher. Considering the scarcity of gold in Yemen and the chronic money shortage in the Turkish government, this was extraordinarily obliging, certainly an auspicious sign.

The officials still insisted that the Germans could continue by land. They had worked out various plans for it. The trek should skirt the areas of revolt as well as the Holy Land. No nonbeliever could set foot in the latter. Preparations for the journey took much too long in Mücke's estimation. He had the distinct impression that they were carelessly or deliberately drawn out. Since none of his pleading brought results, he was determined to apply pressure on the Turks by staging a march to San'a—the seat of the local government where, Mücke felt, things might go more quickly. Moreover, concerned with the health of his people, he wanted to reach a healthier climate. Since their arrival in Hodeida there had continually been five or six cases of fever and malaria among them. There had also been cases of diarrhea, which Dr. Lang blamed on a diet of too little European food. From the first day, Mücke insisted that more nutritious food be furnished them, yet despite many promises, nothing happened. Only after a requested payment of gold did the food improve.

From all sides, particularly from Turkish doctors, came assurances that San'a had a very healthy climate, almost European. Even the sick crewmen would recover there within a few days. After endless difficulties, the march was scheduled for 27 January. At that time the caravan would be ready. Three patients and the doctor would remain in Hodeida.

### 27 January 1915

In the desert travel was only possible at night; during the day it was much too hot for man or beast. Travel on foot was out of the question; they would have to ride. There were many animals available: horses, mules, donkeys. The baggage was carried by a caravan of camels. It wasn't easy for the impatient lieutenant to keep the newly formed caravan together. It was the first time many of the seamen had ever attempted to sit on the back of a four-legged animal. First they had to be held, these suspicious mules with their batting eyes and flapping ears. On being mounted, they turned into veritable carrousels, turning continually. Some of the men had used the predeparture time to practice getting on and off, sometimes taking the saddle along in the process. When everyone seemed to have mastered it, they set in motion, following the tracks of a previous caravan. Because the nights were moon-bright, the tracks were easy to see.

Soon the sailors were in the midst of the desert. As far as the eye could see there was nothing but sand, low dunes sprouting sparse grass tufts. The first few hours they had to make frequent stops, for, while used to the sea, they found it difficult adjusting to the swaying motion of saddles. Men would slip off, whereupon their mounts scampered away and had to be collared again with great patience. This occupation fell mostly to the officers, since they were the only ones who could actually ride. But catching mules and donkeys was no easy job. On being approached, they turned around and with sturdy hind legs kicked energetically.

### 28 January 1915

The area was not safe. Attacks on small caravans were frequent. It was only their second night out when, in the bright moonlight, they spotted about a dozen men on camelback by the side of the road. Turkish gendarmes provided by the army identified them as robbers and readied their guns. Upon seeing the strength of the caravan, the strangers vanished behind the sand dunes.

### 29 January 1915

By the third day they approached the foothills of a mountain range. Uncompromisingly steep and rugged, the mountains soared vertically from the desert bed to a height of 3,600 meters. The way became more difficult. Over rubble and rolling boulders, through dry riverbeds, the road slowly led up the mountain. Finally they saw trees and bushes, vegetation grew more abundant. If their mules had allowed them time to dream, the sailors would have felt themselves transported to the Middle Ages and an oriental fantasy, for wherever there was an obstacle such as a steep grade to make the road more difficult, an impressive Arab castle rose above it.

They stopped at several wayside stations in search of shelter and water. In the city of Manakha, anxiously awaited by the officers and an honor guard from the garrison, they were escorted into the city with great pomp and circumstance. There, in the barracks, everything had been prepared for them, including a sumptuous feast. The *Emden* crew was most grateful to the garrison commander, Major Abdullah Djelil, a Mesopotamian. After several calls on dignitaries and local sheiks in Manakha, Mücke concluded that they were sympathetic to Germany. The landing party remained there for two days so the men could rest. Continuing their journey, they had to leave two patients behind. These men would catch up several days later, escorted by Turkish guides.

*6 February 1915*

The German seamen were heartily welcomed in San'a. For their reception, an elaborate program had been worked out, but it did not take place because the Turks had figured on a much later arrival. Nonetheless, a whole battalion stood in formation to honor the men. A military band played a rousing welcome which some of the sailors recognized to be "Deutschland, Deutschland über Alles." Many officers, high officials, and countless onlookers lined the streets or streamed ahead of the approaching marchers.

Now the negotiating, the waiting, and the delays began again. After two weeks it was decided that the land route was impenetrable, that they would have to return to Hodeida and attempt a sea voyage. Mücke met with stiff-necked resistance from the

Turks. In many conversations with Tewfik-Pasha, the supreme commander of Yemen, he made it quite clear that he and he alone was responsible for his men. But the Turkish high command wanted to strengthen its own garrison by detaining the German troops. To cut this Gordian knot, Mücke wrote one of his diplomatic letters. The answer pointed politely to all difficulties as mere misunderstandings. The bottom line was that no animals would be available for riding and baggage transport. Without animals, a trek through the desert was impossible. The German officers came to regard their Turkish hosts as nothing short of adversaries. It was time to become self-reliant. But they had run out of money. All that remained was an English shilling found in the purse left behind by the former captain of the *Ayesha*. In southwest Arabia only two types of money were in use, Maria Theresa talers and gold. They had to find one or the other. Mücke succeeded in persuading an old retired Turkish general to lend him most of his savings by pointing out that in the near future the revolutionaries would take over San'a and his beautiful money would be lost. He, Mücke, would give him a voucher for the loan, which at the end of hostilities would be paid by Berlin. The man could save his money in that way. He fell in with that plan. (The old general would soon join his ancestors, but his heirs demanded that the voucher be redeemed in the spring of 1925. Since it did not involve a personal loan, Mücke left the settlement in the hands of the finance ministry.)

Through an Austrian windmill engineer in the city, they made the necessary contacts for renting animals. When the governor was informed of their plan, new tactics arose to delay the departure. Elaborate farewell celebrations were scheduled to last at least eight to ten days. The German sailors declined politely. Their mission was to leave as quickly as possible. Finally the Turks gave up, the ban was broken. The return to Hodeida took place without further interruption or delay.

Mücke learned that at Resil Kutup there was anchored a freighter that was to supply a projected Turkish-Italian-built railway. In San'a, he met the Turkish engineer responsible for the ship's upkeep. According to him, it was ready to go, though the engines were packed and the boilers dry. The vessel had no coal, but there were two hundred tons on the beach. Mücke decided this was the ship he wanted to take over, make ready for sea with a few of his men. Then, instead of going to Hodeida, he would divert the rest of the crew and disappear without a trace. The Germans could smell the ocean air already. Maybe they would seize something even larger. This seemed necessary, as the Turkish forces could no longer be trusted and there were spies crawling all over the place.

Mücke took the engineer along. He told the Turkish authorities that he wanted to continue with sailboats and requested sambuks in the Ysa Bay and near Khor Ghuleifaka. In reality, he had no intention of putting to sea from these places.

What was the condition of the freighter which, according to the Turk, was in the best of shape? Initially, Mücke saw only her funnel, sticking above the waterline. She turned out to be a wreck, six to seven years old, deeply embedded in sand, and overgrown with algae. The engineer had known all of that, as he finally admitted. Shrugging his shoulders, he said you couldn't report such things to the authorities or to Constantinople. They didn't want to hear bad news.

*8 March 1915*

Secure in the knowledge that the scuttlebutt concerning a German departure from Ysa Bay had made the rounds, Mücke secured two sambuks, which he brought to Jabana. The boats arrived there at noon, and that afternoon the lieutenant sailed away with them. He still did not know who had told the English about his preparations for departure from Ysa Bay. A British gunboat had entered the wrong bay and patrolled the coast all night with its searchlights ablaze. Perhaps it had not been through malice that the British had been informed; perhaps someone had had the decent intention of keeping the Germans from venturing out to sea so that they would voluntarily remain to defend Arabia with the Turks.

*10 March 1915*

Back in Hodeida, Mücke made a new and remarkable acquaintance. He had been surprised to see on his return a house flying a large German national flag. Now he learned that there actually was a German consul in residence. When the *Emden* party had come through Hodeida the first time, the consul was living in the Italian ship *Juliana* because of a quarrel with Turkish authorities. He was an Italian, acting as both Italian and German consul. Since March 1915 there had been no doubt as to the leanings of Rome in the matter of war; it seemed ludicrous to the German sailors that an Italian consul could at the same time be the German representative. The Italian, however, proved himself most useful. He had an ice machine, and connections with Massawa. Thus he could supply Mücke with information as well as a much-coveted whiskey and soda on the rocks. He asked lively questions regarding the plans of the *Emden* sailors and Mücke, with nothing more pressing to do, gave a "detailed" account. He explained that the caravan had been catching up slowly. All possiblities of continuing on land had been exhausted. They were simply cut off and had to remain until the end of the war. Still, they wanted to return to the mountains because the climate was better there.

The consul conceded that the continued march was hopeless. He was prepared to do everything to alleviate the situation for the Germans. It would be his proud duty to give a gala dinner immediately. Guests from the surrounding areas would be invited. When would be the best time to hold such a feast?

The first officer of the *Emden* always let a few seconds elapse before making a statement or decision. Considering the spies lurking about and the lightning speed with which gossip spread, it was clear everybody would know about the feast. On the evening of the celebration the enemy would certainly have his guard down. That would be the best time to get away! The lieutenant thanked the consul for his generosity and asked him to wait a few days. At the present time Mücke was tired. For the celebration, he would prefer Sunday, 14 March.

The consul made all the preparations, invited the entire neighborhood, and ordered a gigantic banquet. To keep up the appearance of wanting to return to the mountains, Mücke sent Dr. Lang and the now-recovered patients to the waiting caravan. With his plans arranged and well broadcast, it was time to act.

*11 March 1915*

Now Mücke was alone in Hodeida. Both of his sambuks had been sent posthaste to Jabana, a small inlet not too far from Hodeida. The caravan received orders to pack up immediately and hasten to Jabana, arriving there on 14 March at 1600.

*14 March 1915*

Everything came together. The boats were there when Mücke arrived in Jabana. Soon the caravan hove into sight. Provisions, supplies, ammunition, weapons, water, rags, everything was stowed on the boats. Flag on high, with three cheers for the emperor, off they went, that *Emden* crew. In spite of the extreme heat in Hodeida, the feast hosted by the German-Italian consul was bound to turn cold.

# CHAPTER FIVE

# AT SEA AGAIN

*14 March 1915*

At 1700 Lieutenant von Mücke and his men departed Jabana. The German battle flag was fluttering at the stern of his flagship. The "flagship of the second admiral" was commanded by Ensign Geerdts. The second sambuk was somewhat larger than the lead boat, and thus it became a refuge for the sick. Malaria, dysentery, and typhus, still wracking the party, gave cause for great concern. There was no question of leaving the sick behind. Only a change of climate could bring improvement.

Mücke intended to head north along the western side of the Farasan islands. For that purpose he had asked for two native pilots some time before. The Turkish authorities had vouched for them, but only one came, and in any case, there was no interpreter.

The sambucks were twelve to fourteen meters in length, each equipped with a dhow sail. According to their Arab guide, they had a capacity of twenty-two to twenty-five tons.

Up to the last minute they had tried to keep abreast of British activity in the region. At the moment British blockade ships, two gunboats and the auxiliary cruiser *Empress of Russia,* formed a line from Al Luhayyah via Kamaran Island to Zugar. Their main objective was to stop Turkish communications carried by sambuks after the land routes had been made impassable through uprisings. The English had pressed war sambuks from the Idris tribe into service; according to sources, there were seven boats of about ninety tons each plying the coastal waters. It was rumored that they were each armed with a seven-cm Italian gun. The boats and guns had been delivered to the Idris tribe during the Turkish-Italian war. Those were the blockade forces that the German sambuks had to break through. Ensign Geerdts received orders to sail at a distance from the lead boat so that if one was caught, the other might go free. They agreed on a rendezvous farther to the north, a place where one sambuk was to wait for the other. In the descending darkness, the second sambuk soon fell out of sight.

*15 March 1915*

At daybreak it was calm. To their great consternation the men discovered that they were exactly where they didn't want to be—in the middle of the English blockade line. Any moment they expected the mast heads of the British ships to appear. The situation was very tense. The calm kept the boat in a tighter spot than any enemy action could. But, with foresight, they had planned their sailing for the weekend; on weekends the British played golf at Luhaiya. Nothing came in sight that entire day.

In the course of the afternoon a welcome breeze drove the boat forward again. At sunset they could relax with the comforting thought that in a sailboat, making hardly any time at all, they had broken through the British blockade line.

Sometime during the day the second sambuk came into view again. It now received orders to stay close by the lead boat. The two flat-bottomed vessels held themselves between the dangerous reefs of the Farasan islands, a huge, 350-nautical-mile-long coral bed.

Life in the sambuks was almost comfortable. At last they were aboard ship again, thought the men. There wasn't much room, however. Along with the fishermen and pilot taken on to work the boat, there were some thirty-five men aboard, which meant that at fourteen meters' length and four meters' width there wasn't much space for the individual man. A greater part of the boat had to serve as a supply, water, ammunition, and machine-gun storage area. Against the burning heat of the day they stretched wool blankets over the ship; at least their heads were sheltered from the sun. Housekeeping was minimal. On each sambuk was an open, tin-lined stove for cooking. One day they had tough and stringy mutton with rice, the next, boiled rice, lard, and mutton, the third day, tough fat with mutton and rice. At night, cockroaches, bedbugs, and lice were particularly active. In the morning at sunup they began their communal delousing. The top catch was seventy-four lice on one shirt.

They proceeded very slowly. Most of the time there was a dead calm, opposing winds, or a countercurrent.

### 17 March 1915

Lieutenant von Mücke signaled the other sambuk, "Intend to anchor tonight." According to the pilot, the boats were now entering an area of reefs where it was dangerous to proceed at night. About 1800 they neared Marka Island. The pilot guided the lead boat to the anchorage; about two hundred meters off, the second boat followed. With a stiff breeze and rough seas, they still hoped to reach the protected side of the island. But they had not reckoned on their expert Arab pilot, who maneuvered the craft so that it suddenly piled up on a coral reef. Not once but three times the boat crashed into the reef. They were relieved to see that it had not sprung a leak, but it could free itself and head for deeper water to anchor. The second boat was forewarned with semaphore and shouts, but it had already entered the area and, in turning about, hit a reef itself. The crew hoisted a flag, a sign that something was amiss. Almost at once the boat started to list. Those in the first boat could see by the mast that the second had grounded on a reef. Then, abruptly, it slipped farther into the water; now only the masthead was visible angled above the water.

Night was closing in fast. Ten minutes after sundown it was totally dark, without moonlight. They had to have help, fast. On the first sambuk the sail raced aloft and men lay to, literally tearing the anchor out of the depths. With an abrupt turn that almost caused them to ground again, they were free and heading for the stranded boat. They anchored as close to it as possible, which because of the reef, was a distance of some four hundred meters. There were no dinghies or other small craft aboard. Sambuks carried only a hollowed tree-trunk canoe, which at most carried two men. Meanwhile darkness had fallen. There was a lantern on board, but several attempts to light it failed in the blowing wind. "Give me a torch," the commanding officer ordered. From the *Emden* and the *Choising* they had brought some along for emergencies. The lighters worked but the torch would not ignite. During the months of being carried about it had grown moist.

Suddenly out of the darkness voices were heard. The first men from the stranded sambuk were drifting by. With shouts and whistles they were directed to the boat. They had swum away from the sinking craft, their only guide a bright star somewhere in the direction of where they supposed the number-one boat would be. There was great concern, for the area was infested with sharks and, in addition, there were the sick too weak to help themselves.

Since everything else had failed to bring in the stragglers, they gathered wood, doused it with gasoline, and without a second thought about the fire danger, lit it on deck. Damp torches were held in the flames until they dried out and ignited, and flares were shot off which, visible for miles, would no doubt give them away. Finally two canoes approached, rowed by one man each and each carrying a sick man. The remaining sick who couldn't help themselves were tied to the canoes, dangling in the water. The rest of the swimmers came from all sides. The nonswimmers, and there are some in the navy, wore life jackets and made it to the surviving boat by paddling for dear life.

By and by everyone was aboard. There were now seventy men and the vessel sat so low in the water that it could hold no more. Whatever could be spared of water or provisions had to be tossed overboard; in the end, there was only a three-day supply of weapons, ammunition, food, and water.

In the water nearby lay another sambuk, one that belonged to the Idris tribe, an Arab people friendly neither to Turks nor Europeans. This sambuk, seeing the one boat founder, sent its own canoe to the rescue, but as soon as the tropical helmet of the doctor was recognized, they turned tail and left the Europeans to their fate.

The heavily overloaded German boat could not continue to sail ahead, and so before daybreak Mücke sent one of his Arab sailors to the Idris offering a large sum of money, ten thousand pounds in gold, for a few days' loan of the boat. As he had no money to begin with, the lieutenant could afford to make such a high bid. The Idris captain, however, declined. He would do nothing for the Christian dogs.

It would have been easy to take the foreign sambuk with an armed assault. Lieutenant Mücke considered this possibility for the following morning. It would, however, have had far-reaching repercussions, being viewed as an attack on an ally. It would also have been grist for England's mill; Britain had already assured the Idris tribe that it was their friend, while Turkey and Germany were their enemies. Still, there seemed no alternative. In a crosswind with a normal load, as they knew from experience, you need a week to reach the next port. Their provisions would last only three days.

*18 March 1915*

But Aeolus intervened. At sunrise he blew a stiff, fresh, southerly breeze that filled the sails and whisked the heavy boat off. The Idris boat did not become the *Emden* crew's last prize after all.

Quickly they saved what they could from the sinking sambuk, which during the night had slipped down the reef, lodging more deeply in the water. The mast had broken and the boat had capsized. By diving, they managed to salvage two machine guns, a few revolvers, and some of the ammunition. Provisions and clothing as well as pharmaceuticals were lost.

The brisk south wind allowed the overloaded sambuk to cover in one afternoon a distance that normally would have taken six days to sail. In the evening the *Emden* crew reached Qunfidha, where they were welcomed most warmly. An impressive Turkish feast was hastily thrown together and, according to local custom, the hungry men ate without knife or fork or plate. A whole mutton stuffed with rice filled the table. Anxious hands tore the meat and scooped handfuls of rice.

There was a larger sambuk available in Qunfidha. They rented it and continued on their journey, all in one boat. Without further incident they reached Al Lith in the afternoon of 24 March. This was the northern terminal of the Farasan islands, the coral reef that hitherto had given them protection from their British pursuers.

Now the route would have to continue on land or the open sea. One could assume the English would do everything in their power to capture them at sea. In Al Lith Mücke received a letter written by a merchant from which he learned that his next port of call, Jidda, was blockaded by three British warships. Until a short time before, the British had not appeared off Jidda. Hostile confrontations on the coast had been carefully avoided by them, for they wanted to win over the population at the expense of Turkey. Mücke reasoned that the blockade was a sign of England's determination to capture the Germans. By last report, even the smallest sambuk running into Jidda had been thoroughly searched.

Thus the sea route was ruled out. It was necessary to continue on land. They remained in Al Lith for two days to gather caravan animals, replenish water, and make other preparations for the march ahead.

It was in this port that the landing party suffered its first death. One of the sailors had been ill with a case of typhus since leaving Hodeida, and he died on 27 March at about 0300. At his bedside two comrades stood constant watch. A rowboat was prepared, the corpse was sewn into sailcloth weighed down with stones. Upon it, they placed a hat with the German cockade and a bare bayonet. After a short memorial service, the body was placed in the boat and rowed out to the deep sea for burial. Three volleys rolled through the air. Burial on land was impossible, for the fanatic population would not have let the unbeliever rest in peace.

# CHAPTER SIX

# RAS AL ASWAD: BATTLE IN THE DESERT

In the small city of Al Lith camels for the continuing journey were hard to come by. Lieutenant von Mücke called on the sheik of Al Lith; it was the first time a Christian had ever entered his house. He was able to help, and in two days they had assembled some ninety camels. Mücke purchased straw mats to serve as protection against the fierce sun.

On the evening of 28 March the caravan left the city and began its trek through the desert, laden with supplies, particularly water. The march with camels proceeded slowly, along a coastal route where attacks by marauding bands were common. The Germans kept their rifles in a state of constant readiness. As a rule, the troop marched from 1600 to 0900 or 1000, on the average riding fourteen to eighteen hours a day. The trip was enervating. Watering holes dug into the desert sand to a depth of ten meters produced rank brown water.

On 31 March the column, nearly a day's march from Jidda, reached an oasis at 1100. As customary, the men made tents out of their straw mats and covered them with wool blankets. There wasn't room for everyone under the roof, but at least their heads would be protected against the sun. Cooking began almost immediately. They had already gathered dry wood along the way, and soon a fire was going. Mutton was the menu of the day.

The area was inhabited by a tribe claiming to be directly descended from Mohammed and notorious for its bloodthirsty and ruthless pillaging. The area was called Father of Wolves.

As usual, the detachment continued its march at 1600. The route led from the sea through blowing sand dunes, with visibility down to about four hundred meters. Once they had ridden over one dune, another would bar the way and the view. The ground was covered with dry, sparse tufts of grass, sixty centimeters high. In the moonlight the caravan plodded slowly ahead. All at once a band of twelve to fifteen Bedouins rode up on the right, then disappeared. It was a startling thing, over in a moment. To be prepared for what might come, Mücke formed two columns out of the single line of camels. Sleeping on the animals was prohibited. Rifles were readied, and all officers took up position at the head of the caravan.

As the first sign of dawn appeared over the mountains to the right, all immediate signs of danger seemed to have passed. Bedouins were not known to attack in daylight. Mücke had his rifle over his saddle. He now unbuckled the heavy cartridge belt and slowly rode toward the rear of the caravan. He was about halfway there when he heard a sharp whistle. This was followed by a volley of fire, then a barrage of lead coming from all sides. Mücke raised his rifle high in the air, leapt from his camel, and returned to the front of the troop. There a fire skirmish was in progress. In the early morning light, gun flashes were gauged at a distance of about eighty meters.

Neither the snipers nor the members of the formation were in sight. Mücke's tall camels, on the other hand, were quite visible and had become the main target of enemy fire. By now most of the *Emden* men were positioned near the lieutenant, while a small detail had been ordered to the rear. Carried on the camels, the machine guns were set up, two in the front and two in the rear of the caravan. Without further delay the Germans commenced firing. Immediately the opposition was quieted. Those camels still standing Mücke ordered pulled down, out of the line of fire.

German armament consisted of four machine guns, thirteen German rifles, and ten old and three new Turkish rifles. The latter were distributed among the officers. In addition, there were twenty-four pistols, but they were useful only in close combat. Though it was discovered that the enemy's heaviest fire had been concentrated on the left front, his strength was still unknown. They could be dealing with seventy men, perhaps even more. As it became lighter the dunes were seen to be black with Bedouins, about three hundred men.

The German sailors showed no signs of uncertainty. Without waiting for an order they fixed bayonets. "Forward at the double!" cried the lieutenant. With a loud yell the *Emden* crew stormed toward the enemy line. Hardly any shots were fired from the opposition; the enemy was in flight. First the sailors attacked to the left, then to the center, finally to the right. When they had pushed the enemy back about twelve hundred meters, the shooting stopped entirely.

Lieutenant von Mücke gathered his people near the caravan. The machine guns remained posted. Only one sailor had been wounded. As he looked about for his Arab guides, Mücke could account for only seven out of the twenty-four that had been with them before. There were no dead. The missing were later located in Jidda.

A great number of camels had been shot. Supplies and water were unloaded from the fallen beasts. Less vital objects were left behind. Mücke wanted to turn off the route, left, toward the sea shimmering in the distance. There the van would be relatively safe. Unfortunately the machine guns could not be used en route; without carriages, they had to be transported by the swaying camels. The caravan was now arranged in four to six columns. As before, two camels carrying machine guns were in the lead, two were in the rear. An advance guard of ten men in wide-spaced formation preceded the van. A guard of another ten men secured the rear. Another nine men armed with rifles formed a flank guard on both sides. Those armed only with pistols stayed close to the caravan. The advance detail was led by Ensign Geerdts, the rear guard by Ensign Schmidt, the flankers by Ensign Gyssling. The caravan itself, transporting the sick, the wounded man, and Dr. Lang, was led by Ensign Wellmann.

The train started to crawl along again, flag flying. Hope that their adversaries had given up was soon dashed. About ten minutes into the march an almost invisible enemy peppered the column from all sides. Sand dunes concealed movement up to a distance of about four hundred meters, but here and there, over the mounds, the occasional covered heads popped up and then vanished again. A volley descended on the caravan, raising small sand clouds and flinging pebbles into the men's faces. Before they could return the fire the attackers had disappeared again, resuming fire from the other side. Soon the entire area was filled with Bedouins. Then word came that one of the machine-gun-carrying camels had been shot. The rear guard had halted to secure the downed gun. Quickly Ensign Schmidt requested a fresh camel and the gun was in action once more. The caravan was brought to a halt. This was not easy because, along with the gendarmes, most of the camel drivers had disappeared.

Presently Mücke was informed that one of the sailors had fallen and that Ensign Schmidt had been seriously wounded. Command of the rear guard was now assumed by Ensign Wellmann.

Enemy fire intensified. Soon a fierce battle was raging, and just as soon, it stopped again. What had happened? Two of the remaining gendarmes were running toward the firing line waving white flags. A third one explained to Lieutenant von Mücke that his friends wanted to enter into negotiations. Meanwhile, it had become quite clear that this was not a robbery, and that, being outnumbered at least ten to one, they could not continue the march in slow camel step over open ground; they would be under steady enemy fire.

They used the lull to fortify their position. With sand-filled camel saddles, with coffee bags, rice bags, and provision sacks, the *Emden* men built a fortification of encircling walls. Feverishly they dug pits and foxholes and buried the water supply.

With sand-filled petroleum cans they built a second ring of for-
tifications in the center of the encampment, one and a half meters high. They placed the sick, the wounded, and the doctor in
this inner circle. The camels provided cover toward the rear. The
four machine guns were emplaced at each corner of the camp
and protected by sand ramparts. Around the camp men armed
with rifles were placed at regular intervals; those with pistols
filled the gaps. Ammunition was handed out to everyone. The
camp was battle ready when the demands came across from the
other side: surrender of all weapons, ammunition, camels, provisions, and water, as well as payment of eleven thousand pounds
in gold. If these conditions were met, the German troops could
proceed unmolested.

"They must be mad," was the conclusive opinion of all the
*Emden* sailors. Lieutenant von Mücke replied, carefully and politely, "In the first place, we have no money; in the second place,
the surrender of weapons is not customary with German troops."
With that, the last Turkish officer took off after his already
departed men. Some of the remaining camel drivers also used
the cease-fire to disappear. Now only nine remained with the
caravan.

Once more the shooting resumed, lasting until darkness descended. The German group lay well protected behind camels
and saddles, but there was not a great deal of ammunition left
and the water-logged cartridges produced a lot of misfires. They
tried to save the machine-gun ammunition in case of a night attack. The rest of the ammunition was divided among the rifle-
men. There was no loss of life in this part of the battle, but a few
camels were hit. In terms of protection, a dead camel was as
valuable as a live one.

The hard work began right after dark. In the camp everything
was readied to beat off an attack. All rifles and pistols were
loaded, the machine guns continually manned. Men kneeled next
to the outer wall. Nothing moved. Part of the water was un-
earthed and hard tack was passed around. Some men remained at
the guns and the rest fell to digging deeper trenches. The dead
camels had to be dragged away. In the hellish heat cadavers de-

composed rapidly. They bloated and the stretched skin burst, causing the entrails to spill forth. Since the wind blew from the north, the corpses were hauled to the camp's southern end.

The rifles and pistols had been much affected by the constantly drifting sand. They were taken apart and cleaned, one group of guns at a time. Handkerchiefs were wound around the trigger mechanisms to keep them clear of sand. A watch was posted so that the rest of the men could sleep. They cradled loaded guns in their arms. The night passed without further incident.

Earlier, Ensign Schmidt had died of his wounds and been buried in the center of the camp. Mücke had sent a runner, a reliable Arab, to Jidda before the moon rose. He was to steal through enemy lines and report their desperate situation to the military authorities.

Half an hour before sunrise all the men were awake. Everyone was given a cup of water. The next opportunity to drink would not come until after sunset. They could not even cook at night, as their first attempt to do so had resulted in the wounding of two men. The inevitable hardtack was passed around. Men loaded their pockets with it.

With sunrise, lively fire resumed from the other side. Because all of the Germans were under cover, they saved their ammunition and fired only on definite targets. This was no robbery or holdup but a carefully planned attack. Along the coast in the distance two sambuks lay at anchor. Between them and the attackers there was regular relief traffic. The greater part of the enemy must have approached in these boats.

That day they had two further casualties, and their stoker died the following night. The wounded could only receive minimal care because medical supplies had sunk with the sambuk. Only first-aid bandages from the *Emden* were still at hand, along with a few bottles of cognac. Aggravating matters, an unpleasant odor wafted over the camp from a decomposing camel upwind of the encampment. The stench attracted unwanted guests, thousands of black beetles that crawled in the trenches and into their clothes. For every one crushed, a new one appeared. There was no thinking of further sleep. This was an undeniably dangerous situation for the wounded, for tetanus bacilli breed in the horse and camel dung carried by black beetles.

Their bright headdresses used to stave off the heat could not be worn; they offered too tempting a target to the enemy. The glaring sun irritated their eyes and caused headaches. It was so hot the men burned themselves when touching their gun barrels. Grease-soaked camel saddles began to smolder in the heat. A light whiff of smoke permeated the encampment and the glowing saddles were covered with sand to prevent fire. An unending wind blew a fine sand shower over the whole fortification. Sand-filled trenches had to be continuously shoveled. Sand blasted the eyes, ears, mouth, and nose. A thick layer of it accumulated on their sweaty faces. Above them, twenty to thirty carrion kites circled.

At dusk they resumed ready alert. The enemy ceased fire. Two gendarmes disguised as Bedouins were sent to Jidda.

In the middle of the night a noise like a sudden sharp shot came from the direction of the guard posts. In a flash, all the *Emden* hands were in position. But it turned out to be only a band of hyenas and jackals attacking the camel cadavers.

The sun rose for the third time since the battle began. Their situation was serious. They had received no news from the Turkish garrison. Their water was running out and at noon the thermometer stood at 65° Celsius. Mücke issued an order that, come what may, at nightfall they would break for Jidda, even if there was no relief in sight. A few would make it through; unfortunately, the sick and wounded would have to be left behind.

Not far from the camp they could hear the rattle of rifle fire, a number of volleys fired by a strong column. Then a man appeared waving a white flag. He reported that the opposing side no longer wanted the surrender of weapons and supplies; all it demanded now was twenty-two thousand pounds in gold. The enemy must have noticed Turkish troops riding up and decided to salvage at least something of his former demands. It was imperative to draw out the negotiations as long as possible while awaiting the relief detachment. Mücke's answer was a clear, decisive no. The enemy negotiator was not discouraged. He withdrew, returning within a half hour with the same demand. Stalling, Mücke declared that he was prepared to deal only with the ringleader. The leader, naturally, did not appear; he sent a wild threat instead: if the payment was forthcoming, there would be much more fighting. This was followed by a few volleys.

Finally there was silence, though no sign of a relief column. Slowly, deliberately, the *Emden* men peered over their camel saddles, then let their heads show. There wasn't anything to be seen. When nothing happened, they knelt, then stood. They searched up and down with binoculars. Still nothing. The desert seemed to have swallowed up the enemy.

About two hours after the last shots were fired, two camel riders waving a white flag rode toward the camp. As a sign of recognition the sailors hoisted their battle flag. The riders closed to within fifty meters, dismounted, pulled a prayer rug from their bag, sat on it, and began smoking cigarettes. The Germans were used to all sorts of odd behavior, but what could this be? Mücke sent an Arab to question them. They wanted to speak to the commander of the group. They were emissaries of the emir of Mecca, who had heard of their predicament and with his followers come to their rescue.

Lieutenant von Mücke was suspicious. He strolled toward the emissaries, bared saber in his fist. Behind him the men of the *Emden* lined up with guns in firing position. The two arrivals explained that Abdullah, second son of the emir of Mecca, would be there shortly at the head of his troops. A half hour later about seventy camel riders appeared. With their elegant clothing and decorated animals they were easily recognized as no ordinary Bedouins. The *Emden* men were astonished. Without cover, the exotic group rode up in two rows of thirty-five men each, across the sands where only recently hundreds of the enemy had been. They had their guns strapped to their backs, triggers wrapped and stoppers sealing the muzzles. Amid them waved a large red banner covered with verses in gold from the Koran. Under it rode Abdullah and his trusted aides. The troops were singing a rousing song, and ahead of them strode several men beating large drums in accompaniment. A good volley would have sufficed to cut them all down, so the robbers must have disappeared after all.

Abdullah approached Lieutenant von Mücke and greeted him, explaining that he had come with his best troops posthaste as soon as he heard of the attack. He bemoaned this unfortunate incident but was delighted that he had arrived in time to chase off the attackers, with whom he had engaged in a lively skirmish. The "Aleman" could now peacefully proceed to Jidda. He would lead them and supply them with more water. Even with these explanations the Germans were still suspicious. Was it another trap? But their water supply was exhausted, and they had to continue on their way.

With great effort they began loading the camels. Without drivers for the animals the work was not easy; loading camels had never been included in the training manuals of the German navy. Of the 110 animals, 40 had been shot, so numerous sacks and boxes had to be left behind.

Within a few minutes they had crossed the deserted position of their former enemy. Riding over these trenches, the *Emden* men looked back at their abandoned camp and saw streaming toward it from all sides an army of armed Bedouins, about three hundred of them. They swarmed over the stores and plundered what was left behind. It seemed now as if there was a link between the emir's group and their enemy. Mücke's hand touched his pistol holster. Abdullah quickly reassured him that no more shots would be fired. On edge, the *Emden* men went forward. The desert changed from hilly sand dunes to flat rocky desolation.

Were the emir's troops really playing it straight? Mücke would test them by and by. After a few hours he told Abdullah that his men were exhausted and would have to take a short rest. Abdullah declared that the German's wish was his command. The men encamped while their lieutenant joined Abdullah on the prayer rug. As the Bedouin spoke excellent French, a lively conversation developed. Mücke made several flattering remarks about Abdullah's men; he had never expected to meet such excellent fighters in the middle of the desert. He particularly admired their weapons. The Arabs were delighted to hear these compliments. Every single one of them wanted to show off his rifle. With undivided attention Mücke listened and watched, using the opportunity to examine the bores. All were spick and span, not a single shot had been fired from any. The battle in which Abdullah had routed Mücke's enemy had been an outrageous invention. So the mystery was solved; the Germans had before them both enemy and friend in one man.

# CHAPTER SEVEN

# ON TO THE HEJAZ RAILROAD

The next forenoon the *Emden* train reached the fortress of Jidda. The population, which had heard of the desert battle, greeted them with rousing cheers of welcome. On the parade ground before the barracks the entire Turkish garrison as well as Arab auxiliary troops lined up in review. A Turkish colonel greeted the men and expressed his outrage over the attack. He was indignant that the affair could have happened in the shadow of his city's walls, only an eight-hour march away. Mücke thanked him, then rode by inspecting the Turkish troops. Seventeen of the men looked familiar. Only four days before they had been with his beleaguered troops.

The events of the last few days seemed to have been a perverted, ironic farce perpetrated by all sides. The plan of attack, Mücke suspected, had originated with a highly respected ally of Germany, the emir of Mecca. His son Abdullah, their rescuer, had been the enemy leader. After the third day of battle he had become convinced that it was impossible to annihilate the small German unit. In fact, the situation had become seriously embarrassing for him, with forty dead and thirty-six wounded. Thus he had decided to turn about and save face.

Three British gunboats lay anchored off the harbor of Jidda. Here, in the land of the "venerable allies," at least there was a true enemy. It was not easy to find a way out of this delicate situation. Further desert skirmishes they could not endure; their ammunition had been cut in half, and much of it had been rendered useless by the shipwreck. Nor could they depend on the Turkish garrison for support. The Turks must have known about the battle even before it had begun, but they hadn't budged from their fortress.

His second day in the city Mücke picked up a useful Egyptian, a former Suez Canal pilot now sailing sambuks between Jidda and Egypt. He spoke fluent English, certainly a great advantage. He had secured a good sambuk for the *Emden* detachment, and it now lay waiting in the harbor—where the masts of blockading English gunboats were visible every day just outside the coral reefs. After Mücke had planted a rumor that he hoped to undertake a land march again, he took to sea in a motorboat for an exploratory trip. There were no English ships in sight. Did they too believe the rumor?

The night of 9 April the wind was favorable. The Germans prepared to steal away. This time no one would inform the British ahead of time. The emir would find out soon enough, but that was now immaterial. Just as they were about to cast off the Turkish colonel appeared. Wringing his hands, he implored them not to travel by sea; they should take the safe, secure land route. He gave his word of honor that everything was in order. But the Germans didn't listen. The sails billowed on the masts and a beautiful stiff breeze carried them off, direction north.

The protective reefs that were to shelter them from the British lay thirty nautical miles away. With the uncertainty of the wind it was questionable whether they could be reached by daybreak, and so, right after darkness, the Germans anchored in a deeply cut, mountain-ringed bay near Jidda. The next forenoon they continued their journey. When the sun went down they anchored again, not having seen one enemy ship. Their position now lay between sheltering reefs some thirty-eight nautical miles from Jidda.

Two hours later the lookout reported a light outside the reefs passing slowly to the south. As expected, the British gunboats had got under way immediately upon being informed of the

German departure. They had expected to capture the sambuk just outside the reefs, certain that the *Emden* crew would use the opportune breeze to head north.

There was only one way to foil the enemy: go more slowly or anchor. The gunboats steamed uselessly back and forth the whole day, giving up the search between dangerous coral banks. They could not anchor there, and in the dark, passage through the reefs was out of the question. They had to remain in open sea at night. But before they could resume their search, the sambuk had found its way between the banks and hidden. The Germans had finally given their enemy the slip.

The sambuk continued its journey close to shore and used every reef to conceal itself. Slowly but surely it made headway. Only now and then were they delayed by storm and fog. They entered several ports, very briefly, sometimes only for hours, in order to gather information and fresh supplies. Most of the nights were spent at anchor, for dodging reefs was impossible at night.

The nightly anchorage was an unusual maneuver. Around the coral reefs the sea was very deep, so that anchoring in the normal sense was not possible. They had to approach the reefs, lowering sails. Two Arabs standing on the bow would leap overboard, taking along a thin rope threaded with iron hooks. This was deeply embedded in hollows found in the coral blocks just below the waterline. It wasn't always easy work; changing winds threatened a treacherous pileup on the bank.

In Sherm Rabigh they had to change sambuks, the one they were using being too small. The new boat had to be fitted with sand ballast to make it seaworthy.

The entire stretch of coast was sparsely settled. Now and then they sighted small canoes on fishing expeditions and used the opportunity to exchange rice for fresh fish.

The Arab part of the crew was entertaining. They liked to steal by night, and on one occasion this tendency backfired on them. In Jidda Doctor Lang had secured a huge bottle of castor oil for the men sick with dysentery. One morning it had disappeared without a trace. The Arabs became more silent and ashen as the day went by. The result was anything but inspiring. "Allah is righteous! He punishes all those who steal," they sighed, and spent the entire day retching. Apparently they had finished off the whole bottle.

On 28 April, without a particularly eventful passage, their sambuk reached Sherm Munnaiburra, a small sheltered cove about ten nautical miles south of their final destination, Wejh. From here on there were no sheltering reefs; the deep water extended all the way to the coast. Having pushed and battled their way forward for almost six months, and because danger still lurked on the high seas, the *Emden* men did not want to cross this last small stretch of sea by sailboat. From Sherm Munnaiburra, therefore, they would go by land.

Local officials, already notified through runners, had sent several gendarmes to the coast. One of them was to procure camels for the trip. During the night bonfires lit the way to the assembly spot on shore; the awaited camel caravan had arrived. The Germans took provisions for one day along with their weapons and ammunition. Everything else was sent ahead in a sambuk, which fortunately arrived without ever having sighted an enemy ship.

On the evening of 29 April the *Emden* landing party finally arrived at Wejh. Here they washed themselves thoroughly and slept around the clock. Arrangements for another caravan took two days. On 2 May, at about 0800, the party marched off on the last leg of its journey toward the long-sought railroad.

Under the direction of Sheik Suleiman, a resident of Wejh, the caravan marched into an all too familiar sandy desert landscape. Soon, however, the scenery became more pleasant. Mountains loomed ahead of them, and the road started to lead through a picturesque region. The water situation was much better than in the desert; the wells were in better shape and delivered water which, if not entirely clean, was at least potable. Their Arab escorts informed them that there was actually running water at the mountain ridge. But those who dreamed of taking a mountain bath were disappointed. The little stream did actually ripple, but at such a leisurely pace that it could be brought to a stop simply by standing in it.

Here, in the mountains where it was cooler, the Germans traveled in daylight and rested at night. Because of bitter experience they entrenched themselves in their camp, much to the amazement of the Arab escorts. But when the territory of Suleiman Pasha ended—it did not reach Al 'Ala, where the *Emden* crew hoped to find the terminal of the Hejaz Railroad—the sheik himself expected trouble. During the day his followers came from every part of the mountains and formed small groups around him. The caravan reached a strength of four hundred, an inspiring scene: men armed with long Arab flintlocks rode like the wind in billowing brown robes and fluttering headdresses.

The railroad terminal was now only a day's distance away. The road led through high mountains and narrow passages, made for surprise attacks, and passes could only be crossed single file. The caravan slowly drew apart. To prevent surprise attack, Suleiman formed a regular reconnaissance unit whose men galloped into every valley and hunted all the nooks and crannies. A few hours from Al 'Ala they brought letters stating that the sheik to whom this territory belonged was fighting another group to the north, so they could proceed unmolested.

Lieutenant von Mücke now rode ahead of the caravan to order a special train in Al 'Ala and to make arrangements for quartering his men. At a brisk gallop lasting several hours he covered the last stretch of the journey, in the company of Suleiman Pasha, his two sons, and several dignitaries. The Arabs showed the deepest curiosity when he paused on the mountain ridge to observe the roofs of Al 'Ala with his binoculars. They were totally unknown in this area, and everyone wanted to take a look.

Mücke used the large expanse of plateau through which they rode to explain to Suleiman Pasha what a great and mighty nation Germany was. He astonished the Arabs when he explained that German warships could attack their enemy from a distance greater than the length of the plateau they were now on. Gun barrels, he explained, were large enough to hold a galloping ram.

Mücke reached Al 'Ala about noon and was surprised to see that everything had been prepared for him and his crew. A special train was standing by, the locomotive only waiting for a signal to depart. Two German newspaper reporters as well as a number of Turkish officers were waiting for the *Emden* crew to arrive. There were letters from the German colony in Syria, along with cold Rhine wine, champagne, peaches, and many other long-dreamt-of delicacies.

A few hours later Mücke's men arrived. The lieutenant rode out to meet them, surrounded on all sides by a crowd busy photographing their triumphant entry into town. The sailors could hardly believe that here were railroad tracks, a sign of the yearned-for link to civilization. For the next few hours there was sumptuous eating, drinking, and bathing. Then the train rolled north. Now they could indulge in the luxury of stretching out on soft, red velvet cushions. They could finally sleep without a care in the world.

The train traveled through Damascus and Aleppo and on to Constantinople. In two places, where the tracks had not been completed, they had to leave the train and travel by wagon and on foot. Wherever they went, they were greeted jubilantly by the German community and Turkish officials. At every railroad station it was the same story, crowds of people all straining to catch a glimpse of the heroes. They were received with flying flags, rousing music, and roses. Gifts, showered upon them, began to crowd the railroad cars. Without tears, they left behind their old rags and donned new uniforms. Near every wayside their train was surrounded by hordes of Bedouins galloping alongside and doing fancy stunts.

In Aleppo the sailors would finally receive their first news from home in ten months. Letters and an Iron Cross awaited each of them. The next few days were spent reading that wonderful mail from home and the many letters and poems sent by their fervent admirers the world over.

Whitsunday, 23 May 1915, the special train stopped at the station in Haidar-Pasha, the Asiatic terminal of Constantinople. The chief of the German Mediterranean Squadron, also chief of the Turkish fleet, Admiral Souchon, would not be denied the pleasure of greeting the *Emden* men personally. The crew quickly assembled, their flag with them. It had come a long way. Attached with rusty nails to a boat hook, it had flown from SMS *Emden* in the waters of the Far East and the Indian Ocean; it had been planted among the rustling palms of Keeling Island; atop the mast of SMS *Ayesha*, it had been shredded by a howling monsoon; it had fluttered on the stern of the *Choising;* it had led them through cold nights in the Yemen mountains; and through dead wind and shipwreck, it had waved from the stern of clumsy sambuks. Their flag had been the pathfinder in both glittering moonlight and burning desert sun; it had been an inspiring symbol in the red-hot battle waged in the sand dunes of Ras al Aswad. After a ten-month journey in wartime a handful of men had brought the flag back. They were the last of the German cruiser squadron, and the only German unit lucky enough to find its way home with flag flying.

A few short, sharp commands. Their execution showed that months-long deprivation had not dulled these sailors of the Imperial Navy. Lieutenant von Mücke lowered his dagger before the admiral. "By your leave," he said, "landing party from SMS *Emden,* five officers, seven petty officers, and thirty-seven seamen, at your service, reporting for duty."

# Five

# Epilogue

News of the light cruiser *Emden* first reached the German public at the end of August 1914, when the seizure of the Russian vessel *Rjäsan* in Tsushima Strait was reported. In the middle of September an enthusiastic country learned that the cruiser was carrying on a raider war in the Bay of Bengal, capturing British merchant ships. After the announcement of the bombardment of Madras on 22 September, the press could not tear itself away from the exploits of the small German warship. Enthusiasm for the actions of the independently operating cruiser peaked after reports of the successful attack on Penang and the sinking of two enemy warships. On 30 October 1914 a pleased Emperor Wilhelm II dispatched a telegram to the lord mayor of the city of Emden: "I congratulate Emden on its godchild in the Indian Ocean, a godchild whose daring cruiser exploits bring pride and joy to every German heart." On 4 November an official German report announced that the *Emden*'s commanding officer had been awarded the Iron Cross, First and Second Class. All other commissioned and warrant officers and fifty petty officers received the Iron Cross Second Class. Throughout the world a heady *Emden* spirit prevailed. Innumerable poems and songs were dedicated to the ship at home and abroad. The newspapers were full of laudatory articles. Even in the United States an *Emden* club was formed.

The joyful mood, however, was of short duration. At the beginning of November came the good news of Admiral Graf Spee's victory at Coronel, only to be followed by the bad news that Tsingtao, the support base of the German cruiser squadron and the *Emden,* had fallen in an overwhelming Japanese-British assault. And on 11 November 1914, the press announced the honorable but conclusive demise of the German cruiser *Emden.*

The London *Times* found these words for the German ship:

> The dispatch that the *Emden* finally found its inevitable end was received in this country with great relief. She inflicted heavy casualties on British trade. Her skillful and inconceivable appearance on important trade routes spread a fear which influenced the insurance rates most unfavorably. But her fate has awakened other feelings. Since the first September days when the *Emden* appeared in the Gulf of Bengal, her daring and enterprising actions have shown her to possess attributes which people with England's naval tradition must admire. Cut off from all logistical support and with poor prospects of gathering supplies, the *Emden* traveled alone on the wide oceans of the world. Her destiny was an honorable fight for existence. She lead it with a daring which friend and foe alike had to acknowledge. If she ran out of coal, she caught a coal ship; if she required provisions, she fetched them from merchant ships on the high seas. Nevertheless, there is no charge of violence that can be held against her. As reported, Commander von Müller treated the crews of his captured ships nobly and evenhandedly. At no time did he destroy human life unnecessarily. As far as it is known, he strictly obeyed and observed the code of international law. At Madras, he let his crew fire only on oil tanks and the fort. The next morning, as the fog lifted, his ship lay at anchor off the undefended city of Pondicherry. He departed without firing a single shot . . . We are pleased that the cruiser *Emden* was finally destroyed, but we acknowledge Commander von Müller as a valiant and chivalrous adversary. We hope that his life was spared, for should he come to London, we would prepare for him a rousing welcome. Our seafaring nation knows how to admire a daring and resourceful seaman, and there are few events in the new history of sea warfare which are more remarkable than the bright career of the little *Emden.*

News of the valiant end of the glorious career of the light cruiser *Emden* caused deep sorrow in Germany, but it was sorrow mixed with pride over the accomplishments of the ship and her brave crew. The *Emden* phenomenon surged in Germany. For weeks every German paper was full of poignant obituaries.

In neutral countries, too, sympathetic voices arose. The Norwegian *Aftenposten,* in Oslo, rendered its judgment as follows:

> What the *Emden* performed is unmatched in the history of warfare. No one could have believed that a single modern cruiser could against so many overwhelming enemies cause as much damage as she was able to inflict. During this war, very few names were heard as often from the mouths of nations as that of the *Emden* and her courageous commanding officer. How the cruiser succeeded over an extended period in capturing the most essential supplies is a question about which many suppositions have been formed, and on which new light can now be shed. However it may be, these actions testify to the great intelligence, far-sightedness and ability of her captain.

A collection of similar obituaries on the cruiser *Emden* would fill countless binders. In them would be represented newspapers the world over.

On 14 November 1914, in the east Frisian city of Emden, the city council met in a solemn session to honor the cruiser. They directed a telegram to the emperor: "Deeply grieved by the destruction of Your Majesty's glorious ship, the light cruiser *Emden,* and by the large number of casualties which must be mourned by that sinking, we, Your Majesty's most obedient city council of Emden, request that you accept our humblest sympathy as conveyed to Your All Highest Self." The next day the emperor answered the council of Emden from General Headquarters: "My sincerest thanks for your telegram concerning the untimely and yet so heroic end of my cruiser *Emden.* In her last battle against a superior enemy, the brave ship still won laurels for the German battle flag. A new and stronger *Emden* will arise and on her bow we will place the Iron Cross as a remembrance of the glory of the old *Emden.*"

On 1 December 1914 the city of Emden awarded Commander von Müller honorary citizenship. Soon efforts were under way to

honor the survivors of the famous cruiser in a special way by al-
lowing them to add *Emden* to their family names. This thought-
ful initiative floundered in the jungles of bureaucratic regulation,
yet eventually it led to an act which, after the war, allowed more
than a hundred survivors to take the additional name.

In February 1915 initial reports about the landing party's escape from the Cocos and subsequent voyage to Arabia reached
Germany. On 11 February 1915 the leader of that group, Lieutenant von Mücke, was awarded the Iron Cross First Class; the
rest of the men received the Iron Cross Second Class.

Beginning on 11 May 1915 the *Berliner Tageblatt* published
the enthusiastic reports of its renowned correspondent Emil
Ludwig, who had encountered the *Emden* troop at the Ma'an.
A new *Emden* euphoria broke out in Germany when it became
known that on Whitsunday, 23 May 1915, Lieutenant von
Mücke had reported to Admiral Souchon in Constantinople
that the landing party of SMS *Emden* was present and ready for
duty. Mücke was the hero of the day. He and his men received a
rousing welcome wherever they went. His arduous journey from
Turkey via the Balkans and Austria to Germany became a triumphant procession. For the publicity-conscious German pa-
triot, the event came at a welcome time, during a hiatus in the
war when the German army's initial offensive had ground to a
halt. The terrible war of attrition had not yet begun. News of the
adventures and return of the *Emden* crew were seized only too
willingly by the press. Except for a few individual heroics, there
was not much to report from the war at sea. Graf Spee's squadron had met its end near the Falkland islands, and in an unlucky
battle at the Dogger Bank the Imperial Navy had lost the armored cruiser *Blücher.* How welcome it was, therefore, to be
able to remember again the short but splendid career of the
*Emden,* to milk the story for all it was worth. How welcome a
relief was Mücke's adventurous, romantic *Ayesha* story, which
diverted everyone from the chilling army reports about violent
battles in a deadlocked war.

But all was not glory for Lieutenant von Mücke. What naturally did not reach the public was that this young naval hero had
upset the delicate machinery of diplomacy as he and his men

fought their way through "allied" Turkish territory. There had been a clash of opinion between the efficient, adventurous lieutenant and the painfully cautious German career diplomats who wanted to avoid any imprudence that might lead to diplomatic or political ill-will in Turkey.

He who in his professional lifetime learns to spout unctuous courtesies may very well blanch in the face of a vociferous, piratical but charming hotspur. The young officer was bound to be angry when, after his long and strenuous travels, he once again confronted weak-kneed bureaucrats. He himself was not weak-kneed, this enterprising and energetic first officer of the raiding cruiser *Emden*. Had he played so many tricks on the English and sailed the oceans in his fragile craft, forged so many deals with Bedouins, sheiks, and phlegmatic Turks, only to be reprimanded by high-collared diplomats? All of a sudden he should obey their orders? Certainly not! Both he and the navy shrugged off diplomatic rebuffs when it came to a head-on clash with the Foreign Office regarding his actions and words. He who through self-reliance had conducted his own war was not to be intimidated.

What had happened? As stated in Mücke's reports, the probable instigator of the surprise attack against his little unit near Jidda had been the emir of Mecca, at that time much celebrated in Germany as one of the mainstays of the so-called Holy War between the Mohammedans and England's allies. But Mücke knew from his own experience that this Holy War, of which he had read long dissertations in the German press, in reality had never taken place. In fact, eventually it became known that from the beginning the emir had supported England, and at the start of 1915 he had concluded a formal alliance with the British government. In Mücke's opinion, the emir had made detailed plans to let the landing party of the *Emden* vanish in the desert and thereupon collect the five thousand pounds that British agents had placed on Mücke's head. (The son, Abdullah, who had "liberated" the *Emden* group after the battle near Jidda, would be crowned by the English.) With ill-concealed bitterness, the young lieutenant tried to correct the curious views held by the experts in the Foreign Office. Arriving in Constantinople, he felt it necessary to warn the German ambassador of his misgivings about the emir. The information was passed on to the Arab specialist at the embassy, Max Baron von Oppenheim, who attempted to persuade Mücke to change his mind. The latter responded by declaring, "We soldiers, of course, understand nothing of diplomacy; we are, however, permitted to lay down our lives for its mistakes." Since the diplomat could not achieve anything with his cajolery, he submitted an official report to Berlin's Foreign Office, whose apprehensive staff passed it on to the chief of the navy's Admiralty Staff.

This report, composed on 6 June 1915, read as follows:

> On the basis of detailed information concerning the surprise attacks near Jidda related to me by Lieutenant von Mücke and Sami Bey, I cannot agree with the opinions expressed by these two gentlemen that the attack was instigated by the emir of Mecca or his son Abdullah. Circumstantial evidence instead convinces me that Bedouins launched the attack for money and weapons. One must also assume that they had hoped to gain large sums of money and, later, ransom money. This is a rather routine occurrence in the Arab world, where government is not strong enough to prevent it. It is by no means impossible that certain followers of the emir initiated the raid on their own, but it appears to me completely illogical that the emir instigated the attack on the heroes of the *Emden*. Apart from all other considerations, he is politically much too clever to get involved in such folly.
>
> The circumstance that with the simple appearance of Prince Abdullah and the discharge of a few blind shots the whole battle suddenly ceased, and that with the departure of the *Emden* men from the camp the former attackers overran and plundered it, is, as stated before, no more than a routine event. Similar attacks have occurred in Mesopotamia. Sami Bey is particularly furious because on this occasion the sacks of coffee he had brought from Yemen disappeared. The entire attack, carried on in spite of the presence of government policemen from Jidda, as well as the explanations of the affair by Jidda, is for me but further proof of the extraordinarily poor relationship that exists between the rightful Turkish government and the Sherifat. It has also made me aware of the political power the latter wields over Jidda and its surroundings.

The Turkish government allowed that the attack, like many others, had been launched by robbers and Bedouins. Perhaps this one was engineered by our English enemies. There is no doubt that the timely intervention by the son of the emir is what saved the crew of the *Emden.*

At Your Excellency's suggestion, I did request Herr von Mücke to adopt this version which, by the way, his interviewer, Herr Emil Ludwig, telegraphed to the German newspapers, and to let it be with that. In the interest of continued better relations with the emir—and his possible utilization for a large-scale propaganda campaign aimed at hostile Islamic countries—it would in my opinion be desirable for the appropriate authorities in Berlin to order Lieutenant von Mücke to align himself with these thoughts.

This appears to me all the more important since Herr von Mücke has announced that in the near future he will lecture on the exploits of the *Emden,* on his wanderings and his rescue.

The appropriate authority, the Admiralty Staff, passed a copy of the report on to the Office of the Secretary of the Navy and so informed Lieutenant von Mücke. He fumed about the "experts" in the diplomatic service, and made the following official report:

It did not take the intervention of Herr von Oppenheim to alert me to my responsibility of exposing events in Arabia to the outside world; present circumstances and political alliances demand it. I refer you to my telegram from Jidda, which distinctly states the official Turkish position. Moreover, the observations the reporter, Herr Emil Ludwig, gave to German newspapers came from me alone and, without delay, were okayed by German and Turkish censors. My reports were made over the course of many weeks, long before I came to Constantinople. I cannot help but express surprise that Herr von Oppenheim used my purely personal information in an official report so that my superiors would order me to adopt a position concerning events that I had observed long before the appearance of Herr von Oppenheim. I could offer additional observations, unknown to Herr von Oppenheim, but they would require more political discretion.

It was clear that the Admiralty Staff would support its young naval hero. In his official reply the chief of staff elaborated on Mücke's defense of himself:

May I humbly observe that in Lieutenant von Mücke's telegram from Jidda only an attack by an Arab gang is mentioned, Arabs most likely bribed by the British. The lieutenant gave no further report to the public. He has grasped the true situation from the beginning, in full knowledge of the consequences of his statements. He has understood what was expected of him and avoided making remarks unfavorable to Turkish forces. Your Excellency may conclude from this report that special orders or instructions for Lieutenant von Mücke are not required.

Copies of this report to the Office of the Secretary of the Navy were sent the Foreign Office, Lieutenant von Mücke, the German embassy in Constantinople, the commander of the fleet, Germany's Mediterranean division, and Herr von Oppenheim. Small wonder that the lieutenant's return home was a bitter experience. Hounded by painful official action, he now wanted nothing more than to receive a quiet command in the North Sea.

Meanwhile, the crew of the *Emden* was scattered all over the world. Lieutenant von Mücke's men all received assignments aboard warships. Many of them died during the war. The survivors of the *Emden* and the prize command of the *Buresk* were prisoners on Malta. Lieutenant (j.g.) Geerdes and the forty-nine wounded crew members had been taken ashore in Colombo and become Australian prisoners of war.

But where had the other prize crew of the *Emden* gone? On 8 November 1914 Lieutenant (j.g.) Julius Lauterbach had received command of the captured coal ship *Exford* near North Keeling Island. With his sixteen men he was supposed to take her in the direction of Socotra, ahead of the *Emden*. The cruiser had planned, after the action against the radio station in the Cocos, to operate at the mouth of the Red Sea. The *Exford* waited in vain at the agreed rendezvous until the end of November, whereupon she steamed as directed to Padang, on the west coast of Sumatra. Sighting the offshore islands on 11 December 1914, she approached the coast and was within five miles when, suddenly, in front of Padang, a smoke cloud reared up and headed directly for her. It was the British auxiliary cruiser

*Himalaya.* Presently a prize boat arrived, bringing one of the English officers. Because the *Exford* was in Dutch territorial waters, Lieutenant Lauterbach demanded that neutrality be observed. To this, the British officer merely shrugged his shoulders. Any resistance would have been useless, and as the *Exford* could no longer be sunk, she had to be left to the English. The seventeen *Emden* men were transferred to the auxiliary cruiser *Empress of Japan* and on 15 December 1914 brought ashore at Singapore. They were taken to the Tanglin Barracks, where they were joyously welcomed by *Emden* men from the *Pontoporos* and merchant sailors of the *Markomannia.*

On 16 September the *Pontoporos,* under the military command of Vice Quartermaster Meyer and thirteen men of the *Emden,* had been detached from the cruiser in the Bay of Bengal and ordered to meet the *Emden's* tender, the *Markomannia,* near Simeulue. On 29 September, near the Maldives, the *Markomannia* was sent to this rendezvous to consolidate supplies and personnel. On 12 October, in Dutch waters near Simeulue, the British cruiser *Yarmouth* took both ships by surprise. The *Markomannia* was sunk by her own crew, and the *Pontoporos,* with prisoners aboard, was taken to Singapore.

On 15 February 1915 a British-Indian regiment, the Fifth Indian Rifles, revolted in Singapore and liberated German prisoners. Eventually, loyal British troops suppressed the revolt and recaptured most of the Germans, who in April 1915 were shipped to Australia in the freighter *Montoro.* During the voyage the ship ran aground and could only be salvaged with great effort. The *Emden* prisoners, deposited in the Australian camp along with others, were allowed to board the former Russian transport *Kursk* on 1 June 1919. On 21 July 1919 they landed in Rotterdam, whence they were taken to Germany in a special internment train.

During the revolt Lieutenant Lauterbach had been lucky enough to escape from Singapore. After many adventures he succeeded in reaching the Dutch Indies, and from there the United States. On the last leg of his journey he sailed across the Atlantic to Germany, where he arrived in October 1915. From January 1916 to November 1917 he commanded the auxiliary ship *K*. Thereafter he was administrative officer of the First Trade Defense Demi-Flotilla. On 24 December 1915 he was promoted to lieutenant in the reserves. Several books were published about his adventures, written in part by him.

Of the *Emden* personnel on Malta who led the bleak existence of prisoners of war, one, Lieutenant Fikentscher, made a risky escape, from Fort Verdala. In Valletta he went into hiding, and finally, in a desperate attempt, escaped to Sicily in an open rowboat. But Italy, having declared war on Germany in 1915, held runaways captive. Through an exchange of prisoners arranged by the Red Cross, Fikentscher arrived home, in Augsburg, on 21 October 1917.

The imprisoned crew on Malta did not return to Germany until the fall of 1919.

During the first part of his stay on Malta, the commanding officer of the *Emden* had complained not about his own treatment but about that accorded his men by the British guards. After a sudden and unexpected transfer to England, he wrote about the change in the way he was being treated:

> In the morning of 8 October 1916, as I sat eating my breakfast, Major Jellicoe arrived and said that at 0900 I was to report to the governor of Malta. Remembering an earlier conversation with the governor, I knew that they had something special in mind, but I had no idea that I would be removed from Malta that morning. In clothing suited to the climate of Malta—white flannel pants, thin blue coat, tropical helmet—I walked to the gate at the designated time, and Major Jellicoe came to meet me. Soon the camp commander joined us and we drove down to the harbor, where we had to wait a long time for a steam pinnace. I deliberately avoided asking him the reason for this unexpected turn, but the camp commander informed me that I would be taken aboard an English warship. After some time the pinnace arrived. Major Jellicoe and I boarded it; we proceeded across the harbor and approached a battleship, which was ready to depart. Coming aboard I saluted, as was customary. The commanding officer did not return my salute, but with a brisk movement of the hand pointed aft to the companionway, which I was to follow. I was escorted by four men whose guns had fixed bayonets. I was led to a cabin on the afterdeck of the ship, where the win-

dows were secured with thick iron bars. In front of it, a guard paced up and down. After about half an hour the ship, the battleship *London,* steamed out of the harbor. None of my personal belongings could possibly have been brought on board by then.

After a while the commanding officer came and told me that, regretfully, none of my things had come along, but that they would follow on the next postal ship. He would make my stay on board as comfortable as possible, he said, and as a special privilege would allow me to move about the afterdeck one hour in the morning and one in the afternoon.

Presently I informed a guard that I would like to go to the lavatory, whereupon he called two other guards who came with fixed bayonets and escorted me, one a step in front of me, the other one step behind. In the afternoon the commanding officer came to my cabin once more and asked if I had any requests. I explained to him that my treatment had been insulting and totally different from that given me in the *Hampshire,* which had brought me from Port Said to Malta. It was unthinkable that a captured English officer would receive such shabby treatment in a German warship. He explained that the uncommonly severe custody resulted from particularly harsh orders regarding my transport to England. The following morning he informed me that from now on, going to and from my cabin, I would be escorted by only one guard. He grew more friendly, giving me reading material and furnishing me with clothes and toilet articles. I cannot complain about the accommodations or the food.

I was informed that I was being taken to England. On 16 October, after a short stop for coaling in Gibraltar, we arrived in Plymouth. Two English army officers and a noncommissioned officer came to take me off the ship. At the prison I was instructed to get out and was escorted to a soldier's cell. In answer to my question whether this was the customary accommodation for an officer, I was told that no other room was available. I was given a chance to speak to the commander of the prison, to whom I submitted my objections; my treatment was a violation of the customs and regulations of the Hague Convention. Moreover, a British officer, especially one of my rank, would be treated quite differently as a prisoner of war in Germany. He told me that he would try to have a room prepared for me. After a while he returned and asked me for my word of honor, for without that he could not lodge me in a less secure room. I would not give my word. If he thought the cell was a suitable accommodation, I would have to stay in it. I would, however, complain through the American embassy. He repeated that without my word of honor, he could do nothing more. Nonetheless, after a while I was escorted to a room in the administration building, which was located in a courtyard surrounded by a high wall. My room was locked at night, and I had to surrender one boot so that an escape would be even harder. In front of the window a guard marched up and down. Several times during the night a lantern was flashed in my face to determine if I was still there. I was held in this prison for two days. On 18 October I was taken to the railroad station and from there I traveled to Keyworth.

In September 1917 Müller succeeded in an attempt to escape from his camp. Soon recaptured, he was sentenced to fifty-six days' solitary confinement in November 1917.

Because of his seriously deteriorating physical condition—he had suffered from malaria attacks ever since a tropical assignment in SMS *Seeadler*—Commander von Müller was released from British custody in January 1918, taken to Rotterdam, and interned in the Netherlands. Plagued by thoughts of how his command of the *Emden* in her last battle would be judged by the German Admiralty Staff, he received leave, after giving his pledge of honor, to travel to his home town of Blankenberge, in the Harz.

What a different country it was that the commanding officer of the *Emden* was allowed to visit in the beginning of 1918. The enthusiasm of August 1914 had died. Memory of the *Emden*'s glorious actions had faded. His home was haunted by the ghosts of Verdun and Jutland, of the massive battles fought in the west with automatic fire and gas, a mutiny in the navy, ammunition strikes in factories, the hunger blockade. And now the United States had entered the war. The desperate U-boat war had passed its zenith. Privation and sacrifice had changed the land and its people. Ebullient patriotism belonged to the past. The land struggled for survival in the midst of an increasingly uncertain political situation.

The papers gave scant coverage of the return of the once famous commanding officer of the *Emden*. Why bother? Hadn't the last survivors returned home years before? And wasn't the captain's name Mücke anyway? In the navy only the U-boats counted now. Would the massive spring offensive bring results before the Americans added their enormous material and troop strength to bear in the west? How soon after the collapse of Russia could German troops be withdrawn from the eastern front, and how long before the Ukrainian wheat harvest could be used to feed hungry Germany? Those were the great unanswered questions. The commanding officer of the *Emden* practically had to sneak back to his birthplace, still a prisoner on furlough because he had given his captors his word of honor.

But his Admiralty Staff had not forgotten him. At the end of 1917, when his return seemed likely, the navy had set in motion plans to award him the highest decoration for valor, the Pour le Mérite. This most famous of German commanders should receive the decoration, especially now that the Iron Cross First Class had been awarded en masse to privates first class who had destroyed the tracks of British tanks and to sergeants, storm troop leaders, who had taken enemy trenches.

The Admiralty Staff had submitted an application to the emperor's Navy Cabinet, under whose jurisdiction promotions, personnel matters, and decorations came. On 18 January 1918 the chief of the Navy Cabinet, Admiral von Müller—no relation of the *Emden*'s captain—replied to this with cautious inquiry:

> Before I present your request for the awarding of the Pour le Mérite to the Emperor for a decision, may I ask you to clarify several disturbing points?
> 1. Was it not a mistake to make for the Cocos?
> 2. Can the grounding of SMS *Emden* be defended militarily and in terms of seamanship?
> 3. Did the commanding officer fully preserve the honor of the flag when—in all probability to protect the lives of his crew—he hoisted the white flag?
> 4. Was there no opportunity for the commanding officer to destroy the ship and its weapons so that nothing could fall into the hands of the enemy?

I would also be grateful to you for a short and graphic report of the last battle of SMS *Emden,* which would provide
me with additional data for presentation to the Emperor.

This cool reaction surprised the Admiralty Staff, which, nonetheless, proceeded with the request. Another entreaty for favorable action was sent to General Headquarters. To this Admiral
von Müller reacted even more cooly. In a letter of 6 February
1918 he insinuated that if the commanding officer of the *Emden*
were not so popular, he would have to answer to a court-martial
because of his last operation and the demise of his cruiser. Only
by imperial grace would this painful proceeding be avoided.
Still the annoyed Admiralty Staff did not relinquish its position.
On 15 March 1918 the chief of the staff, Admiral von Holtzen-
dorff, directed the following letter to Admiral von Müller:

Sir, I transmit herewith the report of the commanding
officer of SMS *Emden* concerning the landing on the Cocos
and the battle with the Australian cruiser *Sydney*. In it, you
will find answers to four questions posed in your letter of
18 January 1918. To this I add the following in particular:
To 1. For the landing on the Cocos, the stated reasons
justified the execution of this undertaking. The risks connected with this undertaking and correctly weighed by the
commanding officer were no greater than those taken for
the bombardment of Madras or the run into Penang Harbor. Considering the possibility of running up against a superior enemy, I cannot see any error in deciding to land on
the Cocos.
To 2 and 4. When the commanding officer decided to
beach his ship on the reef, none of his guns was capable of
firing. The torpedo room, because of an underwater hit,
was flooded and had to be abandoned. The large number of
casualties and the battered condition of his ship, slowed
down and burning, precluded further opportunity of dam-
aging the enemy ship. Under these circumstances, the decision to beach the ship on the reef instead of sacrificing the
rest of the crew by sinking her was justified. Whatever
might fall in the hands of the enemy was so riddled and
militarily worthless that preservation of the rest of a valiant
crew was the highest duty the commanding officer could
have performed.
To 3. With regard to hoisting the white flag, this was not
done to terminate an ongoing battle; the flag was raised ap-

proximately five hours after its end, when the returning cruiser *Sydney,* through misunderstood signals, once more opened fire on the wreck. The survivors, many wounded among them, were on the stern expecting to be rescued. This measure, then, was aimed solely at preventing the useless sacrifice of defenseless men. . . . It would have been more appropriate for the commanding officer to lower the battle flag in the absence of the British cruiser. Commander von Müller himself later expressed his concern that the use of the white flag as a signal might be misinterpreted. . . .

I hope that His Majesty, the Emperor, on the strength of this report, has the grace to award the recommended decoration to Commander von Müller, who has returned from a long and most difficult imprisonment.

The original draft of the reply, in the kaiser's handwriting, contains the marginal comment, "Yes, it is perfectly justified."

It was not a broken man but a veteran of three years of imprisonment who had returned. He was a fellow sufferer, witness to the flagging destiny of his country—radiant hero no longer, but an internee on leave, a reflective, melancholy man consumed by self-reproach and guilt. Thus it was with a sense of great relief that on 21 March 1918 he received an imperial telegram that read as follows:

On the basis of the report presented to me by the Admiralty Staff concerning the last days of my cruiser *Emden* and her final battle, I hereby award you the Order Pour le Mérite. The efficient and valiant conduct of you and your crew is commendable. You have given your ship's name a place of honor forever, and you have given the world a shining example of gallant and vigorous cruiser warfare. Proposals for the decoration of the ship's staff and crew, mentioned at the end of your report, I accept with pleasure.

—Wilhelm I. R.

An officer could not thank the emperor personally for a decoration, but he could express appreciation to his superior officer. And so Commander von Müller wired a telegram to the chief of the Admiralty. Staff on 22 March 1918: "Sir: I obediently express my heartfelt gratitude for the good wishes of the Admiralty Staff and the very kind words you transmitted to me along with His Majesty's decree."

Modestly, but with pride and gratitude, Commander von Müller accepted the decoration that signified the appreciation of his country and its navy. Above all, it confirmed that he was a good officer who had commanded his cruiser honorably and dutifully.

The great world war moved toward its climactic end. In the fall of 1918 Müller returned for good from his internment in Holland. He was promoted to captain and appointed to the Navy Office in Berlin, where, many years before, he had worked with Grand Admiral von Tirpitz, now in political disfavor. He spent the last years of his life in Blankenberge, in almost total seclusion. Modestly, he resisted offers from publishers who wanted to bring out his memoirs. He remarked about it in private circles: "I have not accomplished anything particularly great, but only did my duty. If I wrote about it, I could not help feeling that I had made money from the blood of my comrades. This I cannot do." And so he never published a single line about his adventures. His thoughts we know only from preserved official reports and private letters. He declined an invitation to join and promote the German Society of Nobility, informing them that, to his mind, the most important task was the reduction of class conflict; Germans needed a greater sense of unity. He dedicated himself to the well-being of the survivors of his crew, whom he joined in a reunion celebration. With Grand Admiral von Tirpitz he maintained a correspondence, also with Captain Erich Raeder, who was working for the Navy Archives on the official history of the cruiser war. The empire had fallen, but he did not turn away from his country; rather, he wanted to work for the establishment of a greater Germany. As a German National delegate, he was elected to the Diet of Braunschweig.

Captain Karl von Müller died on 11 March 1923, not yet fifty years old. His name is remembered today in the Karl von Müller Barracks in Emden, no longer a naval but an army unit of the Bundeswehr. On a bronze plaque emblazoned with the *Emden*'s coat of arms stand the following words:

> SMS *Emden,* Commander Karl von Müller, sank numerous merchant ships in the Indian Ocean, destroyed the tank installation of Madras, and destroyed the Russian cruiser

*Zhemtchug* and the French destroyer *Mousquet* in the port of Penang. On 9 November 1914, pursued by a superior enemy and after a raging battle with the Australian cruiser *Sydney,* Commander Müller's ship was beached on Keeling Island. Nearly one-half of the crew died for the Fatherland. Glorious ship—yours is the city whose name you carried around the globe.

The name *Emden* would not be forgotten. On 16 December 1916 the light cruiser *Emden* (ex–*Ersatz Nymph*) had been commissioned and assigned to be the flagship of the torpedo boat flotillas. From 11 to 19 October 1917 she had participated in the German fleet's seizure of the Baltic islands of Dagö and Ösel, one of the largest amphibious operations of the naval war. On 19 November 1918, along with other modern units of the German navy, she departed Wilhelmshaven and proceeded to the Firth of Forth. There, in accordance with the armistice, Admiral Beatty interned the German fleet, unfortunately turning the event into a humiliating spectacle. On 26 November 1918 the *Emden* was interned in Scapa Flow. At the start of 1919, when the nucleus crew of the fleet flagship *Frederick the Great* proved unreliable, the commander of the interned units, Rear Admiral von Reuter, transferred his flag to the cruiser *Emden.* Thus the second cruiser with the celebrated name became the last flagship of the fleet that had formed the core of the Imperial German Navy.

On 21 June 1919 the men of the *Emden* opened the seacocks on their ship. On that day the German High Seas Fleet sank in the bay of Scapa Flow. While going down, the *Emden* was towed into shallow waters by British patrol ships. On 11 March 1920 she was awarded to the French navy, which used her in explosives experiments. Finally, in 1926, she was scrapped in Caen, France.

In Wilhelmshaven on 7 January 1925, the first cruiser to be built after the war received the traditional name. It was a distinction for an officer of the Republic's navy to command the *Emden,* particularly because she was the training ship for future officers and embarked on long world cruises. On her first voyage (1926–28) she was commanded by Captain Foerster, a future fleet chief; on her second voyage (1928–29), by Captain (later

Admiral) von Arnauld de la Perière, who in 1912 had served in the old *Emden;* and on her third (1930–31), by Captain Witthoeft, also a member of the crew of the first ship. During her world tour of 1934–35, Captain Karl Dönitz had command.

On her first voyage, the newest cruiser of the Republic's navy visited the Cocos. The commanding officer wired the city of Emden, "At the grave of the first *Emden* we stand in silent commemoration of you, the sponsor city." On this voyage the cruiser took soundings at the deepest spot in the Pacific Ocean, which hydrographic charts label the Emden Deep.

In the last days of World War II, after numerous combat actions, the third cruiser *Emden* succumbed. Hit by bombs and burning, she was beached in Heikendorfer Bay, near Kiel. On 3 May 1945 she was dynamited, and finally, in 1949, dismantled. Meanwhile, the wreck of the first *Emden* lay rusting, plundered and battered by the sea on the coral reef off North Keeling Island. For a while, souvenirs were made from her parts; natives especially treasured knives that came from the steel plates. After 1950, the hull was cut up by a Japanese salvage company.

Time obliterates much. In our fast-moving world constitutions, flags, and colors change, along with predominant spiritual and political values. But everything connected with the cruiser *Emden* is honorably acknowledged—by friends and former enemies, by all political camps, by this and the other side. Today there is the frigate *F 221,* or *Emden,* commissioned on 24 October 1961 under the black, red, and gold flag of the Federal Republic of Germany. The congratulatory telegram quoted words of the president of the Weimar Republic, who, on 6 January 1925, when the third *Emden* was christened, had sent the following message to the Navy Office in Wilhelmshaven:

> On the occasion of the launching of the cruiser *Emden,* I send my heartiest congratulations and good wishes. May the spirit that pervaded the old *Emden,* a spirit of self-sacrifice, love of the Fatherland, and seamanship, continue to live in this ship. May this youngest member of our growing navy always be blessed with a happy voyage.
> —President of the Reich Friedrich Ebert

# THE SHIP

Official records describe the light cruiser *Emden* as follows:

**Principal Dimensions**

Capacity in British register tons was 2,624.303.

Overall length in meters between perpendiculars was 111.0. Length from the after part of the stern to the forward edge of the ram was 118.3. Length on the designed waterline was 117.9. Greatest designed beam was 13.5 to the outer edge of the frame. Greatest beam for docks and locks was 13.56. Compartment depth from the upper edge of the double bottom or bottom stringer to the upper edge of the top deck beams amidships between perpendiculars was 7.1. Height from the upper edge of the horizontal keel plate or outer edge of the rabbet to the upper-deck beams amidships between the perpendiculars was 7.8. Designed draft forward was 5.127, aft, 4.527. Average draft was 5.270.

Displacement was 3,664 tons (specific weight of sea water, 1.015) with the following load in tons: 102, provisions and materials; 22, drinking water; 65, fresh water in the double bottom; and 400, coal. Each 10.59 tons brought an additional draft of one centimeter on the outer plating. Maximum displacement was 4,100 tons.

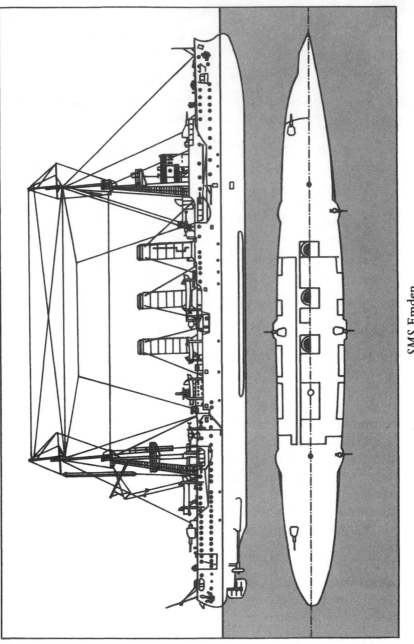

*SMS* Emden

The ship's hull was constructed with Siemens-Martin mild steel. The interior watertight bottom reached from frame 21 to 74 to the fourth, from frame 74 to 80 to the second longitudinal frames. Twelve watertight bulkheads divided the ship into thirteen compartments. From frame 21 to 40 a central bulkhead was constructed to provide watertight separation between the main engine and auxiliary engine rooms. On each side of the ship, a gangway/coal-bunker bulkhead reached from frame 21 to 74, from the double bottom to the armored deck. Below the armored deck, passageways between frames 40 and 74 served as a center coal bunker. They in turn were bounded by frames 40/41 and 73/74, forming transverse bunkers. In addition, there was a center bunker between the armored deck and the upper deck from frame 33 to 75.

The ship had a long, rounded bow and a long poop. Behind the bow was the conning bridge and, below it, the conning tower. A bridge connected poop and bow; between them was the open main deck, covered with 75mm, midship with 65mm, teakwood boards. Besides that, bow, poop, main deck, middle deck, and platforms had steel plates covered with linoleum. The ship's bottom was steel. A triangular cross-section bilge keel was connected on both sides of the bilge; its length was 35 meters, center height, 0.6 meters. Bilge plates were made of steel; pine wood and glue filled the space between plates. The sternpost was cast steel. The rudder was a forged piece of Siemens-Martin mild steel with alternating ribs and a 15mm rolled steel rudderblade between. The stem was also of cast steel.

The ship's main steering gear was steam powered. The auxiliary steering gear consisted of a hand-operated wheel connected to the screw spindle through line shafting, coupling, and drive chain. The main steering gear had a maximum rudder angle of 40°. The turning radius with all engines forward and a rudder angle of 35° was 455 meters to starboard (460 meters to port) at 11 knots and 550 (543) meters at 7 knots. At 20 knots it was 550 (515) meters.

The cruiser had two steel masts with topmast and yardarms; the mainmast had a gaff. Each mast carried a wooden radio antenna. Both masts carried a top on the trestletree, a crow's nest on the forward side of the mast top, and a platform for two searchlights each. The foremast and the mainmast were 41.3 meters in height, measuring from the designed waterline to the masthead. The following heights are also given in meters above the designed waterline. The tops are measured from the underside of their platforms. Foremast: top, 23.1; crow's nest, 33.6; searchlight platform, 16.1. Mainmast: top, 23.1; crow's nest, 33.6; searchlight platform, 13.1. The upper edge of the funnels was 18.2 meters above the designed waterline.

## Armor

The armored deck extended from frame 3 to the stempost with a level center part and 37° sloped, standing side sections. The after end was connected to the higher central section between frames 10/11 by an 80mm beveled glacis plate, the forward end between frame 80 and 87 by 80mm armored sill plates. The intersection of the beveled molded edge and the outer edge of the frame angle bar was in the middle, 1.2 meters below the designed waterline.

1st layer: In the horizontal parts, ship construction steel was 15 millimeters from stem to sternpost except from frame 10½ to 87, where it was 10 millimeters thick.

2nd layer: Ship construction steel (low-percentage nickel steel) was of 10 millimeters diagonally from frame 10½ to 87; 15 diagonally aft of frame 10½; 25 diagonally forward from frame 87.

3rd layer: Low-percentage nickel steel was 25 millimeters thick in the slopes to the cork dam and on the inside edge of the transverse frame angle from frame 10½ to 87.

## Ammunition Shafts

Ammunition shafts were not protected. The four guns on the poop and the forecastle as well as both medium guns on the upper deck had armored shields 50/25/20 millimeters thick. None of the remaining four guns had shields. The conning tower was constructed of 100mm tempered armor plate with an 80mm shield. Floors and decks consisted of 25% demagnetized nickel steel. The 0.5-meter interior diameter pipe for the communications lines was made of soft nickel steel of 25mm thickness. The armored deck had a cork dam on both sides from frame 21 to the sternpost.

## Armament

Armament consisted of ten 10.5cm rapid-firing guns on MPL C/1904 mounts. The gun barrels elevated to 30° and depressed to 10°. Range at 30° elevation was 12,200 meters; the maximum rate of fire was sixteen rounds per minute. Of the ten guns, two were located on the bow to port and starboard behind the wave breakers; two on the forward upper deck in blisters behind the forecastle to port and starboard; two on the middle upper deck, port and starboard; two on the after upper deck in blisters below the poop port and starboard; and finally two on the poop deck to port and starboard.

The bearing arcs of each pair of guns was as follows (0° clockwise to 360°):

1. Starboard 340°–145°, port 215°–20°
2. Starboard 360°–155°, port 205°–360°
3. Starboard 23°–158°, port 197°–337°
4. Starboard 25°–180°, port 180°–335°
5. Starboard 40°–220°, port 140°–320°

## Ammunition

Ammunition supply for overseas duty consisted of 750 high-explosive (Jz) shells, 720 high-explosive (Kz) shells, and 30 steel shrapnel shells—150 shells per gun. The ship had four magazines, two fore and two aft. There were eight ammunition hoists aligned on double shafts at frames 86/87, 80/21, and 18/19. The shafts opened in and under the bow and under the poop. Ammunition was hoisted by electric winch.

On overseas duty, light cruisers carried four machine guns on deck. The guns' maximum range at the highest possible elevation was 2,400 meters; the maximum rate of fire was 250 rounds per minute. For each machine gun, ten thousand live cartridges were carried, kept in the forward ammunition chambers near frame 85/86 and between frames 80 and 85. Light cruisers on foreign duty also carried one or two 6cm SBts L/21 cannon on Bts LC/1900 mounts; there was, in addition, one LLC/1900 mount as well as two machine-gun mounts. For the 6cm boat gun also used as a landing gun, 341 shells were on hand.

### Torpedo Armament

Torpedo armament consisted of two 45cm underwater broadside tubes with a minus 2° launching angle. The tubes were located under the armored deck near frames 74 (starboard) and 80 (port). Measured abeam, line of fire and arc of aim were 20° ahead. The height of the firing tubes in relation to the designed waterline (above the lower edge of the keel) was minus 2 meters. Torpedo target controls were located in the conning tower on the quarterdeck and on the aft searchlight stand. The cruiser carried five 45cm C/03 torpedoes.

### Searchlights

Four strong 150-ampere searchlights swept the whole horizon. Two sat side by side on a double platform on the foremast, two were set up one abaft the other on a double platform on the mainmast. The ship also had a 17-ampere unmounted signal searchlight.

### Power Plant

The plant consisted of two vertical triple-expansion engines with three cylinders each and of four fore and aft boiler rooms with twelve small-bore water-tube marine boilers; there was a high-limit boiler pressure of 16 kg/cm². A coal supply of 790 tons could be stored under normal conditions. The electrical plants were fed by three Elektra turbodynamos of 110 volts and 45kw output. Two were located in the auxiliary engine rooms on the upper platform deck, one was mounted on the middle deck, port side, between frames 25 and 29.

## Ship's Screws

There were two four-bladed propellers, 4.3 meters in diameter, with an adjustable rise of 6.3 meters.

## Coal Consumption

Based on averages obtained during the ship's sea trials in 1910, total coal (and coal-oil) consumption during twenty-four hours at 8 knots was 34 tons; at 12 knots, 60 tons; at 20 knots, 205 tons; at a top speed of 23.85 knots, 371 tons.

## Crew

Under normal conditions the *Emden* crew consisted of 365 men, including 16 officers, of which 10 were line officers and 2 were midshipmen. There were rifles for 120 men. The landing party was composed of 5 officers and 140 men; 87 men were armed with rifles and 30 served the landing gun.

## Drinking Water and Provisions

There was a normal drinking water reserve of 21.2 tons, which lasted seven days. Provisions for the crew consisted of the following, given in tons: meat, 5.65; preserved foods, 9.95; bread, 11.5; alcohol, 0.7. These provisions were for a period of ten weeks. Additional provisions for the commanding officer amounted to 2.5 tons; for officers, 10.08; for warrant officers, 10.92; and for stewards, 1.2. Total weight of provisions, including packing material, was 58.08 tons.

## Trial Runs

The trial runs were successful. In a six-hour test under forced draft on 10 August 1909, the new cruiser, with 15,683 of shaft horsepower and 134.75 revolutions per minute in the main engines, reached a speed of more than 23 knots. On 30 and 31 July 1909 the *Emden* steamed at 17 knots, on 11 and 12 August 1909, at 12 knots. On 17 and 18 August 1909 she embarked on a twenty-four-hour coal-measuring cruise at 20 knots. On 20 August 1909, near Neukrug, she reached a top speed of 24.014

knots on a measured mile. The average maximum speed on the measured mile was 21.121 knots.

The *Emden* received the following operating orders: most economical speed, 8 knots; cruising speed, 12; highest endurance capability, 20; forced performance, 23.85.

Her turning and maneuvering qualities were good. In heavy winds she turned rather heavily in place, particularly when her bow was against the wind. For the ship to pivot, her backing engine had to turn at higher speed than the one going ahead. Stopped, she drifted slightly athwart the wind. She performed badly in swells coming from abeam or astern; in a pitch she took on water quickly. In heavy seas or running against the waves, the *Emden* operated best at a medium speed range of 12 to 14 knots.

# BIBLIOGRAPHY

*Official documents and related materials at the Bundesarchiv/Militär-archiv, Freiburg/Breisgau*

RM 92/2370    Kriegsakten SMS *Emden*. Band 1, Rekonstruktion des Kriegstagebuchs usw. (War documents SMS *Emden:* Reconstruction of the combat log, etc.)

RM 92/2371    Kriegsakten SMS *Emden*. Band 2, Verschiedene Berichte über Kriegstätigkeiten. (War documents SMS *Emden:* Diverse reports about war activities.)

RM 92/2372    Kriegsakten SMS *Emden*. Band 3, Offizielle Korrespondenz, Presseberichte usw. (War documents SMS *Emden:* Official correspondence, press reports, etc.)

RM 99/605    Kriegsakten SMS *Ayesha*. (War documents SMS *Ayesha*.)

RM 3/3407    Admiralstabsakten SMS *Emden*, 1909–September 1914. (Admiralty Staff documents SMS *Emden*, 1909–September 1914.)

RM 3/3408    Admiralstabsakten SMS *Emden*, Oktober 1914–1921. (Admiralty Staff documents SMS *Emden*, October 1914–1921.)

RM 3/862        Bauakten Kleiner Kreuzer *Emden*, Juli 1905–Juni
                1907. (Construction documents light cruiser
                *Emden*, July 1905–June 1907.)

RM 3/863        Bauakten Kleiner Kreuzer *Emden*, Juli 1907–
                Dezember 1908. (Construction documents light
                cruiser *Emden*, July 1907–December 1908.)

RM 3/864        Bauakten Kleiner Kreuzer *Emden*, Januar 1909–
                1914. (Construction documents light cruiser
                *Emden*, January 1909–1914.)

RM D3/149       Dienstschrift DE 146/IV H.14: Technische Daten
                und Details mit einer Zeichnung 1:1000;
                Schiffsbeschreibung. Band enthaltend SMS *Em-
                den*. (Official record DE 146/IV H.14: Technical
                data and details with a drawing 1:1000; ship's
                description. Volume contains SMS *Emden*.)

SZ 185/186      SMS *Dresden/Emden*. Pläne 1:100, Seitenriss,
                Decksplan und Detailzeichnungen. (SMS *Dres-
                den/Emden*. Plans 1:100, profile deck plans and
                detail drawings.)

RM 5/6127       Indiensthaltungsakten SMS *Emden:* Stapellauf,
                Ausreise, Reiseberichte, Mai 1908–Mai 1914.
                (Commission documents SMS *Emden:* launch-
                ing, departure, cruise reports, May 1908–May
                1914.)

RM 3/155        Stapellaufakten SMS Kleiner Kreuzer *Ersatz Pfeil*
                (*Emden*), 1907. (Launching documents light
                cruiser *Ersatz Pfeil* [*Emden*], 1907.)

RM 40/661       Akte betr. Rückkehr des Landungszuges SMS *Em-
                den* (*Ayesha*) über Konstantinopel. (Documents
                on the return of the landing troop SMS *Emden*
                [*Ayesha*] through Constantinople.)

RM 6/234        Kreuzergeschwader, Bl. 121. (Cruiser squadron,
                Bl. 121.)

DZ II/M 55/1    *Emden* III Akten, 1927–28. (*Emden* III docu-
                ments, 1927–28.)

RM 2/825        Qualifikationsberichte. Band 7, Oktober 1912 bis
                März 1914. (Fitness reports, October 1912 un-
                til March 1914.)

RM 2/834        Auszüge aus den Qualifikationsberichten der Fre-
                gattenkapitäne. Band, 1906–18. (Excerpts

|  | from the fitness reports of the commanders, 1906–18.) |
|---|---|
| RM 2/835 | Auszüge aus den Qualifikationsberichten der Korvettenkapitäne. Band 1, 1906–18. (Excerpts from the fitness reports of the lieutenant commanders, 1906–18.) |
| RM 2/837 | Auszüge aus den Qualifikationsberichten über Seeoffiziere vom Kapitänleutnant abwärts. Band 2, April 1910–1915. (Excerpts from the fitness reports of naval officers from lieutenants down, April 1910–1915.) |
| RM 3/60-66 | Akten über die Belagerung Tsingtaus. (Documents on the siege of Tsingtao.) |
| RM 3/3152-3167 | Akten des Kreuzergeschwader betreffend. (Documents on the cruiser squadron). |
| RM 5/5370 | Akten über Übungen des Kreuzergeschwaders. (Documents on the exercises of the cruiser squadron.) |
| RM 38/161-172 | Akten des Kreuzergeschwader betreffend, insbesonders Band 161 und 166. (Documents on the cruiser squadron.) |
| RM 5/5984-6062 | Akten über die ostasiatische Stationen. (Documents on the east Asian stations.) |

### Printed Works

Anon. *Das* Emden-*Spiel im Indischen und Grossen Ozean.* Stuttgart: Frankh, 1915
———. *Unsere* Emden. Berlin: Hillger, ca. 1916.
Ardoin, Paul. *L'Emden: Ses croisières et sa fin.* Paris: Challamel, 1920.
———. *L'Escadre allemande du Pacific.* Paris: Challamel, 1920.
Assmann, Kurt. *Deutsche Seestrategie in zwei Weltkriegen.* Heidelberg: Scharnhorst, 1956; Heidelberg: Vowinckel, 1957.
Baer, C. H. *Der Völkerkrieg: Eine Chronik der Ereignisse seit dem l. Juli 1914.* Vol. 1. Stuttgart: Julius Hoffmann, 1917.
*Bangkok Daily Mail.* 22 November 1914. 16 November 1914. 2 December 1914.
*Bangkok Times.* 4 November 1914.

Bartz, Karl. *Der Kommandant der* Emden: *Das Leben des Kapitäns v. Müller.* Berlin: Deutscher Verlag, 1939.

Baumbach, Norbert v. *Ruhmestage der deutschen Marine: Bilddokumente des Seekrieges.* Hamburg: Broschek, 1933.

Baynham, Henry. *Men from the Dreadnoughts.* London: Hutchinson, 1976.

Belot, Admiral de, and A. Reussner. *La puissance navale dans l'histoire de 1914 à 1959.* Paris: Editions maritimes et d'outre-mer, 1971.

Bennett, Geoffrey. *Coronel and Falklands.* London: B. T. Batsford, 1962.

———. *Naval Battles of the First World War.* London: B. T. Batsford, 1966.

*Berliner Tägeblatt.* 5 November 1915.

Bermbach, J. *Zittere England: Unsere* Emden *ging nicht unter.* Parts 1 and 2. Dietrich and Brückner, 1914, 1915.

Bess, Freg. Kapt. a. D. "SMS *Emden* während des zweiten chinesischen Bürgerkriegs vor Nanking und den Tung-Lean-Chan-Forts im Jahre 1913." *Marine-Rundschau* 30 (1925): 83–90.

Bingham, Edward Barry. *Falklands, Jutland and the Bight.* London: John Murray, 1919.

Blond, Georges. "Le dernier corsaire." *L'océan indien: L'océan des perles et du Pétrole.* Paris: Presse de la Cité, 1975.

Brechenmacher, J. K. *Die Heldenfahrten des Kapitänleutnants v. Mücke-Schilderungen aus dem Weltkrieg.* 1916.

———. *Heldenfahrten und Untergang der* Emden-*Schilderungen aus dem Weltkrieg.* 1915.

Busch, Fritz Otto. *Admiral Graf Spee Sieg und Untergang.* Berlin-Leipzig, 1943.

———. *Die* Emden *jagt.* Berlin and Leipzig: Schneider, 1935, 1941.

Busch, Fritz Otto, and Georg Günther Frh. v. Forstner. *Unsere Marine im Weltkrieg.* Berlin: Brunnen Verlag Willi Bischoff, 1934.

Busch, Fritz Otto, and Gerhard Ramlow. *Deutsche Seekriegsgeschichte.* Gütersloh: Bertelsmann, 1943.

Bywater, Hector C. *Cruisers in Battle: Naval Light Cavalry Under Fire, 1914.* London: Constable, 1939.

Cardwell, Robert. "The History of the Raiding of the Cocos and the Capture and Sinking of the *Emden. The Zodiac: The Submarine Cable Service Papers.* Vol. 13, no. 148 (Nov. 1920): 117–35.

Casey, Lord. "The Cruise of the *Emden." Royal Australian Navy News,* 22 November 1968.

*Ceylon Times.* 29 September 1914.

Chack, Paul. *La guerre des croiseurs, du 4 août 1914 à la Bataille des Falklands.* 2 vols. Paris: Soc. d'editions géographiques, maritimes et coloniales, 1922–23.

Chack, Paul, and Jean-Jacques Antier. *Histoire maritime de la Première Guerre Mondiale.* 3 vols. Paris: Editions France Empire, 1969, 1970, 1971.

Chatterton, E. Keble. *Gallant Gentlemen.* London: Hurst and Blackett, 1931.

Cheret, G. K. *Der Emden letztes Gefecht-Heldenkampf des deutschen Kreuzers im Indischen Ozean.* 1941.

*Chronology of the War.* 3 vols. and 1 atlas. London: British Ministry of Information, 1918–20.

Churchill, Winston S. *The World Crisis, 1911–18.* 3 vols. London: Thornton Butterworth, 1923, 1923, 1927. Revised and condensed, 1931.

*Coast Seaman's Journal.* 24 March 1915.

Copplestone, Bennet. *The Secret of the Navy.* London: John Murray, 1920.

Corbett, Sir Julian. *History of the Great War: Naval Operations.* 5 vols. London: Longmans, Green, 1920–31.

Cornford, L. Cope. *War.* New York: George H. Doran, 1918.

Cranwell, J. P. *Spoilers of the Sea: Wartime Raiders in the Age of Steam.* London, 1942.

Dane, E. *The British Campaigns in Africa and the Pacific.* London, 1919.

Daniell, David Scott. *Sea Fights.* London: B. T. Batsford, 1966.

Darby, Leonard. "The Official Report of the *Sydney-Emden* Engagement on November 9, 1914." Part 2. *Mufti* (December 1937, January 1938).

Daveluy, Admiral. *L'actions maritimes pendant la guerre anti-germanique.* Paris: Challamelt, 1920.

Dick, C. *Das Kreuzergeschwader: Sein Werden, Sieg und Untergang.* Berlin: Mittler, 1917.

Dixon, Campbell. "How the *Emden* Went to Her Doom." *Epics of Empire.* London: Dean, 1936.

Dohm, Arno. *Geschwader Spee.* Gütersloh: Bertelsmann, 1939.

Dupuy, Trevor Nevitt. *Naval and Overseas War, 1914–15.* New York: Franklin Watts, 1967.

Ekman, Per-Olof. "SMS *Emden:* En sjöfartsräd för 50 år sedan." *Tidskrift i Sjöväsendet.* Stockholm, June 1964.

———. "*Emden.*" *Sveriges Flotta.* Stockholm, 1964.

"Emden III." *Marine-Rundschau* 30 (1925), 40–41.

"Emden III." *Marine-Rundschau* 30 (1925), 440–41.

Erdmann, Gustav Adolf. *Die Taten der deutschen Flotte im Weltkrieg.* Bielefeld and Leipzig: Velhagen & Klasing, 1915.

———. *SMS* Emden *und sein Kommandant.* 3rd ed. Leipzig: Fock, 1916.

Fanthorpe, Lionel. "The Cruise of the *Emden.*" *Warships of the First World War.* London: Phoebus, 1973.

Farrère, C. *La mort de l'*Emden. Paris, 1934.

Farrère, Claude, and Paul Chack. *Combats et batailles sur mer.* Paris: Flammarion, 1925.

———. *Sur mer 1914.* Paris: Flammarion, 1925.

Fayle C. Ernest. *History of the Great War.* 3 vols. London: John Murray, 1920–24.

———. *Seaborne Trade.* 3 vols. London: Longmans, Green, 1920–24.

Feuga, Jean. *L'*Emden-*Croiseur Corsaire.* Paris: Librairie Alphonse Lemerre, 1931.

Fikentscher-Emden, Erich. *Aus Malta in die Freiheit.* Berlin: Berliner Illustrierte, April–May 1942.

———. *Erinnerungen aus unserer* Emden-*Zeit.* Augsburg: Selbstverlag, 1964.

———. *Ostasien und die Südsee, 1912–14: An Bord des Kreuzers SMS* Emden. Münich: Selbstverlag, 1976.

Floericke, Kurt. *Der Schiffsjunge der* Emden: *Erzählung aus dem grossen Weltkrieg für die reifere Jugend.* Stüttgart: Frankh, 1915.

Floerke, G., and G. Gärtner. *Unserer Flotte Heldentaten-Seekriegserlebnisse.* Münich, 1915.

Floerke, H. *Von der Nordsee zu den Dardanellen: Neue Heldentaten unserer Flotte.* Münich: Georg Müller, 1916.

Forstmeier, Friedrich. *Warships in Profile.* Vol. 3. Ed. by Antony Preston. Windsor: Profile Publications, 1973.

Freisburger, W. *News about the* Emden. 1936.

Frothingham, Thomas G. *The Naval History of the World War.* Vol. 1, *Offensive Operations, 1914–15.* Cambridge: Harvard University Press, 1925.

Funke, A. *Ayesha-Fahrten und Abenteuer der* Emden-*Mannschaft von den Kokosinseln bis Konstantinopel.* Berlin: Volkraft-Verlag, 1915.

Fürbringer, Oberbürgermeister. *Die Stadt Emden in Gegenwart und Vergangenheit.* Emden, 1892.

Galle, Josef. *Der Krieg auf dem Meere.* Langensalza, J. Beltz, 1916.

Garnham, S. A., and Hadfield, Robert L. *The Submarine Cable*. London: Sampson Low, Marsten, 1930.

Garcia, C. R. "An Account of the *Sydney-Emden* Action." In *The Times* (London), 15 December 1914.

Gellert, Georg. *Heldenfahrten der* Emden *und* Ayesha-*Abenteuer und Kämpfe der* Emden-*Mannschaft in dem Weltkriege, 1914—15*. Berlin: Meidinger, 1915, 1917.

Glossop, John A. Letter of Proceeding, Colombo, 15 November 1914. Official battle transcript. Naval Secretary, Navy Office, Melbourne. NO 14/9318, 8 December 1914.

Gottberg, Otto v. *Die Helden von Tsingtau*. Berlin: Ullstein, 1915.

———. "SMS *Ayesha*." In *Kreuzerfahrten und U-Bootstaten*. Berlin: Ullstein, 1915.

Gröner, Erich. *Die deutschen Kriegsschiffe, 1815—1945*. 2 vols. Munich: J. F. Lehmanns, 1966, 1968.

Hagqvist, Wilhelm. *Kryssaren* Emden, *tropikernas kaparkonung*. Stockholm, 1915.

*Handbook for the East-Indian Archipelago*. Part 1. Hamburg: Hydrographic Institute Berlin, 1933.

Heichen, Walter. *Helden der See-Heldentaten unserer Marine, 1914—18*. Berlin: Aweichert, n.d.

———. *Unsere* Emden. Berlin: Hillger, n.d.

Henningsen, N. *Unserer Auslandskreuzer Ruhm und Ende, 1914*. After accounts and letters of eyewitnesses. Cologne, 1935.

Heuler, Felix. *Mit Volldampf ran an den Feind: Ein Heldenbuch der deutschen Marine aus den Kriegsjahren 1914—15*. Würzburg, 1916.

Hildebrand-Röhr-Steinmetz. *Die deutschen Kriegsschiffe*. Vol. 2. Herford: Koehler, 1980.

Hirst, Lloyd. *Coronel and After*. London: Peter Davies, 1934.

Hislam, Percival H. *The Admiralty of the Atlantic: An Inquiry into the Development of German Sea Power*. London, 1908.

Hoecker, O. *Die falsche* Emden: *Eine heitere Seegeschichte*. Leipzig: Hesse, 1915.

Hoehling, A. A. *Lonely Command: The Epic Story of the* Emden. London: Cassell, 1957.

Hohenzollern, Franz Joseph Prince v. Emden: *Meine Erlebnisse auf SM Schiff* Emden. Richard Eckstein Nachf., 1925.

———. Emden: *My Experiences on SMS* Emden. London: Herbert Jenkins, n.d.

———. *L'Emden*. Paris: Payot, 1929.

Hough, R. *The Pursuit of Admiral von Spee*. London: Allen and Unwin, 1969.

Hoyt, Edwin P. *The Fall of Tsingtao*. London: Arthur Barker, 1975.

————. *The Last Cruise of the* Emden. London: André Deutsch, 1966.

Hubert, F. *La guerre navale, mers du nord, mers lointaines*. Paris: Payot, 1916.

Hurd, Archibald. *From Helgoland to Keeling Island*. London: H. C. Bywater, 1914.

————. *Sons of the Admiralty: A Short History of the Naval War, 1914–18*. London: H. H. Batsford, 1919.

————. *The British Fleet in the Great War*. London: Constable, 1919.

————. *The German Fleet*. London: Hodder and Stoughton, 1915.

————. *The Merchant Navy*. Vol. 1. London: Longmans, Green, 1921–29.

Irving, J. *Coronel and the Falklands*. London: A. M. Philpot. 1927.

————. *La chasse aux croiseurs allemands*. Trans. from the English. Paris: Soc. d'editions géographiques, maritimes et coloniales, 1928.

Janson, General v. *Tsingtau, Erwerb, Blüte und Verlust*. Berlin: Mittler, 1915.

Jellicoe, John. *Lord Jellicoe's Erinnerungen: England's Flotte im Weltkrieg, zwischen Skagerrak und Scapa Flow*. 2 vols. Berlin: Vorhut Verlag–Otto Schlegel, 1937.

Jose, A. A. *Official History of Australia in the War of 1914–18*. Vol. 9. Royal Australian Navy, n.d.

Kalau vom Hofe, Eugen. *Kampf und Untergang des Kreuzergeschwaders*. Berlin: Verlag Kameradschaft, 1915.

————. *Kriegszug des Kreuzers* Emden *und seiner Helden weitere Fahrt*. Berlin, 1916.

————. *Unsere Flotte im Weltkrieg, 1914–15*. Berlin: Mittler, 1915.

Kirchhoff, Hermann. *Der Seekrieg, 1914–15: Schiffspost und Feldpostbriefe, sowie andere Berichte von Mitkämpfern und Augenzeugen*. Leipzig: Hesse and Becker, 1915.

————. *Maximilian Graf von Spee, der Sieger von Coronel: Das Lebensbild und die Erinnerungen eines deutschen Seemanns*. Berlin: Marinedank, 1915.

Koerner, Peter. *Der Erste Weltkrieg, 1914–18*. Vol. 4, *Der Krieg zur See*. Munich: Wilhelm Heyne, 1968.

*Kölnische Zeitung* (Cologne). 22 November 1914.

Koop, Gerhard. Emden: *Ein Name-fünf Schiffe*. Munich: Bernard and Graefe, 1983.

Laar, Clemens. *Die grauen Wölfe des Grafen Spee.* Berlin: Scherl, 1940.

Langmaid, Kenneth. *The Sea Raiders.* London: Jarrolds, 1963.

Lauterbach, Julius. *1,000 Pf. Sterling Kopfpreis: Tot oder lebendig.* Berlin: Scherl, 1917.

————. *Mis adventuras de guerra en el mar, 1914–18.* Madrid: Joaquin Gil, 1936.

Lehfels, G. *Der Herr des Meeres: Fahrten und Abenteuer der Emden im Weltkrieg.* Bielefeld: Velhagen and Klasing, 1915.

Liersemann, Heinrich. *Klar zum Gefecht: Unsere blauen Jungen im Weltkrieg, 1914–15.* Berlin: Weichert, 1915.

Lietzmann, Joachim. *Auf verlorenem Posten: Unter der Flagge des Grafen Spee.* Ludwigshafen/Bodensee, 1922.

Lockhart, J. G. "Of the Company of the Privateers: SMS *Emden.*" In *Strange Adventures of the Sea.* London: Philip Allen. Reprinted in *Great Sea Stories of All Nations.* Ed. by H. M. Tomlinson. 1st ed. London: George H. Harrap, 1930. 2nd ed. London: Spring Books, 1967.

————. *The Sea, Our Heritage.* London: Geoffrey Bles, 1940.

Lowell, Thomas. *Lauterbach Frän Kinesiska Sjön.* Helsingfors: Holger Schildt, 1933.

————. *Lauterbach of the China Sea.* London: Hutchinson, 1939.

Luckner, Graf Felix v., and Julius Lauterbach. *Mein Freund Juli-Bumm: Die Abenteuer des Kapitän Lauterbach von der* Emden. After the American edition by Thomas Lowell. Leipzig: Koehler and Amelang, ca. 1934.

Ludwig, Emil. "Berichte über *Emden*-Landungsmannschaft in Arabien." *Berliner Tageblatt.* 11 May 1915.

————. *Die Fahrten der* Emden *und* Ayesha: *Nach Erzählungen des Kapitän-leutnants von Mücke, seiner Offiziere und Mannschaften.* Berlin: S. Fischer, 1915, 1916.

Mäkelä, Matti e. *Liehuvin Lipuin.* Jyväskylä/Finnland: Gummerus, 1965.

Mantey, Eberhard v. *Les Marins allemands au combat.* Paris: Payot, 1930.

*Marine Journal.* Emden roster. No. 6/1971, year 18, p. 6.

Middlemas, Keith. *Command the Far Seas.* London: Hutchinson, 1961.

*Morning Post* (London). 23 August 1916.

Mücke, Hellmuth v. *Ayesha.* Berlin: Scherl, 1915. Revised edition, 1926.

————. "Bericht über den Landungszug SMS *Emden.*" In Raeder, *Der Kreuzerkrieg in den ausländischen Gewässern,* vol. 2, plan C (q.v.).

————. "Der Durchbruch des Landungszuges SMS *Emden* nach Konstantinopel." In Reinhard Scheer and Willy Stöwer, *Die deutsche Flotte in grosser Zeit.* Braunschweig and Berlin: Westermann, 1926.

————. *Die Abenteuer der* Emden-*Mannschaft.* Reutlingen: Ensslin, 1921.

————. "Die Kreuzerfahrten SMS *Emden.*" In Reinhard Scheer and Willy Stöwer, *Die deutsche Flotte in grosser Zeit.* Braunschweig and Berlin: Westermann, 1926.

————. *Die Taten der* Emden *und anderer Kreuzer.* Leipzig: Hesses Volksbücherei no. 1031, 1915.

————. *Emden.* Berlin: Scherl, 1915.

————. "Emden-Ayesha." In *Unsere Marine im Weltkrieg, 1914–18.* Berlin: Eberhard von Mantey, 1927.

————. *L'equipage de l'*Ayesha. Paris: Payot, 1930.

————. Tagebuch des Landungszugs SMS *Emden-Ayesha.* In BA-MA RM 99/605. Excerpts printed in Schlieper, *Klar Schiff* (q.v.).

————. *The* Emden. London: Ritter, 1917.

Mücke, H. v., and A. Funke. Ayesha-*Fahrten und Abenteuer der* Emden *Mannschaft von den Kokosinseln bis Konstantinopel.* Berlin: Marinedank, 1915.

Müller, Karl v. Official reports of the commander of the *Emden.* Partially covered in Raeder, *Der Kreuzerkrieg in den ausländischen Gewässern.* Vol. 2.

Nagel, Alfred G. Emden: *Ein Gedenkbuch deutschen Heldentums zur See.* Kiel: Mühlau, 1927. Berlin: Lichtenfelde, 1934.

Nauheimer, A. M. SMS Emden: *Unter Benützung des gesamten zur Zeit erreichbaren Materials von Tagebüchern, Briefen und Berichten zum Besten der Invaliden der* Emden. Leipzig: Xenien, 1915.

*Navy News* (Canberra). 11 November 1961, 30 October 1964.

*The New York Times.* 24 December 1934.

Noble, Edward. "The Transport." In *The Naval Side.* London: C. P. Hayward, 1918.

Oellers, Heinrich. *Wehe dir England.* Leipzig: Xenien, 1931(?).

Oesterwitz, H. *Auf der* Emden *und* Ayesha: *Erlebnisse eines Teilnehmers.* Berlin: Wallmanns, 1916.

Ottinger-Emden, Hermann. *Das Buch von der* Emden. 1936.

————. *Die glückhafte* Emden. Stuttgart: K. Thienemanns, 1936.

————. *Kampf und Untergang der* Emden. Stuttgart: K. Thienemanns, 1936.

Phillip, O. *Englands Flotte im Kampf mit der deutschen Flotte im Weltkrieg, 1914–16.* Leipzig, 1920.

*Pinang [Penang] Gazette.* 28 October 1934.

Pinckert, Chief Petty Officer. "Der Überfall auf die *Ayesha*-Leute." In G. v. Dickhut-Harrach, *Im Felde unbesiegt,* vol. 1. Munich: J. F. Lehmanns, 1921.

Pitt, Barrie. *Coronel and the Falklands.* London: Cassel, 1960.

Plötz-Emden, Hugo. *Toteskampf des Kreuzers* Emden. Emden: Rhein-Ems-Zeitung, 1954.

Pochhammer, Hans. *Graf Spees lezte Fahrt: Erinnerungen an das Kreuzergeschwader.* Leipzig: K. F. Koehler, 1924. English ed., *Before Jutland: Admiral Spee's Last Voyage.* London: Jarrolds, 1931.

Poggi, Marco. *Le Navi fantasma, gli ultimi Corsari: La Guerra di corsa degli incrociatori tedeschi, 1914–18.* 2nd ed. Naples: Bianco, 1960.

Raeder, Erich. *Der Kreuzerkrieg in den ausländischen Gewässern.* Vol. 1, *Der Krieg zur See, 1914–18.* Berlin: Mittler, 1923. Vol. 2, *Die Tätigkeit der Kleinen Kreuzer* Emden, Königsberg, *und* Karlsruhe. Berlin: Mittler, 1923.

Ratman, R. "Costly Russian Love Affair That Ended in Disaster." In the *Straits Echo and Times of Malaya* (Pulau-Penang). 14 January 1970.

Reincke, Ewald. "Wir fahren gegen England: Die Geschichte eines *Emden*-Matrosen." In *Unser Seekriegsbuch,* ed. by Walter Stein. Berlin: Montamus, 1915.

Reussner, André, and L. Nicolas. *La puissance navale dans l'histoire de 1915 à 1914.* Paris: Éditions maritimes et d'outre-mer, 1974.

Reventlow, Ernst Graf zu. *Der Einfluss der Seemacht im Grossen Kriege.* Berlin: Mittler, 1918.

Roehle, R. *Als Flüchtling um den halben Erdball: Die abenteuerlichen Erlebnisse des Prisenoffiziers SMS* Emden, *Kptlt. d. R. J. Lauterbach.* Münster and Stuttgart: Verlag v. Müller, n.d.

———. Emden-Ayesha: *Heldenfahrten und Abenteuer deutscher Seeleute im Weltkrieg.* Stuttgart: Union, 1915.

Scheer, Reinhard. *Deutschlands Hochseeflotte im Weltkrieg: Persönliche Erinnerungen.* Berlin: Scherl, 1920. English ed., *Germany's High Sea Fleet in the World War.* New York: Peter Smith, 1934.

Schlieper, Rear Admiral. *Klar Schiff: Unsere Seehelden im Weltkrieg.* Leipzig: Buchh. Gustav Fock GmbH., 1915 (?).

Schoen, Walter von. *Kreuzerkrieg führen.* Berlin: Deutscher Verlag Ullstein, 1936.

Schultze-Jena, Kurt. *Der Kampf um Tsingtau.* Jena: G. Fischer, 1916.
Selow-Seman, K. E. *Kapitänleutnant v. Müllers letzte Fahrt.* Berlin: Scherl, 1917.
*Siam Observer* (Bangkok). 9 November 1914, 12 November 1914.
*Singapore Free Press.* 8 February 1935.
Southworth, John van Duyn. *The Age of Steam.* Vol. 1. New York: Twayne, 1970.
Spencer-Cooper, H. *The Battle of the Falkland Islands.* London: Cassel, 1919.
Steen-Steensen, R. "Emden i Diego Garcia." In *Sveriges Flotta,* no. 4. Stockholm, 1965.
Stegemann, Hermann. *Geschichte des Krieges.* 3 vols. Stuttgart and Berlin: Deutsche Verlags-Anstalt, 1919.
Sternau, Th. v. *Die Siegesfahrt der* Emden, *nach Schilderungen des Kapitänleutnants v. Mücke.* Leipzig: Graph. Werke, 1916.
Stevens, W. O., and A. Westcott. "The Cruise of the Emden." In *A History of Seapower.* New York, 1942.
Stoelzel, Rear Admiral, ed. *Ehrenrangeliste der kaiserlich-deutschen Marine, 1914–18.* Berlin: Verlag Marine–Offizier-Verband, 1930.
*Sunday Gazette* (Pulau-Penang). 15 July 1973.
Teltz, Camillo. *Zur See-Erlebnisse eines Seeoffiziers auf Schiffen und Meeren.* Minden: Köhler, 1930.
*The Times Diary and Index of the War, 1914–18.* London: Times, 1921.
Tirpitz, Alfred v. *Der Aufbau der deutschen Weltmacht.* Stuttgart: Cotta, 1924.
———. *Deutsche Ohnmachtspolitik im Weltkriege.* Hamburg: Hanseatische Verlagsanstalt, 1926.
———. *My Memoirs.* London: Hurst and Blackett, 1919.
Toesche-Mittler, Siegfried. *Die deutsche Kriegsflotte sechs Monate im Kampf.* Berlin: Mittler, 1915.
———. *Unsere Auslandskreuzer im Weltkrieg, 1914–15.* Berlin: Mittler, 1915.
Tramond, Loaunès, and André Reussner. *Elements d'histoire maritime et coloniale contemporaine, 1815–1914.* Paris: Soc. d'éditions géographique maritimes et coloniales, 1922–24.
Tuchman, Barbara. *The Guns of August.* New York: Macmillan, 1962.
Urban, W. *Die Kriegsfahrten der* Emden: *Erzählung für die Jugend.* 9th ed. Stuttgart: Union, 1918.
Vat, Dan van der. *The Last Corsair: The Story of the* Emden. London: Holder and Stoughton, 1983.

Vollerthun, Waldemar. *Der Kampf um Tsingtau*. Leipzig: Hirzel, 1920.

Waldeyer-Hartz, Hugo v. *Der Kreuzerkrieg, 1914–18*. Oldenburg: Gerhard Stalling, 1931.

———. *Kreuzertaten der Weltgeschichte*. Potsdam: Rütten and Loening, 1942.

———. *Männer und Bilder deutscher Seefahrt*. Braunschweig: Vieweg, 1934.

———. *Ran an den Feind*. Berlin: Jugendhort Walter Bloch, 1915.

———. *Von Tsingtau zu den Falklandinseln: Eine Erzählung von den Heldenkämpfen um Tsingtau und der ruhmreichen Fahrt des deutschen Kreuzergeschwaders im Weltkrieg*. Berlin: E. S. Mittler, 1917.

Weyer, Bruno. *Taschenbuch der Kriegsflotten*. Munich: J. F. Lehmanns, 1900–.

Wheeler, Harold F. B. "The Exploits of a Modern Corsair: Rounding up the Exclusive *Emden*." In *Stirring Deeds of Britain's Sea Dogs in the Great War*. London: Harrap, 1916.

Winter, Government Head of Clergy. *Tsingtau: Eine Erinnerung an Ostasien*. Tsingtau: Haupt, 1911.

Witthoeft, Robert. "Die Vernichtung des russischen Kreuzers *Zhemchug* durch SMS *Emden* in Penang am 28 October 1914." In Reinhard Scheer and Willy Stöwer, *Die deutsche Flotte in grosser Zeit*. Braunschweig and Berlin: Westermann, 1926.

———. "*L'Emden* dans le détroit de Tsoushima et dans le port de Penang." In v. Mantey, *Le marins allemands au combat*. Paris: Payot, 1930.

———. *Unsere* Emden: *Erlebnisse auf den Kaperfahrten im Jahre 1914*. Berlin: Reimar Hobbing, 1926.

———. *Unsere* Emden: *Kaperfahrten im Indischen Ozean*. Revised ed. Berlin: Ernst Steiniger, 1938.

Wolff-Emden, R. *Von den Kokosinseln nach Deutschland: Meine Erlebnisse beim Landungszug der* Emden-Ayesha, *1914–15*. 1940.

Wolflast, Wilhelm. *Der Seekrieg, 1914–18*. Leipzig: Hase and Koehler, 1938.

Woodward. *Great Britain and the German Navy*. Oxford, 1935.

Wyllie, W. L., and M. F. Wren. *Sea Fights of the Great War*. London: Cassell, 1918.

Zimmer, G. "Mit SMS *Emden* auf Kriegsfahrt." *Marine Rundschau* 29 (1924), part 3, 125–31.

The Naval Institute Press is the book-publishing arm of the U.S. Naval Institute, a private, nonprofit, membership society for sea service professionals and others who share an interest in naval and maritime affairs. Established in 1873 at the U.S. Naval Academy in Annapolis, Maryland, where its offices remain today, the Naval Institute has members worldwide.

Members of the Naval Institute support the education programs of the society and receive the influential monthly magazine *Proceedings* and discounts on fine nautical prints and on ship and aircraft photos. They also have access to the transcripts of the Institute's Oral History Program and get discounted admission to any of the Institute-sponsored seminars offered around the country.

The Naval Institute also publishes *Naval History* magazine. This colorful bimonthly is filled with entertaining and thought-provoking articles, first-person reminiscences, and dramatic art and photography. Members receive a discount on *Naval History* subscriptions.

The Naval Institute's book-publishing program, begun in 1898 with basic guides to naval practices, has broadened its scope to include books of more general interest. Now the Naval Institute Press publishes about one hundred titles each year, ranging from how-to books on boating and navigation to battle histories, biographies, ship and aircraft guides, and novels. Institute members receive significant discounts on the Press's more than eight hundred books in print.

Full-time students are eligible for special half-price membership rates. Life memberships are also available.

For a free catalog describing Naval Institute Press books currently available, and for further information about subscribing to *Naval History* magazine or about joining the U.S. Naval Institute, please write to:

Membership Department
**U.S. Naval Institute**
291 Wood Road
Annapolis, MD 21402-5034
Telephone: (800) 233-8764
Fax: (410) 269-7940
Web address: www.navalinstitute.org